# CHANGE FROM WITHIN

# CHANGE
## *from* WITHIN

### REIMAGINING THE 21ST-CENTURY
### PROSECUTOR

## MIRIAM ARONI KRINSKY

THE
NEW
PRESS

NEW YORK
LONDON

Requests for permission to reproduce selections from this book should be made through
our website: https://thenewpress.com/contact.

Published in the United States by The New Press, New York, 2022
Distributed by Two Rivers Distribution

ISBN 978-1-62097-736-1 (hc)
ISBN 978-1-62097-774-3 (ebook)
CIP data is available

The New Press publishes books that promote and enrich public discussion and
understanding of the issues vital to our democracy and to a more equitable world. These
books are made possible by the enthusiasm of our readers; the support of a committed
group of donors, large and small; the collaboration of our many partners in the
independent media and the not-for-profit sector; booksellers, who often hand-sell
New Press books; librarians; and above all by our authors.

www.thenewpress.com

*Book design and composition by Bookbright Media*
*This book was set in Avenir and Bembo*

Printed in the United States of America

2 4 6 8 10 9 7 5 3 1

# CONTENTS

# Introduction:
# A New Vision for Justice

MIRIAM ARONI KRINSKY

Founder and Executive Director, Fair and Just Prosecution

"Safety means no more empty porches. It's the ability
to feel like you can go out on your porch and have a
glass of lemonade and not be concerned. Your children can be jumping rope, your elders can be pulling
weeds in the garden, and you don't have the concern
that harm will come to them. . . . It's not just being
safe, but feeling safe. And for so many families in
neighborhoods that have been impacted by violence,
that's all they want: to be able to be free in their communities, to do the things that so many of us take for
granted, which is to just sit on your porch."

—*State's Attorney Kim Foxx*
*Cook County (Chicago), Illinois*

Throughout the United States, people are demanding justice.
They want fairness, accountability, healing, and an end to the
kind of policing and prosecution that causes harm, especially in

communities of color and among people living in poverty. As organizers, advocates, and local leaders have long argued, harsh and racially biased approaches haven't made our neighborhoods stronger or safer. Instead, these practices have fueled mass incarceration, wasted billions of taxpayer dollars on jails and prisons, and frayed our social fabric.

In increasing numbers, voters are embracing the need for change, delivering that message at the polls, and propelling mandates for reform. As a result, we are seeing a new generation of elected prosecutors use the immense power of their office to move in a different direction, toward a smaller and less punitive criminal legal system. This book features oral histories of thirteen of these leaders, adapted from interviews conducted with them.

These reformers are fundamentally reimagining and re-creating their role as prosecutors.* They envision a system in which everyone is respected and heard, whether they are community members; people who are arrested, charged, or convicted; survivors or witnesses of crime; loved ones; or some combination of these roles. As a former federal prosecutor, I know that the changes underway are long overdue—and that they aren't simply theoretical or mere tinkering around the edges. Elected leaders in this movement are overhauling policies and practices in significant ways that will make their communities safer and healthier. And these vital reforms will move us closer to a criminal legal system that is fair and just.

---

* Many elected prosecutors are district attorneys, though some have other titles such as state's attorney, commonwealth's attorney, or prosecuting attorney. Throughout this book, these titles are used interchangeably; the terms district attorneys, DAs, and chief prosecutors refer to head prosecutors in charge of a local prosecuting office.

## Upending the Status Quo

District attorneys wield tremendous power to change our criminal legal system. As its gatekeepers, they exert enormous influence over who comes into the system and every critical decision thereafter—the charges people face, if and how cases proceed, whether mandatory minimum sentences or death sentences (where allowed by law) will be pursued, and the ultimate dispositions of cases. But too often prosecutors have used this discretion to ramp up penalties in response to human struggles that are the manifestation of poverty, substance use disorder, and/or mental health issues.

Elected prosecutors haven't traditionally welcomed the perspectives of, or engaged in meaningful dialogue with, those impacted by the system, most notably people of color and their communities. District attorneys rarely come from these communities; the overwhelming majority of chief prosecutors in the United States have long been middle- and upper-class white men. Not surprisingly, their policies have favored people like them. These paradigms have started to change, particularly since the 2016 elections. A growing number of chief prosecutors are now people of color, women, and others who haven't typically held these positions, and they are driving critical reforms in their jurisdictions.

The leaders who tell their stories in this book are a diverse group.[1] Some grew up poor. Some have had loved ones who were arrested or incarcerated. Some have lost people they cared about to overdose or health problems resulting from substance use. Some have lost family and friends to gun violence. Some have personally experienced violent crime or other trauma. Some have loved ones who grapple with serious mental illness. Some have been arrested. Some used to be public defenders and never worked a day as a prosecutor until they were elected to this office. Some are the descendants of people who were enslaved. Some grew up with parents or other family members who were police officers. These leaders hail from red, blue, and purple states. They represent vastly different jurisdictions, including rural, urban, and suburban areas throughout the country.

They also have a lot in common. They have stood with the Black Lives Matter movement, regardless of their political party, and have called for our nation to reckon with racial injustice.[2] They have banded together to help protect the bedrock of our democratic processes and urge other prosecutors to discontinue practices and policies that have driven mass incarceration. And they have been harshly criticized for voicing and acting on their deeply held principles; some have even been threatened with violence.

These leaders also share a steadfast commitment to changing the status quo. For many of them, this means transforming their offices' culture, enhancing transparency, and embracing prevention-oriented approaches to public safety that are sensible and data-driven. They are rethinking how their jurisdictions prioritize the use of limited resources, often taking less punitive (and less costly) approaches to lower-level charges and focusing instead on preventing and responding to the most serious types of crime. They are adopting restorative justice† approaches, which bring together someone who was harmed and the person responsible for the harm, thereby stressing accountability and often avoiding

---

† Restorative justice "brings together those directly impacted by an act of harm to address the impact of the crime, hold the person who did it accountable, and make things as right as possible for those harmed." See Common Justice, "Restorative Justice: Why Do We Need It?," common justice.org/restorative_justice_why_do_we_need_it; and *Fair and Just Prosecution, Building Community Trust: Restorative Justice Strategies, Principles and Promising Practices*, (San Francisco: Fair and Just Prosecution, 2017), fairandjustprosecution.org/wp-content/uploads/2017/12/FJP.Brief_ .RestorativeJustice.pdf.

not only incarceration but the traditional criminal legal process altogether.

# Capturing the Essence
# of Reform-Minded Leaders

Fair and Just Prosecution (FJP) launched in early 2017 to bring together and support mutual learning among more than a dozen reform-minded DAs. Within five years, that number had grown to more than seventy elected local and state prosecutors who collectively represented about 20 percent of the United States' population. *Change from Within* shares the stories—in words and images—of some of these innovative leaders who are redefining the landscape of prosecution.‡

Thanks to a vibrant partnership between FJP and the public art program Mural Arts Philadelphia—and with the generous support of the Art for Justice Fund—nine artists were selected to create visual works that accompany the first-person stories of the prosecutors profiled in this book.[3] These portrayals were partly in response to each DA's answer to the question "What does justice mean to you?" The artists come from various parts of the United States and work in a broad range of styles and mediums. All of them were once incarcerated, underscoring how important it is to amplify the voices of those who have firsthand knowledge of the system and whose ideas often go unheard or unacknowledged. In many cases the artists' work reflects their personal experience with the criminal legal system, sometimes overtly and sometimes subtly, in ways that may not be obvious to the beholder. Five of the contributors had pieces in the acclaimed 2020–21 MoMA PS1 exhibition *Marking Time: Art in the Age of Incarceration* in New

---

‡ Although we could not include all of those leaders in this book, we have endeavored to feature a representative cross-section of this broad and growing movement.

York City.[4] Many of them are well-known in the art world and
have had their work shown in galleries and museums, as well as
acquired for various collections.[§]

One of the artists is Antonio Howard, who received a life sentence as a juvenile and was able to return to the community at age
forty-one. He describes himself as "shelf-taught": he kept developing as an artist by studying instructional books he bought with
money from selling his paintings.[5] Another participating artist,
Tameca Cole, of Birmingham, Alabama, is on parole after spending more than twenty-five years behind bars. She has written that
the outlet of art gives her the ability and power to show others
"how degrading it feels to be Black in America . . . under systemic
racism."[6] James "Yaya" Hough, also a former "juvenile lifer," was
the first artist in residence at the Philadelphia District Attorney's
Office, through a program sponsored by FJP and Mural Arts with
support from the Art for Justice Fund.[7] Talking about the work he
created as part of that project, he said, "I want people to see themselves reflected in the eyes of the portrait subjects. . . . Whether
we know it or not, we are all justice-impacted."

Like the artists, each prosecutor profiled here has had an exceptional journey, and many threads connect these leaders champi-
oning reform. When the DAs tell their stories, they use words
like *respect*, *accountability*, *compassion*, *dignity*, *fairness*, and *humanity*. They emphasize data-driven and other evidence-based policies and practices and are expanding those capacities in their
offices through online dashboards, the public sharing of information, and other mechanisms that seek to shine a light on what
was previously a black box of prosecutorial decision-making.
They are reconceptualizing how their successes are defined and
measured—downplaying the criteria prosecutors have historically

§  To learn more about the artists and see other images, go to fairandjust
   prosecution.org/ChangeFromWithin.

used that often emphasized sheer volume, such as the number of cases filed, conviction rates, and sentence length. They are creating and adopting metrics that help capture holistic concepts such as community engagement, procedural justice, and racial equity. And they are embracing principles focused on reducing the footprint of the justice system and promoting fairness and accountability.¶

## Rejecting Failed Practices

Research shows that skyrocketing rates of imprisonment in the United States since the 1970s "have had a limited, diminishing effect on crime."[8] Studies have also described the fiscal repercussions of mass incarceration's dwindling returns at the local, state, and federal levels.[9] And in recent years we have seen a growing divide between law enforcement and some communities—particularly communities of color and LGBTQ+ communities—as well as an erosion of trust in the criminal legal system.

Given their immense power, elected prosecutors are well positioned to reform the system. They can improve its fairness, promote racial equity, and prioritize policies and actions that foster the safety and well-being of their communities. Reform-minded prosecutors think about and use their power and discretion in new and different ways, recognizing that mass incarceration is unjust, inhumane, and inequitable, with insidious consequences for individuals, families, and entire communities across generations.

---

¶ Fair and Just Prosecution, Brennan Center for Justice, and The Justice Collaborative, *21 Principles for the 21st Century Prosecutor* (San Francisco: FJP, 2018), fairandjustprosecution.org/staging/wp-content/uploads/2018/12/FJP_21Principles_Interactive-w-destinations.pdf. The prosecutors interviewed for *Change from Within* discussed many of the principles that the 2018 publication emphasizes, among them addressing racial disparity; encouraging the treatment—not criminalization—of mental illness and substance use disorder; treating kids like kids; holding police accountable; and creating effective conviction review units.

The damage that prosecution can do became obvious during the 1980s and 1990s.[10] But by 2016, so had the prospect of chief prosecutors shaking things up. Kim Foxx's victory in the Democratic primary in Chicago that March—and a handful of other local elections around the country that November—signaled a turning point: voters had chosen new leaders who had run for office on a promise of real change.

In addition to aligning on some fundamental principles—including shrinking the justice system's footprint, making communities safer while relying less on incarceration, and advancing transparency and racial equity—these prosecutors also face similar challenges. Each one of them is attempting to push a boulder up a hill, and their jobs can be isolating and lonely, especially for those elected leaders who are people of color, women, or both. As these DAs develop and adopt new strategies to make their criminal legal systems fairer and more equitable, FJP seeks to highlight successful reforms and lessons learned while generating resources to propel broader change in the field.

This progress is powerful but fragile. The outcome of one election can jeopardize a jurisdiction's momentum toward justice. But that fragility challenges us to grapple with how to hard-wire change, quantify the damage done by past practices, and both document and communicate the benefits of reform. And as community members demand bold thinking and the protection of voting rights, these elected leaders are responding. Many DAs have joined with other law enforcement officials in speaking out against states that promote voter suppression.[11] The voice of the people has always been critical to advancing justice—and progress will continue only if communities keep pushing for the basic rights and profound changes we all deserve.

Reformers in this movement are often referred to as *progressive prosecutors*. But that is a misnomer that suggests a political label of *progressive* instead of the more apt focus on *progress*: the essence of reform. This movement is broad and bipartisan. Republicans, conservatives, and others who might not describe themselves as progressive are vital to transforming prosecution and making the criminal legal system smaller, fairer, and more accountable to everyone, including taxpayers. District attorneys with a broad range of political ideologies are rallying around those objectives and the need for transformation.

## Lessons from the Past

I come to this work not only with decades of professional experience, but with a personal desire and drive to make things better. My father and the members of his immediate family survived the Holocaust. They made it through concentration camps, detention camps, and death marches. I bring the perspective of an immigrant; my children are the first generation in my family born in this country. My father ingrained in me the abiding need to work with and for the community, a principle that guided me toward public service and to become a federal prosecutor. But too often I have witnessed a justice system that isn't fair or just. And I know that there is much to learn from history and from mistakes of the past.

In the summer of 2019, FJP staff traveled to Berlin with a group of reform-minded prosecutors. We went to learn from a country that has significantly lower incarceration rates, shorter prison sentences, more humane conditions of confinement, and compassionate, age-appropriate responses to children and young adults—in short, a far less punitive system.

We observed the many ways that German society has acknowledged and confronted its horrendous past. We talked about the parallels between Nazi concentration camps and how people of color have historically been treated in the United States. As part of the trip, we visited the villa in Wannsee, along a picturesque river on the outskirts of West Berlin, where German leaders crafted "the final solution."[12] That site is now a museum, and we used those reminders of the past to embark on a timely and challenging dialogue about the need for prosecutors to be courageous leaders—not simply in the fight for justice reform, but also more broadly as the final bulwark against injustice.

Scholars of the Nazi regime describe the complicity of inaction by judges, lawyers, and other esteemed community members who sat by silently and enabled horrific things to happen. The antidote is *Zivilcourage*, "everyday moral courage," or the willingness to speak out and work to defy injustice, even at personal risk.[13] In the face of unjust laws and our own country's history of atrocities, we are all called to have the *Zivilcourage* to reckon with the past and work toward a more righteous future.

Since that trip, in the tumultuous years that followed in our own nation, many who went with us to Berlin have taken steps to answer that call. In the face of false narratives, disruption of the democratic process, and laws and executive orders attacking people based on their race, ethnicity, country of origin, religion, sexual orientation, or gender identity, reform-minded prosecutors spoke out and took action. They pledged to not enforce biased laws, demanded a transformation of policing, fought to protect immigrants and voting rights, and stood up for the rights of transgender people and reproductive health care choices.[14] They joined millions of demonstrators in calling for racial justice and an end to police violence. Through these and other acts, they helped make their communities fairer, safer, and stronger.

## Looking Forward

It is likely that future election cycles will bring more reform-minded prosecutors into office and into the public eye. While it's impossible to foresee the full trajectory of change that might lie ahead, some things seem likely—or at least we can hope and work for them to come to fruition.

As more DAs push for a smaller, more equitable, and more transparent system, those objectives should become the norm rather than remarkable. Ideally, more voters of every political stripe—and in an even broader spectrum of jurisdictions—will support candidates who have a plan for meaningful change. More prosecutors will leverage their power and focus on how to use their discretion most efficiently to help create a less punitive system that truly promotes justice for all. Some may even join community activists and other reformers who seek to reduce DAs' budgets and invest more in communities instead.

I hope we will see an increasing number of elected prosecutors adopt a philosophy that resembles that of the medical profession: *First and foremost, do no harm.* If the criminal legal system deflects more cases, we may see other systems—including public health and social supports—step up and engage more people who need their services and assistance. I also hope we will see more DAs work to break down barriers and make the system more collaborative and more restorative, with new ways to envision and measure success.

Over time, better data collection and analysis can help guide DAs' offices on what's working and what isn't. Conviction integrity units will continue to remedy past wrongs but should also help improve practices in a way that reduces the chance of unjust convictions happening in the first place. More prosecutors will likely go beyond simply conducting conviction review and establish broader "post-conviction justice" processes that include taking a second look at past extreme sentences. And more DAs will respond to the fact that many crimes occur because of untreated substance use disorders, mental illness, or both—and they will embrace public health approaches rather than punitive ones as a result. Reforms will focus on compassionate, effective, data-driven ways to address the underlying human struggles and conditions involved.

Our country is just beginning a journey toward justice and healing—and transforming prosecution is only one component of what it will take to get there. The personal stories in this book offer both a road map and a vision for the future. They illustrate the power that communities have to put dramatically different leaders in office. These stories highlight the passion and tenacity of prosecutors who are using their power as a tool for decarceration; advancing fairness, justice, and racial equity; and creating healthier and safer communities for everyone. Perhaps most important, these stories offer hope for a more effective and more meaningful way to think about public safety, as exemplified by State's Attorney Kim Foxx's vision of "no more empty porches."

It is inspiring to picture a future where everyone feels safe in their neighborhood—and where racial injustice and mass incarceration are things of the past. It is my hope that these leaders and their stories will help vividly paint that picture.

# 1

# Chesa Boudin

District Attorney, City and County of San Francisco, California

*In November 2019, Chesa Boudin was elected as district attorney for San Francisco. A Rhodes Scholar and a Yale Law School graduate, he worked as a law clerk and a public defender, ultimately leading the bail reform unit of the San Francisco Public Defender's Office. Criminal justice issues are personal to Boudin; both of his parents spent most of his childhood in prison, and when he took office in 2020, his father had been behind bars for more than thirty-eight years. In his campaign for DA, he ran on a platform to end mass incarceration, center crime survivors, and address the root causes of crime. On June 7, 2022, with only about one in four eligible voters in San Francisco weighing in, Boudin was recalled as DA after a campaign financed by a few affluent special interests.*

Luis "Suave" Gonzalez
*Chesa Boudin*, 2021
Mixed media, watercolors, and acrylic

**Luis "Suave" Gonzalez** is a Philadelphia artist and activist who uses acrylics and mixed media to craft pop-style imagery, collages, and murals that address themes of social justice. He spent thirty-one years in prison, and since his release has served as a TED Talk presenter, a Reimagining Reentry Fellow through Mural Arts Philadelphia, an instructor at the University of Pennsylvania, and cohost of the podcast *Death by Incarceration*. For more insight into Suave's work, find him on Instagram: @the_mad_artist_chunky_papi.

## Artist's Statement

*Inspired by the DA's lived experience with the justice system and his mission of reforming the system in San Francisco, I created a lifelike portrait of Chesa Boudin.*

## Steel Gates and Metal Detectors

When I was fourteen months old, my parents dropped me off with the babysitter and went to participate in an armed robbery of a Brinks truck.[1] Even though my parents were merely the unarmed drivers of a getaway car—a switch car—the robbery went terribly wrong, and a security guard was shot and killed. Two police officers were also shot and killed. My parents never came back to pick me up from the babysitter that day. Instead, my mother ended up serving a twenty-two-year prison sentence, and in 1983 my father received a seventy-five-year minimum sentence.

I don't remember that day, that month, or even that year—I was too young. But my earliest memories are of going through steel gates and metal detectors just to be able to see my parents, just to be able to give them hugs. I spent years of my childhood—and now decades of my life—visiting jails and prisons, just to build a relationship with the people who brought me into the world. I saw firsthand the system's failure to rehabilitate people who have committed crimes; its refusal to invest seriously in victim services or healing; its embarrassingly high recidivism rates; and overall, its failure to make our communities safer. From an early age I wanted to fight to ensure that other people like me had access to the same kind of opportunities and second chances I had as a kid. I wanted to make sure that the criminal legal system was better than the one I saw growing up. I wanted to fight to end the system that is appropriately referred to as "mass incarceration."

## Childhood Challenges and One Friend's Very Different Path

Growing up, I encountered a lot of the challenges that many children with incarcerated parents face. I was angry. I was ashamed. I felt unloved and abandoned. Those feelings often manifested in outbursts, social behavioral problems, learning disabilities, and academic delays. I didn't learn to read until I was nine years old, and in seventh grade I got suspended from school for one of those outbursts.

During that time, I met a young man whose obstacles resembled mine but whose path ultimately differed dramatically. I got to know Lorenzo on visits to my mother's prison, as his mother was incarcerated with mine. His mother had been sentenced under New York State's Rockefeller drug laws, convicted of a nonviolent drug offense.* My mother had been convicted of a felony murder—albeit her personal role was nonviolent and unarmed. Our mothers were serving shockingly similar sentences. Lorenzo was a couple of years older than me, and while I was still struggling in school, he'd already found his stride: he was a straight-A student and the star of his public-school basketball team. When I'd get upset during prison visits, my mom would often send Lorenzo to calm me down. I looked up to him. My mom would sometimes say, "Can't you be more like Lorenzo?"

Over the years, thanks to lots of second and third chances, I was able to get on the right track. Ultimately, I was accepted to Yale College. When I was a freshman, I hadn't seen Lorenzo for four or five years. Over time he had stopped visiting his mother, and we had fallen out of contact, lacking easy ways to keep in touch in the days before the internet and email. One day I got a letter from my father, who said he'd just met someone on his cell block who claimed to be a friend of mine. His name was Lorenzo.

I was stunned that someone I looked up to—someone who was as smart and capable and full of potential as me or anyone

---

* These sentencing laws for drug-related convictions were passed in 1973 when Nelson A. Rockefeller was governor. In 2009 the state legislature agreed to repeal the laws. See Jeremy W. Peters, "Albany Reaches Deal to Repeal '70s Drug Laws," *New York Times*, March 25, 2009, https://www.nytimes.com/2009/03/26/nyregion/26rockefeller.html.

else—ended up in the same prison as my father. I was struck by the harsh realities of our legal system. I came to understand the intergenerational cycle of incarceration and the ways in which our nation's addiction to incarceration makes us less safe, not just by destroying families but by creating future crimes and crime victims. It also forced me to reflect on how I had avoided that path. I became aware of the privileges and opportunities that came with my white skin, with being native born, and with being raised by a stable upper-middle-class family. Lorenzo, by contrast, was Black, an immigrant born in South America, and had been raised by a working single grandmother in a poor neighborhood.

Now I am even more aware of how those differences, which were not any fault of his or credit of mine, affected the directions of our lives. I know that had Lorenzo been given the support and second chances I had repeatedly received, he too could have won elected office and had the opportunity to serve his community. But he wasn't given those second chances. So many children in our system are deprived of their parents due to incarceration and, as a result, are deprived of the opportunity to be successful. And that's because of some mistake their parents made and our society's punitive response, a response that typically harms far more than just the person who committed the crime.

## Realizing That Good People Sometimes Do Bad Things

I struggled with a lot of self-blame for what my parents did, and it took me years to learn to forgive them and even to forgive myself. I never would have gotten to that place of forgiveness and restoration and comfort in my own skin if not for the restorative justice† practices my family used during prison visits and phone

---

† Restorative justice "brings together those directly impacted by an act

calls. Early in their time behind bars, both of my parents made a number of core commitments to help restore my trust in them, to help address the damage of their decisions. They committed to being honest and open with me and to always answer my questions, no matter how hard. They put me and my needs first, to the extent that their incarceration allowed. And they modeled good values and behavior: they dedicated their time to helping those around them through AIDS education, violence prevention work, parenting classes, and more.

I got to know my parents, and I got to appreciate both their complexity and their shortcomings. I recognized their tremendous love for me, for each other, and for humanity, but I also understood that they had done something terrible. That understanding, that nuance, eventually made it possible for me to accept that their decision to participate in the crime wasn't my fault. It took me a long time to overcome my shameful and guilty feelings. It took a multidimensional relationship with my parents, one that allowed me to engage with and learn from them and allowed them to try to heal the harm they had caused. If I had cut my parents off out of anger, if we'd been unable to have visits and phone calls, not only would I still be burdened by resentment and bitterness and anger toward them, but there's no way I would have made it into Yale College or Yale Law School. The challenges I faced as a kid were so great that they would have been insurmountable had I not come to terms with the truth that my parents weren't evil people, but that sometimes, good people

---

of harm to address the impact of the crime, hold the person who did it accountable, and make things as right as possible for those harmed." See Common Justice, "Restorative Justice: Why Do We Need It?," common justice.org/restorative_justice_why_do_we_need_it; and *Fair and Just Prosecution, Building Community Trust: Restorative Justice Strategies, Principles and Promising Practices*, (San Francisco: Fair and Just Prosecution, 2017), fairandjustprosecution.org/wp-content/uploads/2017/12/FJP.Brief_ .RestorativeJustice.pdf.

do bad things. That's part of life, that is part of the world we live in. What's important is how we respond, how we repair the harm that's been done. We can move on; we can move forward together.

## Seeing Justice Abroad

My life gave me space for reflection in other ways as well. I've been lucky to travel, live, and study abroad, including in England, Venezuela, and Chile. I've visited jails, juvenile detention centers, and prisons in nearly a dozen countries. I came to understand that the rule of law is fragile, and that in the United States there is far more respect for the rule of law and faith in the judicial process than in many other parts of the world. At the same time, our country spends exorbitant resources on a wide-reaching, punishment-focused legal system that bears little resemblance to the systems in other countries. The United States has a unique dedication to extreme punishment; in other parts of the Western world, things like solitary confinement and the death penalty and life without the possibility of parole are exceedingly rare.[2] All the while, our crime rates, including violent crime rates, have tended to be higher.[3]

Having seen different approaches in other countries—sometimes born out of corruption or bureaucratic ineptitude, and sometimes because of intentional value-driven choices—I know that we stand out as the only country with the ability to and the interest in spending as much as we do on incarceration. In the state of California, for example, about 10 percent of the general fund budget goes to the prison system. That's unthinkable in other parts of the world, and it is a tremendously flawed approach to public safety. We need to invest in prevention because it is more effective, more cost-efficient, and more humane.

# The System's Revolving Door

Shortly after law school I joined the San Francisco Public Defender's Office, where I spent five years representing clients in cases ranging from low-level misdemeanors to violent felonies. One of the things I saw play out over and over again was how the system is set up to ensure that people who get arrested fail. Rather than promoting individual change, helping people secure jobs, or rehabilitating them, our system does the opposite.

I saw a system that was totally uneven: the odds were stacked. The laws and practices were set up to presume guilt and perpetuate punishment. And they did so without one iota of empirical evidence that more time behind bars heals victims, deters future crime, or even rehabilitates the people who committed a crime. I saw a jail that was—and sadly, still is—San Francisco's number-one provider of mental health services, and I represented people who desperately needed housing and therapy, but instead were treated with cages and handcuffs.

I grew close to some of the individuals caught up in that system. Some of them—called "frequent fliers" by court staff—return again and again with case after case, all of the courtroom players fully aware that whether they're convicted or acquitted, the root cause that led to their arrest will remain untreated. In the courtroom, the sad reality remained unsaid: our city was willing to spend around $250 per night to jail people, but somehow lacked the resources to find them housing when they were released or treatment to recover or case management to help them get on their feet.

Being a public defender reinforced what I had learned from my own life experience visiting my parents in prison: that people who have done bad things are more than their worst mistake. No one should be defined by one crime, one struggle, or one

challenging period in their life. With the right supports, structures, and opportunities, most people can overcome hardship and
succeed. But sadly, once people become entangled in our justice system, the chances decrease of them ever being able to hold
down a job, be attentive parents, or achieve stability. This lack of
security leads people to commit crimes—and the cycle continues.

## The Human Faces of Our Systemic Failures

As a public defender I encountered countless people and stories
that shed light on the failings of our system: problems with overpolicing in poor neighborhoods, the criminalization of poverty,
the misguided choice to invest in cages rather than communities. Back when I was primarily handling misdemeanors, I was
assigned to represent a young man who was smart, quirky, and
thoughtful, but also struggled with serious lifelong behavioral
health issues. He would fixate on certain places like shopping
malls or local swimming pools or restaurants. For hours on end,
he would just hang out in front of those places, sometimes star-
ing at people. He wasn't violent, he wasn't dangerous, he wasn't
committing crimes, but he made people uncomfortable, and too
often the response was to call the police. He would get arrested
for something like trespassing, and the businesses would use that
arrest to obtain a stay-away order. So the next time he went there,
they could immediately call the police and he would be arrested
again.

Over the years, he racked up hundreds of arrests for things that
had nothing to do with legitimate public safety or criminal activity and everything to do with his mental health struggles. But our
society lacked the tools, the creativity, and even the willingness
to engage with this young man in any other way. I saw him come
in and out of the jail over and over again. I struggled to figure out
what it would take to get through to him—and to get through

to the judges, prosecutors, and police officers who repeated the same responses over and over, as if this time there would be a different result. Ultimately, we did have a breakthrough with him because we found a phenomenal case manager to aid him in obtaining mental health services. Those services, combined with some care and compassion, helped this young man finally change his behavior.

My passion for bail reform was also reinforced by specific clients. I once represented a young man charged with felony car theft, and when I first reviewed the file before I met him, it looked like a watertight case. There was video footage of the incident; the car owner witnessed the car drive off; and an additional eyewitness identified my client as the driver of the stolen car. When the police found the car, my client was sitting in the passenger seat—and he had previously been arrested and convicted for stealing a car.

Based on all of that, the judge refused to let my indigent client out and set bail higher than he could possibly afford. When I told my client that he couldn't go home to his family, he implored me to find a way to have him released. He explained that he had a daughter and a girlfriend, and that he needed to be there for them. He had been through the system enough to know that prosecutors are often willing to let someone out if they plead guilty to a serious crime, so he asked me, "Can I plead guilty to a strike?"‡ Bewildered, I said to him, "You're not even charged with a strike—just with stealing a car." He responded, "I know the prosecutor can add a strike, I don't care, tell them they can add a strike and I'll plead to it if I can go home to my family."

---

‡ In California, a strike is typically a conviction for a violent or other "serious" felony. Conviction of a strike results in lifelong consequences, including the possible doubling of all future felony sentences. See "California's Three Strikes Sentencing Law," California Judicial Branch, California Courts, courts.ca.gov/20142.htm.

Luckily, that didn't happen; my investigator found a copy of the video footage and it showed a woman stealing the car—not my client, a man. Ecstatic, I showed my client the video and exclaimed, "Look, you're going home. The case is going to be dismissed." And I asked, "But why wouldn't you tell me you were innocent? Why were you willing to plead guilty not only when you were wrongly accused, but of something even more serious than that?" He said something that has haunted me ever since: "That's how the system works for people like me. I don't have faith that because I'm innocent I'm going to get out. My most likely path to freedom was being willing to plead guilty." He was not wrong. That *is* how the criminal legal system works; that's how it's set up. Without that video, he very likely would have been wrongly convicted, simply because he was too poor to buy his freedom.

## An Unlikely Candidate

The Chesa Boudin who graduated from law school never could have imagined running for district attorney, and the Chesa Boudin who started off as a San Francisco public defender couldn't have imagined even *working* in the San Francisco District Attorney's Office, much less leading it. But I evolved over the years. I grew increasingly frustrated by many of the cases I saw, cases that revealed the broad failings of the legal system. I became disheartened by my own inability as a public defender to change systemic dysfunction. I realized that I could spend my entire career as a public defender and probably serve only five- or ten-thousand people. And I knew that prosecutors have far more power than any defense attorney ever holds. As a public defender you can have an impact on your clients' lives, but your job is to advocate for one person at a time, one case at a time. I recognized that as district attorney I'd be making policies that would affect the entire city and county of San Francisco.

Meanwhile, from coast to coast, from north to south, in places like Philadelphia and Boston and Chicago and so many others, I watched a new generation of prosecutors win their elections and use their positions to change this horribly abusive, unjust system.[4] They did things like committing publicly to reducing the number of people locked up and stopping prosecution of drug possession and working to reduce racial disparities—and they implemented policies consistent with that vision and those values. It was the first time in my life that there was a broad national consensus that the status quo approach to criminal justice—the so-called "tough on crime" perspective—was failing us: it was undermining safety, bankrupting local governments, starving schools and public health budgets, and ignoring the needs of survivors of crime. I wanted to be a part of the movement for change. I wanted to jump in—relying on my life experience and my career as a public defender—to find ways to reinvent this country's approach to crime and punishment.

This epiphany of sorts happened to coincide with the first time in over a hundred years that there was no incumbent running for reelection as the San Francisco district attorney. It was a wide-open race. In January 2019 I announced my candidacy. Eleven months later, in a hard-fought ranked-choice vote—following an election that included around $700,000 in attack ads against me by police unions and a mayor who appointed my opponent as interim DA just weeks before the election—I was elected.

The decision to run had been monumental for me, not only because it meant switching from being a public defender to being a prosecutor, but because of its implications for my fiancée (now my wife), my parents, and my whole family. We had many long, difficult conversations before I made the decision. One of those

conversations was during a prison visit to my father in upstate
New York. We sat across a visiting-room table from each other
one day in the fall of 2018, and I told him that I was considering
a career change. He was curious and wondered if I was going to
do something like work for the ACLU or Civil Rights Corps, an
amazing nonprofit where I had been founding chairman of the
board.

When I told him that I was thinking of running for district
attorney, he was genuinely surprised. His first concern was about
my fiancée and me, and whether this would be compatible with
our lives, whether it would be possible to do this in a way we felt
comfortable. He was also concerned about the extent to which
the system might change me or present insurmountable challenges. He said that although he had great faith in my work ethic,
my intelligence, and my values, he had less faith in any one person's ability to change practices so deeply ingrained in the system. So he worried about me. Ultimately, he was supportive—as
he always has been. I believe the fact that I was able to be fully
transparent and honest during my campaign about what I hoped
to accomplish was a testament both to the values of the people I
serve in San Francisco and to the broader conversation we're having nationally about what effective leadership looks like.

## Changing Practice and Policy in the DA's Office

I've been in office since January 2020, a year that presented
challenges I never could have anticipated. Despite all the obstacles, I am proud of what we have accomplished already. One
of the first things I did when I took office was to establish an
across-the-board, no-exceptions policy that prohibited my staff
from asking for money bail. As a local prosecutor, I don't have
the power to rewrite and entirely eliminate money bail from the

California Penal Code, but I do have the power—and I require my staff—to exercise our prosecutorial discretion in not seeking bail under any circumstances. Doing so promotes justice: money bail is a system that undermines public safety and makes a mockery of the promise of equal protection under the law. It's a system that allows the wealthy to buy their way out of jail, no matter how dangerous they are, no matter how serious the charges of which they're accused, no matter how many prior convictions they have, or how imminent a threat they may pose to the public. But poor people—even when accused of minor offenses like trespassing or shoplifting, regardless of whether they are facing a weak case and have a family at home depending on them—are forced to languish behind bars simply because of their poverty. In short, bail has no place in any criminal system we refer to as *just*.

I instructed my staff not to request money bail. I explained that we would replace a wealth-based system of pretrial incarceration with a risk-based system, one that looks at ways we can mitigate risk, respect the presumption of innocence, and honor this country's fundamental right to liberty. We would ask a court to hold somebody in custody only in those narrow circumstances when there are no conditions or combinations of conditions that can reasonably protect the public. For those cases, it shouldn't matter how much money the defendant or their family has.

We've also changed our approach to dealing with people who engage in misconduct. I've put in place a wide range of policies that focus on the most serious crimes—and allow us to be proportionate in our approach to punishment. For example, we know the justice system is rife with racial bias at every step of the process, and I don't want my office or my charging decisions to exacerbate racial disparities. More than two decades of data show that the San Francisco Police Department disproportionally stops and searches Black and brown motorists. The disparities are greater in San Francisco on a per capita basis than in virtually any other part of California. Yet despite numerous reports, a Department of Justice investigation, and a blue-ribbon panel, the police department didn't change its policies or its practices—and those statistics only seemed to get worse. So in February 2020, after only a month in office, we announced a policy declining to prosecute contraband criminal cases stemming from pretextual traffic stops.§ We refuse to be complicit in encouraging or signing off on racial profiling.

State law allows for increased penalties for so-called "gang enhancements," widely known to be racist laws that target men of color. It also allows for prison sentences to be doubled or even increased to life sentences for people with certain serious or violent prior convictions. In February 2020, I announced a policy that we would focus on holding people accountable *only* for the conduct in the case at hand, rather than also considering sentencing enhancements like gang enhancements or "strikes," which punish people for conduct they have already been punished for.¶ In practice, that means if someone is charged with a crime and there's an enhancement based on their conduct in this crime— such as the use of a gun or committing a hate crime—we would still charge those conduct enhancements. But if they've already

---

§ "A 'pretext' or 'pretextual' stop and search occurs when a law enforcement officer detains a person for a minor offense (i.e., traffic or other infraction) because the officer seeks to investigate the person for potential involvement in another, unrelated crime (i.e., drug possession). . . . The use of pretext stops was sanctioned by the Rehnquist Supreme Court in the 1996 *Whren* decision. *Whren v. United States* (1996) 517 U.S. 806. Justice Ginsburg has . . . suggested that it may be appropriate to reevaluate *Whren* in light of the criticism that the decision promotes improper police arbitrariness." For more, see "Policy Directive: San Francisco District Attorney's Office, Declination of Contraband Charges Based on Pretextual Stops," sfdistrictattorney.org/wp-content/uploads/2020/11/Declination-of-Contraband-Charges-Based-on-Pretextual-Stops.pdf.

¶ Status sentencing enhancements refer to circumstances such as a prior criminal record or alleged gang membership that could allow prosecutors to increase the penalties an individual faces for committing a new, often unrelated, offense.

been sentenced, we would not double or triple that sentence (as the Three Strikes law calls for). We know how ineffective prison is at rehabilitation; when people go to prison, about two-thirds of them will end up back there again. So we would focus on holding them accountable for what they've done, not what they were previously punished for—not who they are, not what neighborhood they grew up in, not their race.

## Enforcing the Law Equally

We've also implemented bold reforms to hold police accountable. I ran my campaign with a commitment to enforce the law equally, and that means approaching incidents in which police violate the law with the same level of scrutiny and severity as any other violation or crime. Sadly, that's not the reality in most parts of this country. The need for this approach became even clearer in light of the killing of George Floyd just a few months into my first term.

Converting that commitment into reality took a lot of work. There are tremendous obstacles to equal enforcement of the law when it comes to police officers. In November 2020, I announced manslaughter charges against a San Francisco police officer who shot and killed an unarmed Black man in 2017. As far as anyone is aware, it was the first time that an on-duty police officer here was charged with homicide. Although police have a very difficult—sometimes impossible—job, when they abuse the trust we place in them, they must be held accountable.

I know police officers are forced to make quick decisions about use of force and that they are often injured on the job; not every use of deadly force is criminal, of course. It is therefore also important to me to exonerate officers who did not break the law. Accordingly, in December 2020, we announced the decision not to prosecute three officers who had used lethal force earlier that year: two officers who shot and killed a suspect and another officer who shot at—but missed—a suspect who was charging at him with a screwdriver.[5] We made that decision because—from looking at video footage and through interviews with witnesses—we believe that while lots of things could have been done differently, and hopefully will be next time, under the circumstances it was lawful for the police to use lethal force in self-defense. I don't make these charging decisions lightly, and I know they will always be scrutinized and criticized, so I stick to what I promised the voters: to enforce the laws equally, no matter what.

Police prosecutions are only a small piece of our police accountability work. We have also worked on numerous internal policy directives—for example, to prevent the filing of cases that rely on the testimony of officers who have prior serious misconduct charges, or that involve resisting arrest charges, without reviewing all available evidence first. We've engaged in external legislative advocacy to prevent prosecutors from accepting law enforcement union money and to compensate victims of police violence like any other crime victim. We have much work to do in San Francisco and as a nation to truly address the systemic racism in our policing, and I am committed to doing that work.

## A Sense of Urgency

As a candidate for district attorney, I focused on what I would do differently: changes to my office, to policies, and to staff. Of course, I didn't think nearly enough about how the job would change me. There is a profound difference in the way I approach a case as a district attorney from the way I did when I was a public defender. As a public defender my ethical obligation was just to that one client, to fight for what was best for them. As district attorney, I am constantly trying to balance competing interests, trying to make sense of this term we call *justice* and ensure that I am pursuing it, not just for the person who was harmed by crime or the person accused of crime, but for all of us who live in the spectacular city and county of San Francisco. To me, justice means fairness and equality and consistency and predictability. In the context of criminal cases, justice means hearing and caring for the people who have been harmed and ensuring that the people who caused that harm are held accountable, not simply punished. We must recognize the full humanity of every single person connected to or caught up in the justice system.

The work is challenging. It's sometimes depressing and frustrating. I know that we don't have the tools, resources, or knowledge to solve every problem, that we can't bring back people who have been killed. I find the job changing me in ways that I hope are mostly for the better, as I think about difficult issues from new perspectives and grapple with steep learning curves and challenges. I try to be vigilant against the easy and constant temptation to fall into the status quo approach to doing business. The system is set up in and has long operated in a particular way. We're trying to fundamentally change it to be more effective at promoting justice. I confront constant resistance to change—bureaucratic, institutional, legal, financial. I want to keep the sense of urgency that I had on day one in office, and I do that by surrounding myself with mission-driven staff, by being personally involved in the day-to-day details of cases, and by staying connected to the communities I serve.

## The New Generation of DAs

I also stay connected with other people who have jobs like mine. The other people who are part of this movement have become friends, mentors, mentees, and allies. They are a source of inspiration, of creativity, of advice, even of laughter. In many ways we are a family and we're there for each other; we've been through similar challenges. We've all gotten the hate mail and the death threats. We've all had folks within our own offices try to undermine and sabotage us. We all struggle with tremendous amounts of misinformation and disinformation about the work we're doing and the status quo we inherited. So it's essential that we do this work together and not be isolated or divided. It's essential that we point to successes in other jurisdictions—for example, in Vermont, where Chittenden County State's Attorney Sarah Fair George recently eliminated cash bail.[6] Successes like that remind us that this is doable, that bold reforms are possible.

Others say, "We can accomplish this if they did it in San Francisco," and then, in turn, I can look at Philadelphia or Chicago and say, "Well, if State's Attorney Kim Foxx [in Cook County, Illinois] can publish all this data and be this transparent with her case-filing information, then we can do the same thing in San Francisco."[7] When naysayers try to cut us off at the pass before we implement a new policy, it's invaluable to be able to refer to other places that have already gone down that road and done it successfully, and in ways that allow us to measure the benefits to public safety.

Having a network of like-minded prosecutors has allowed us to create a safe community, to share ideas and fears, to talk about things we're considering trying, and to learn best practices from each other. We are able to create the kind of support that's typically really evasive when you're in these unique roles—being the head of an office, elected to a role that has historically been defined by how many people you've sent to prison. We're all trying to do the job better and differently and more humanely, and we often come under horrific attack because of that courage. But at least we have each other.

# Confronting a Pandemic, Systemically and Personally

Because I recognize so many of the ways in which mass incarceration undermines public safety, I campaigned on a platform of ending it. But even after a lifetime of visiting jails and prisons, it wasn't until the COVID-19 pandemic that I came to fully appreciate how connected our criminal legal system is to our public health system. I lived every day of 2020 with anxiety for myself, my wife, my extended family, friends, staff, and the people of San Francisco, but especially for my father.

Like so many millions of people behind bars in this country, in prison my father didn't have access to hygiene tools or the social distancing practices that have become normal for many of us. He didn't have access to good health care when he got sick. He didn't have access to easy or regular COVID-19 testing. And even though he turned 76 in 2020, he was tested only once that year, despite the fact that people in the cell next to him tested positive, and that he's in a high-risk group because of other underlying medical conditions. And 2020 was the only year of my life when I didn't see my father. I think about how isolating and frightening the pandemic has been for all of us, but how that is magnified and amplified for people who are incarcerated, especially with conditions that not only make it more likely that they get sick, but make it less likely that they'll get the help they need if they do get sick.

## Achieving the Impossible

My whole life, I thought that my father would likely die in prison, even though he never had a single disciplinary violation on his record. He conducted lifesaving work around AIDS education and anti-violence training. He was a mentor to generations of younger people in prison, many of whom are now out and living productive lives. In 2020, we asked Governor Cuomo of New York to consider granting my father clemency, reducing his sentence, and allowing him to come home and spend his last years with us. On Christmas Eve 2020, our request was denied.

Eight months later, on August 23, 2021—Governor Cuomo's last day in office—I woke up and said to my wife, "Today is the day: either my dad gets a shot at freedom or we've hit a dead end. I'm feeling optimistic." I was working from home via Zoom and kept obsessively refreshing the governor's press page, looking for new announcements about clemency. I was in the middle of a meeting when my phone lit up: my mom. I sent it to voicemail and texted her: "I'm in a meeting, what's up?" She wrote back immediately: "David's sentence was commuted, he's going to the parole board!"[8] I tried to return to the meeting, but it was impossible. I apologized to the folks on the call, left the Zoom, and ran down the hall to my wife's office, screaming out the news. We fell into each other's arms, called my mom, and just sat there, the three of us, weeping in silence.

Governor Cuomo's decision only made my father *eligible* for parole. In October 2021, he was interviewed for about five hours by members of the New York State Board of Parole. We knew we would get a decision any day. On Tuesday, October 26, I was in a meeting in a downtown San Francisco coffee shop. As it ended, I looked at my phone and saw a number of missed calls from my mom. I called her back, still alongside my team. As soon as my mom answered, she blurted out, "He made his board! He's coming home!" I yelled out loud, "YES!" That my father was coming home felt like a massive weight lifted off my shoulders.[9] It felt like a testament to our collective perseverance and strength. It felt like we had achieved the impossible by sheer force of will and determination—it felt like a dream come true. In some ways it was a gradual process: clemency, then parole hearing, then parole decision, then release, all spaced out by weeks or months. In other ways, after forty years of incarceration, of assuming that my father would die behind bars, after a lifetime of thinking that hope was in vain, it seemed to happen suddenly.

When we got the news of his release date, I immediately flew to New York on a red-eye and made it just in time to meet my mother and go to his approved parole address with a bouquet of flowers. We waited for him to get processed out of the parole office in downtown Manhattan, looking eagerly at every approaching car. Eventually, a black car with government plates pulled onto the sidewalk to avoid blocking traffic. My mom and I ran out of the lobby as my father stepped toward us. We all burst into tears in a group hug in the chilly November morning air. When we pulled ourselves together, my mother said to him, "You made it. You made it home." And then I spent three days with my father in freedom. For the next trip? My wife and I plan to fly out with our baby, our first. What a miracle to be able to introduce my son to my father, not in a prison but in a home. And I still have to fight back tears every time I think to myself: *my father somehow made it to the age of 77, through 14,615 days in prison, in maximum security. He made it, he survived, he is home.*

Reentry after incarceration is incredibly challenging. In many ways, the longer you're in, the harder the transition. For more than forty years my father has not been allowed to touch a door-knob or a key or currency; he has not been allowed to use the bathroom behind closed doors or go see a doctor when he has felt ill. While he was gone, the world changed dramatically. When he was arrested there was no such thing as a CD or a cell phone or the internet or an electric car. He is experiencing a rebirth of sorts, but in the body of a seventy-seven-year-old man who has had every aspect of his life controlled and monitored for the past four decades. My father is lucky to have a strong, broad network of family and friends who are totally dedicated to supporting him. And yet it is overwhelming, even as we are overjoyed; it is exhausting, even as we are exuberant; it is impossible, even as we are inspired. My father can't go back and make up for all he has missed. Instead, he can put one foot in front of the other and simply appreciate freedom in every moment of every day.

# 2

# Satana Deberry

District Attorney, Durham County, North Carolina

*Satana Deberry grew up in Richmond County, North Carolina. Her parents instilled in her the value of education and helped guide her to attend Princeton University and Duke University School of Law. After a brief stint working in the federal government in Washington, DC, she returned to North Carolina, where she worked as a criminal defense attorney in her hometown of Hamlet, as general counsel for the state's Department of Health and Human Services, and as executive director for Habitat for Humanity of Durham and the nonprofit North Carolina Housing Coalition. In 2018, local advocates urged her to run for district attorney of Durham County. Since winning that race, Deberry has continued fighting for justice and equality for poor people, communities of color, and other historically excluded groups.*

Jared Owens
*Satana in Situ*, 2021
Acrylic and paper on panel

**Jared Owens** is a New York–based multidisciplinary artist whose practice focuses on bringing awareness to the plight of nearly 2.5 million people who are enmeshed in the U.S. carceral state. He is self-taught during more than eighteen years of incarceration, working in painting, sculpture, and installation, using materials and references culled from penal matter.

## Artist's Statement

*The piece depicts Satana Deberry in her work space, surrounded by books. I used her quotes because to me they are powerful affirmations of her intent as a district attorney attempting to make positive change in the justice system.*

# What It Means to Be
# the Black Mother of Black Kids

It is not insignificant, doing what I do while knowing the jeopardy that Black kids are in. I have three teenagers. During my campaign, I talked a lot about being the Black mother of Black children, because it really does inform how you see the world. You have to think about so many things when you're the parent of children who—if they get pulled over—anything could happen to them.

As DA, I have a specialized license plate so that not everybody can see my information through DMV records. But that means I can't let my kids drive my car. It puts them at risk, because if they are being kids and are speeding or get in an accident—and police run my plates—it could put my kids in even bigger jeopardy because an officer may think they stole the car. I think about what could happen if my kids do get involved in something.

My kids campaigned with me, so they learned a lot about the criminal legal system. For my youngest child, it mobilized her to be more active. She went on to sit on the Youth Steering Committee for the Southern Coalition for Social Justice and is on the county youth advisory board.[1] I'm glad she speaks up. As I tell my daughters, "Closed mouths don't get fed. Women are taught to infer things and not to directly advocate for themselves. You are your best advocate, so be that."

When the protests were happening after George Floyd's murder in 2020, my youngest wanted to be involved. Most of the protests were in Raleigh, and she participated. My daughter was fourteen and she got tear-gassed. She FaceTimed me and was crying, because the tear gas makes your eyes water. Her eyes were watering, her voice was shaking, and her camera was facing the wrong way for most of the conversation. All I saw was smoke and people running. Any mother would have felt fear, but as the mother of a Black kid, it was even worse. At the time, I was post-ing on Facebook, and I got such hate back. The things people said about my kid—it was horrible. And then every day I work with law enforcement as the DA. Every day.

I see a lot of horrible things in this job. I'm never going to say that bad things do not happen, that human beings don't do bad things to each other. We do some horrible things to each other. But that's not mostly what I see. Mostly I see folks who, since they were my daughters' ages or younger, were involved in little things that make it hard for them to *not* get involved in bigger things. As a Black person, I feel as if I literally see those bigger things in every file. I see my kids—and what would happen if they made one or two mistakes or grew up in a different neighborhood.

## Entering a Different World

When I was in high school, I spent one summer at Governor's School at St. Andrew's College in Laurinburg, North Carolina, and they had a big college fair for all the kids.[2] I was about to be a junior, so none of the recruiters were really talking to me. They would kind of shoo me along and tell me to "reach out when you're a senior." So I was waiting for my roommate, and the per-son next to me was an admissions officer for Princeton. She asked me about myself, and we talked for a bit. I come from a family with a long history of going to college, so I knew I'd go too, but at that point all colleges were the same to me. She encouraged me to consider coming to Princeton and promised to send me some information about the school. When I got back home at the end of the summer she'd written me a note, and for the next year and a half we stayed in touch.

I remember distinctly that the application fee for Princeton was $45. Everywhere else it was $15. My parents were public school teachers, so they said I could apply to Princeton or to three other schools. I wrote the admissions officer a note and said thank you, but the application fee is too much. She waived the fee. That should've been a clue about the type of world I was about to walk into, but I didn't think about it that way. I ended up getting in, and my financial aid package made it cheaper for me to go to Princeton than to any other school—even one in my state. I showed up at Princeton in the fall of 1987, sight unseen. Taking me to college became our family vacation that year; it took us a week to drive up the East Coast.

Princeton was a different world. I didn't really understand privilege yet—that's part of being young—but it was a very different place from where I'd come from. Princeton has this reputation for being the most Southern of the Ivies. There's certainly a tradition of the planter class sending their sons there. But as somebody who came from the South, it was not a very Southern place to me. I remember getting there, and I would say "Hey" to everybody I saw, and they would look at me like I was crazy.

It was cold, very cold. I didn't have the right clothes; I didn't have hardly anything. There were kids from places I'd never heard of—Andover or Sidwell Friends—that were feeding people to the Ivy League. I didn't have the background that they had, but I was prepared for the classroom. And I worked a ton of jobs. The 1990s TV show *In Living Color* had a skit with a family called the Hedleys. They were West Indian and they worked all the time—that was the joke; even the little kids had like five jobs—and so all my friends at Princeton called me a Hedley. I literally worked my way through college. I bought the clothes on my back and everything else. In that sense, I was different, but I was always competitive in the classroom. It was always where I excelled.

## An Unexpected Trajectory

When I was young, I never had any intention of becoming a lawyer. From the time I was five, if anybody asked me what I was going to do, I told them I was going to be a pediatric surgeon. All through high school, I took all of the STEM classes available.[3] But when I got to college, I ran into organic chemistry, which I think is everybody's story as to why they're not a doctor!

At that point I didn't know what I was going to do. But I had taken this course called "The Social Basis of Individual Behavior," the introductory sociology class at Princeton. Howard Taylor was the professor, and he was kind of mythological among the Black students on campus.[4] He was very fair-skinned, he had blue eyes, and, at the time, blond hair. After the deadline had passed to drop the class, he would announce to everybody that he was Black, and all the white students—their jaws would drop. I had signed up just to see that show, but that class completely changed the course of my career. It changed how I thought of myself and the world around me.

I had really deep roots in the South. I had grown up in Hamlet, North Carolina, a small town in Richmond County. It was a railroad town, and I had one grandfather who was a Pullman porter on the railroad. Both of my parents were teachers and went to historically Black colleges and universities. But even though I had these roots growing up in a historically Black community in the South, where my family had been for generations—both sides had been enslaved there—race and class and ethnicity had never really struck me until I took that class. It was then, once I took Professor Taylor's class, that I started to realize not only the influence race had played in my life, but how the fact that my parents and grandparents had gone to school placed us in a socioeconomic class that affected the opportunities I had.

There are all these external forces impacting our lives that are wholly out of our control. Especially when you're a smart kid, you think you're the one doing all the work; you think you're succeeding only because of *you*. In that class, I learned that a lot happened in the past four hundred years that allowed me to be successful, just as a lot happened in the past four hundred years that made me less successful than I could have been.

That experience had me thinking about what I wanted to do in the world. And then I went to Yale with a friend who was on the debate team. It turns out that debates are boring, but Yale Law School was fascinating. Before the internet, you would learn about what was happening on campus through the bulletin boards. As I was walking around Yale, I saw so much interesting information and so many opportunities posted on these bulletin boards. I was fascinated.

It was those experiences that led me to become a lawyer: the combination of that sociology class and seeing law school as a place where I could bring all these concepts together and move the world forward.

## Looking for a Place to Thrive

After Princeton, I went to law school at Duke, which was very corporate at that time. Everybody went from law school either to a clerkship or to New York or DC for a big firm job. My first and second summers I tried the big firm thing and, unsurprisingly, hated it. Those firms still aren't diverse places, but in the early and mid-1990s they *really* weren't. At almost every firm where I clerked, all the cleaning staff in the buildings knew me. I'd find that the Black person who cleaned my office would always be helpful. Everyone in my office would ask, "How do you know this person?" And I'd respond, "This is the only person in the building who talks to me." The partners didn't, the other lawyers and law students didn't. But the cleaning staff did.

That also served as one of my first lessons in being a lawyer—always be nice to the administrative and cleaning staff, because they know everything. I would literally hear things that were going to happen to me from them. It made me realize this was not an atmosphere where I would thrive.

After law school I ended up in DC, working in the federal government. And I ran into many of the same problems: lawyers of color were few and far between. So I came back home, where a good friend and I decided to start our own firm. Though she had some clients she brought from her former firm, I didn't. Somebody told me that if I went down to the courthouse and put my name on a list, I would get clients. And it was true: it was a list of people who were charged with crimes and needed court-appointed lawyers because they couldn't afford one. That's how I got my first clients.

Those were informative years. I was representing people I knew from the community. I was in my late twenties and I have younger siblings, so there was about a ten-year age range of folks we grew up with who were coming through criminal court. Because I knew these people and knew their lives, I didn't think of any of them as criminals. I didn't think of them as bad people. While I was at Princeton and Duke building my life, their lives were sinking. They didn't have access to education, there were no jobs, some of them started selling drugs or became substance users and sold drugs for the purpose of continuing their habit. Just person after person after person.

By the time they got to me, bad things in their lives had already happened and put them on this trajectory. I knew that maybe this time I'd keep them out of prison, but there would probably be a next time, because we had done nothing to address their underlying challenges. I ended up leaving that work because it was just demoralizing to see people I knew in that situation.

## Housing Advocacy and a Snarl of Systems

My law partner was mostly a real estate attorney. She was working with Black churches, and church members would often seek her out because they were facing foreclosure or eviction. She didn't do that type of work, but I figured I could learn it—and that was my introduction to housing issues. I started doing foreclosure pre-vention a decade before the housing crisis really happened. From there I went to the North Carolina Department of Health and Human Services, another place where all these systems—the legal system, child welfare, the health department, and so on—are at play in the lives of low-income people and communities of color. I had also joined the board of Habitat for Humanity of Durham, and when the executive director stepped down, I filled that role while they searched for a permanent director.

I really loved housing work. It brought all of my expertise together, and I felt as if I was actually doing something for people. Every day on my way home now, I drive past houses that I helped build, and that's a satisfying and fulfilling feeling. Back then, I was working with community organizations and nonprofits, and all these people were starting to tie their work together. Afford-able housing advocates were starting to understand that there are all these rules that keep people out, and community activists were starting to understand that banks were writing huge loans for white people and none for Black and brown people. Their communities were steadily degrading because people couldn't get home equity and couldn't build businesses. And they couldn't do that because of the criminal legal system, because of credit scores, and because of how developers decide where to develop. It was all of those things and more. It was everywhere—and still is.

Around this time, Nia Wilson, who runs an organization that hires people impacted by the criminal legal system to work in the community, contacted me and told me she'd been working with folks to try to reform that system.[5] They'd gotten pretty far with law enforcement, with the judges, with city and county people, but they could not get the local district attorney to talk to them. So they decided to try to replace him. I asked her how I could help, and she said, "I need you to run."

At first, I said no. It was like that Meatloaf song: "I would do anything for love, but I won't do that." Emily's List says that you have to ask women seven times before they actually run.[6] I don't know how many times they asked me, but it was a lot. Finally, they convinced me.

## Difficult Decisions and Tough Conversations

It turns out that the most difficult aspect of this job—it was true on my first day and continues to be the most difficult thing—is that almost everybody I prosecute is Black. Of course, I knew this before, but as a defense attorney, you just have your clients. You don't have *everybody*. You don't get the bird's-eye view of all the cases. Once I became responsible for every criminal case in Durham County, I saw just how many of the defendants were Black. For example, almost all the kids on our juvenile caseload are Black.[7] That is stunning. I'm still not used to it, and I hope I never will be.

A lot of our victims are also Black, so it is really difficult to be out in your community saying, "We've got to change the way we prosecute." We focus on the least among us: the most vulnerable, the people who have the least money, the people who have substance use problems and other health problems. And on the other side, the victims, the survivors—they look exactly the same. That's really difficult.

It can also be extremely difficult to talk with victims' families, especially when they don't agree with our approach. In 2015, a Muslim couple and the wife's sister were murdered in their apartment.[8] It was long before I took office, but the case was still open when I took over. It was one of the oldest cases in the office at the time, and I had run on closing homicide cases that had been open for years. We had to resolve it, but the Durham District Attorney's Office had announced its intention to seek the death penalty. At this point the family was on their second DA. They'd had different assistant district attorneys, plus the FBI and a U.S. Attorney, and all of them had said they were going to seek the death penalty and that the defendant would pay the ultimate price.[9]

I had been very clear in my campaign that I was not going to seek the death penalty. It's one thing to say that during the campaign—that you object to the death penalty in all the ways in which it is possible to object—but it's another to say that while you sit in front of people whose children have been murdered by somebody who lashed out simply because he hated the way they worshipped.

I had to unwind the family's expectations emotionally. We spent a lot of time in my office, where they'd come by and talk to me and tell me why they wanted the death penalty. We had to get to know each other, so that when my office finally headed into court and said we were no longer seeking the death penalty, they understood why and they trusted me. In the end they did.

Sadly, the death penalty has become one way our system shows victims' families that their loved ones' lives mattered. The death penalty primarily happens to people who kill white people, so when people of color have been killed, their families naturally ask, "Why don't *we* get that?" And that's most of the victims we see in my community. That was the case here: they were people of color. That inequity is the first thing that comes up with people who want me to seek the death penalty. "Is it because my family member is a person of color that you're not pursuing this?"

## A DA's Office That Looks Like the Community

I'm really proud of the diversity in this office—not just racially and ethnically, but also in terms of sexual orientation, gender, and socioeconomic class. It just looks different here. Durham County has a long history of Black power and Black political progress. We have lots of Black people in power in this community, including here in this courthouse: the judges, the sheriff, and me. When you walk in and look at who stands up for the state now, it looks a lot more like the people who are out there in the community. I'm proud of that.

I'm also proud that our prosecutors ask themselves if they are doing the right thing for the right reasons in how they handle their cases—and they feel comfortable coming to me and sharing those concerns. The other day I had a prosecutor who came in with a case that had been charged as a felony. She had already agreed to bring it down to a misdemeanor, but she really felt that this woman needed to take a little more accountability in her life. I asked her, "Are you the one who provides her with accountability? You want her to be a better person? We can't do that; we don't have that power here." But she felt comfortable talking to me and she knew there wouldn't be any impact on her if she disagreed with me. I'm proud of that, too; I'm proud of the way we struggle with each other around this work.

I'm proud that there are twelve thousand people in my community who've had their fines and fees cleared and can get their driver's licenses back.[10] I'm proud that people know who I am, not because they recognize me at the grocery store—which happens a lot—but because they know who their district attorney is and they have expectations of me. Whether those expectations line up with my policies or not, people know who I am and what I do, and I can't say that a lot of people in Durham County knew that in years past, including me.

I want everybody to win. I want everybody to get as much out of their life as possible and I don't want these systemic barriers to prevent that. To paraphrase Rabbi Abraham Joshua Heschel, a great civil rights activist, "I resent other people's injuries."[11] I want people to be able to win and I want their injuries to be acknowledged in a way that allows us all to move forward. That's what justice means to me: everybody wins.

## How Black Women Are Changing the System

I'm a Black woman. What does it mean to me to have this job as a Black woman? It goes back to how so many of our victims and survivors are also Black women. I see myself every day in the courtroom, and I see myself in all the activists who are asking me to do better. It is a challenge to me to know the vulnerability that people face and still say to them that we're going to try to do this differently, we're going to try to do this in a way that will provide a path through this process. We can't make you feel whole, but we can make you feel seen.

That's another thing that Black women in particular bring. I have a lot of colleagues who say, "I'm doing this for the victims." But I know very well that they don't have any connection with their victims; their victims are just a way to prop up their particular policy or political beliefs. For me, the victims and survivors are people I actually know. We have a group here called the Religious Coalition for a Nonviolent Durham, and some of the most active members have been mothers of murdered children.[12] Those Black women push against me all the time, but they also stick up for me when it's necessary.

An important bond has grown between and among elected Black women prosecutors. We're all essentially experiencing the same thing in our communities. Our jurisdictions may be different in size and geography—[Cook County State's Attorney] Kim Foxx runs the second-largest law firm in the world, while Shameca Collins [district attorney in Mississippi's Sixth Judicial District] is in a small place in Mississippi—but we all have the exact same pressures. We all have kids, we're all trying to manage our families, we're all still responsive to our communities *and* we send Black people to prison, which is not an insignificant thing.

Not many people out there experience what we're experiencing. A lot of women are juggling their families and careers, but they're not putting people in prison. They're not the hope and the dream of a whole movement. We sometimes need somebody who will say, "Hey, sis—they *are* picking on you. It's not your imagination; they are picking on you and I know it because I've been through it, and I got you." That's mostly what we're doing with each other.

Aramis Ayala [a former state attorney for Florida's Orange and Osceola counties] said, "It's not just because I am the first Black elected state attorney in the state of Florida that I think differently: it's bigger than that. I have a different concept of justice."[13] I think this is the next level of Black leadership that we are moving into. For a hundred years it was about getting someone who looked like me in the chair, but that didn't change anything. These are big systems, and if I get hit by a bus tomorrow, the system rolls on; the system doesn't really care who's sitting in that chair. You've got to make the system work differently; you need to apply the law in a way that sees the people who are convicted of crimes as members of our community who need help—and not outsiders who deserve punishment. We're just looking at them as people.

## "Who I Work for and Who I Am"

There are experiences in my life, including as a queer person, that inform the decisions I make and the policies our office implements. Given who I am, it never occurred to me that I wasn't going to be out. I believe *queer* is about culture and a worldview—and nowadays, you get to be anyone as a queer woman. It's interesting how rarely this comes up in my role as district attorney. I think what really pisses people off is that I'm a Black woman.

And if you grew up in a Black family, you know the saying "If Mama's happy, everybody's happy." The truth is this: if Black women and Black queer women and Black trans women are safe, everybody's safe.

Progressive leaders of any race or ethnicity need to talk about how we view the system. In my office I have a picture of Barbara Jordan [the late Texan civil rights leader and former member of Congress] and Ann Richards [the former Texas governor]. Barbara Jordan was one of my heroes growing up. I used to watch all her speeches and cut anything I found on her out of the paper. I wanted to *be* Barbara Jordan. She was the first Black woman I saw that I *knew*. I also have paintings of two little Black girls in my office. They are by an artist friend of mine, freedom clay, and they're lovely.[14] I keep them here because they remind me who I work for, and they remind me who I was—and to a certain extent of who I still am. I am still a little Black girl with Afro puffs. I've had a whole amazing life unfold for me. That's what I want for other people—to have that opportunity for an amazing, positive life to unfold.

# 3

# Parisa Dehghani-Tafti

Commonwealth's Attorney, Arlington County
and the City of Falls Church, Virginia

*Parisa Dehghani-Tafti was elected commonwealth's attorney in 2019,*
*defeating the incumbent in a contentious race. After earning a bachelor's*
*degree from the University of California, Berkeley, she attended New*
*York University School of Law. She has worked as an attorney for the*
*District of Columbia's Public Defender Service, as the legal director for*
*the Mid-Atlantic Innocence Project, and as an adjunct law professor at*
*Georgetown University Law Center and George Washington Univer-*
*sity School of Law.*

James "Yaya" Hough
*The Price of Our Ticket*, 2021
Mixed media on watercolor paper

**James "Yaya" Hough** is a Pittsburgh-based artist and painter. He was incarcerated at the age of seventeen and served twenty-three years before being released in 2019. While in prison, he took art classes and partnered with Mural Arts Philadelphia as a muralist. He has contributed to more than fifty murals and was the inaugural artist in residence at the office of Philadelphia District Attorney Larry Krasner. For more on James's work, see his Instagram account: @hough9459.

## Artist's Statement

*Parisa Dehghani-Tafti has said that she was inspired by James Baldwin's book* The Price of the Ticket. *In the painting, brown and Black arms reach upward to grasp a slowly falling ticket with the words "Justice Admit One" inscribed. The arms, emerging from a red-and-white-striped background, symbolize the number of people who—historically and currently—seek just outcomes from the U.S. justice system. In the foreground is a powerful quote from the Commonwealth's Attorney Dehghani-Tafti.*

# "My Parents Often Had to Decide Between Rent and Food."

At the risk of sounding pithy, my "origin story" actually *does* sort of lead to where I am now. I came to the United States with my parents when I was four, and I grew up really, really poor. I didn't realize we were poor until I noticed that I was going to school with apples that weren't whole; they had chunks cut off. All of our fruit had chunks cut off. Later, I realized that it was because my parents often had to decide between rent and food. My mom used to go into the dumpsters of grocery stores and pick out the fruit that had been discarded, fruit that was bruised or had rotten parts.

My parents were really committed to our education, so my mom worked three jobs. During the day, while my sister and I were at school, she was a cashier at McDonald's. At night, she cleaned at a nursing home. And on weekends, she cleaned our schools so that we could go to Montessori without having to pay the normal tuition cost. And though my parents cared deeply about our education, they had no social capital; back then they had no idea how the system worked or that they could meet with one of our teachers and have a conversation and advocate for us in that way. They didn't know what the SAT was. We went through life not really knowing how to advocate for ourselves but understanding that even the smallest mistake could really change our lives for the worse. So I've always had this feeling—there but for the grace of God, as they say. Things just happened to work out.

No one in our family spoke English when we got here, and my parents put me in school within ten days of arriving in this country. I went into pre-K as a four-year-old, not really understanding that I was going to school. Every day I wasn't sure if my parents were going to come and pick me up. It was a pretty terrifying time. I was in this Darwinian hellscape where the kids thought I couldn't intellectually grasp what was going on; they didn't realize that it was a language issue. I got bullied a lot.

## The Unjust Conviction of a Friend

I think my parents always knew that I was going to be a lawyer. One day they got a call from our Sunday school teacher, who basically told them, "Parisa won't stop arguing with me; she's challenging the existence of God. She won't accept any arguments."

I ended up at Berkeley, where I studied philosophy and comparative literature before going to NYU School of Law. My path to law school is where the story really gets interesting. It was because a friend of mine, Brendan Loftus—another philosophy major at UC Berkeley—was convicted of a crime he didn't commit, one that didn't even occur.[1] Along with a friend of his, he was convicted of raping a fourteen-year-old girl. But it never happened. The girl had some mental health issues, and these two young men came under suspicion. Despite all kinds of inconsistencies in the case and a lot of exculpatory material being withheld, they were both convicted.[2] Brendan was sentenced to five years in prison and ultimately served about two years.

While my friend's trial was happening, we could see the injustice of it all and that the story didn't hang together. We all saw that there was something very, very wrong going on with the trial. As I was deciding between going to law school or to graduate school for philosophy, I realized that I had a skill set I could use to help solve this problem.

I was one of many, many people who submitted letters to the judge after the conviction. My letter said things like, "This is not the person I know; there is no way he did this." When I would get sick, this is the person who would bring me soup—and I got sick a lot, because I fed myself very poorly back then. He was always a really gentle and kind person, and it was unfathomable to me that he would ever do anything like that. I just knew that he didn't. His conviction ended up being overturned on the basis of prosecutorial misconduct.

After his release, Brendan worked for a while as a paralegal with the San Francisco Public Defender's Office, and now we touch base on social media every once in a while. He would always reach out when I got an exoneration at the Mid-Atlantic Innocence Project and was very excited when I was elected as commonwealth's attorney. I've always told him, "This is because of you, Brendan. You did this. This is the result of your suffering, so know that something good came out of it."

## Dealing with the System's Wreckage

I went to law school and knew I probably wanted to do innocence work, even though that was really just being defined.* So I got involved with death penalty work, and some of the cases I worked on were cases of actual innocence. The thing that struck me about those cases—and later on as a public defender—was that when the system makes mistakes, it leaves behind an incredible amount of wreckage. It even leaves behind an incredible amount of wreck-age when it *doesn't* make mistakes.

There are clients you'll always remember because of who they are. Then there are cases that stick with you because it could have been so easy to get it right, but the system still managed to get it wrong. I think about the arson cases you see that are based on bad science and really bad application of psychology.[3] In so-called arson cases from the early 2000s and before, you had a perfect storm of a hypothesis posing as science, along with people's per-

---

* The Innocence Project describes its work as exonerating "the wrongly convicted through DNA testing and [reforming] the criminal justice sys-tem to prevent future injustice." See innocenceproject.org/about.

ception of what they would do in that situation. Together those factors created suspicion—and worse, tunnel vision, which frequently led to wrongful convictions. The prosecutors or juries for these cases often thought somebody was too emotional or not emotional enough. The irony is that *you see that* in arson cases; somebody's hysterically trying to break in and save their families, and that's considered "too emotional." But when somebody is just standing there stunned and having sort of a freeze reaction, that's viewed as "not emotional enough." So somehow their reaction to this tragedy determines whether the system goes after them or not. I've seen clients who experienced a loss that was then compounded by being accused of killing their loved ones. That's a heartbreak I can't begin to imagine.

One client I worked with at the District of Columbia's Public Defender Service really sticks with me because it was one of the most egregious things I've seen. He had committed a murder when he was very young and had gotten a lengthy sentence and was out on parole. He kept getting re-incarcerated based on technical violations of his parole supervision terms.[4] When I was representing him, he'd been out for about a year, and it was probably the sixth time his parole had been revoked.

As I was talking with him, I realized something wasn't right. Luckily, I had the resources to get him a whole battery of tests. It turned out that his intellectual functioning was like that of a young child. He couldn't read, he couldn't tell time, he couldn't understand numbers. So when he would leave the Bureau of Prisons and get sent home with fifty bucks and a windbreaker and told to go to DC and see his probation officer at X time on X date, he had no idea what that meant. He didn't know the days of the week, didn't know what Thursday was, didn't know what the fifth of September was; he didn't know how to read a bus schedule to get to an appointment. As a result, he repeatedly didn't show up. But not a single parole officer ever asked him if he knew what he was supposed to do or went out to try to find him. It was incredibly heartbreaking, because this was a man in his seventies who had spent his entire life in and out of jail and prison. He wasn't a danger at this point but was still getting locked up because he literally could not get himself to his parole officer.

That case tells us what we need to do—and how much better we need to be on reentry planning and support if we want to make sure that we lower the prison population and create safer communities. So you won't be surprised to hear that one of the next projects in our office is trying to fix parole and probation.

Another client I can't forget is Troy Burner.[5] I was the legal director at the Mid-Atlantic Innocence Project when his case came through, and I fought for us to take it on. He was convicted as a seventeen-year-old of killing somebody and was given a life sentence. While his innocence claim was pending, the law in DC changed. His litigation team was able to get him released while the court reviewed his innocence claim; he had an excellent record during the decades he spent in prison. In March 2020, he was exonerated.

From the moment he got out, he has been taking care of his mom. He's been working with organizations to help other people get out of prison who were sentenced as youth, and he's been helping folks who are reentering who were also sent to prison while they were young. Troy and I became friends over time. He has come to celebrate my life events, and I got to celebrate some of his. It's at once heartbreaking and heartening to see someone like Troy make his way out in the world again after so much was taken away from him. So when he asked me to officiate his wedding in March 2021, I said yes, because it's important to bear witness to the new life he's building for himself and his family.

## Tackling Problems Upstream

Eventually, I decided to get involved in prosecution and run for office, because I wanted to help build a criminal legal system that keeps people safe without creating so much of that wreckage. I looked at that system and didn't like what I saw. And—similar to when I decided to go to law school—I realized that I had the power to fix it. I credit other people with this idea, but it became clear to me that what was being done in my name, as a resident and taxpayer, was fueling mass incarceration. I kept thinking about that parable about the villagers who see babies coming down the river and pluck them out downstream. The entire village is plucking out the babies, and then somebody thinks to walk upstream to find out why the babies are ending up in the river to begin with.[6]

As a public defender I spent eighteen years working toward a fairer system. I was supporting people downstream, it was fulfilling work, and I was able to help so many families. But I realized that the whole system is just throwing everybody—the innocent and the guilty—into the river, and we're paying a huge financial and human cost for it. The deeper I went into what was happening locally, the more upset I got, and the more it troubled me that this was all happening in my name.

I hate to admit it—because in a way it's so typical—but I had to be asked to run for this office. I wish the story was, "I'm so bold, I made the decision, and I did it myself," but like many women, I was looking for *somebody else* to run. And, like many women, people kept coming back and pointing at me and saying, "Well, why don't you do it?" And I kept saying, "No, no, I don't want to be an elected prosecutor." But ultimately, I decided to do it because of my parents, especially my mom. At her core my mother was a problem solver, and she taught me that when I identify a problem, it's my responsibility to fix it; if I have the skills, I have an obligation to fix it. And that's why I decided to run for commonwealth's attorney.

## A Family Decision

So I jumped in. While I was running, people kept saying, "Even if you don't win, you've started a movement." And I'd respond, "That's really nice, but I'm not going to lose." Of course, I didn't *know* that I would win, and there were certainly moments during the campaign when it felt like I had to be pushed out the door to continue campaigning. But once I set my mind to something, there's pretty much no obstacle I'm unwilling to fight.

I have the most amazing family and support system you can imagine. My husband has always been a huge cheerleader and extremely supportive of my career. We split our childcare responsibilities 60/40, where he does the sixty. We took a long time to decide whether I should run, and again—as so many women do with decisions like this—I brought it to my family to discuss. Frankly, that's what anybody should do before they embark on a campaign, because at the end of the day, everybody's exposed and has to pick up the slack. My kids were young, but I sat down and explained to them how hard it was going to be, how little they were going to see me, how they were going to be dragged to events. And I don't think they quite understood, but we all came to an agreement that I'd run.

Once we made that decision, my husband was set on doing everything in his power to make sure I won, even in the moments when he regretted that I wasn't spending time with our family and felt hurt that I wasn't paying attention to him. He was a rock. All of the grievances he had—he waited until after the election to raise them, which was really nice [*laughing*].

My family got me through a challenging race. At one point I called my dad and said, "We just can't keep this together, I need you to come help me with the kids." The next week he was on a flight from Arizona to Arlington—and he stayed for over a month. He helped with the kids in the morning, picked them up from school, and watched them in the afternoon. He helped around the house. He was incredible. At the same time, my husband was cooking every meal, and he and my sister were out knocking on doors and joining me at events. My sister knocked on a lot of doors!

## Challenges on the Campaign Trail

Campaigning is hard. I'm a really shy person. I'm really reserved. I'm this sort of weird combination of shy and extroverted: I get a lot of energy from people and I'm bubbly and have a great time when I come out of my shell and feel comfortable and trust people. But it takes a while for me to get to that point. I never liked public speaking and I never liked trial work. I liked the intellectual challenge of an appellate argument, but I wasn't one of those people who wanted to be out in front performing. So it was hard to get used to that, and honestly, I wasn't very good at it. The first few speeches I gave were truly awful. My daughter hadn't seen any of my speeches, but the day we launched the campaign, she said, "I'm really nervous." I asked her why, and she said, "I'm afraid that you're going to embarrass me." And I was like, "You don't really say that to people! [*Laughing.*] That's one of the feelings you keep inside."

I was under so much scrutiny and knew that if I made even the tiniest misstep, I would get raked over the coals. I relied on my notes a lot. I sometimes spoke haltingly and hesitatingly, because I wanted to make sure I said the right thing. During debates you have to get all this information across in two minutes. I got made fun of a lot for that. And I hated "call time," which is dialing and asking for money. It's harder than anything else you do on the campaign trail, and I think it's particularly difficult for women. It's one thing to ask for a vote; it's another thing to say, "Invest in me." I had to have a friend come and force me to make calls, but I ended up raising a lot of money from individual donations and locally.

Still, I think the worst part was the harsh attack by law enforcement in response to one of my campaign mailers. In our mailers we always cited everything we said. I got accused of lying, I got accused of mischaracterizing, and people would say, "Well, how do I know who is telling the truth?" My response would always be: "Which mailers have citations? You can disagree with me, but I'm showing my work and not just lobbing insults."

One mailer I sent out talked about how my opponent did not hold the police accountable in two past cases, and the police union supported her.[7] My point was that I'm a more neutral party than my opponent, and that I would hold people accountable: I take to heart the notion that nobody is above the law. That really, really upset the police union. They held a press conference and decided they were going to take me on. It did get my name out there, but they were very aggressive. And I wasn't going to back down.

I was lucky, because by that point Terry McAuliffe, who was governor, had endorsed me. I was worried that he was going to revoke his endorsement, but he said, "No. You go fight the good fight. They're wrong." The *Washington Post* was thinking about endorsing me, and I thought, "Oh, dear, now that's going to explode." Thankfully, they did endorse me. But that week, three county board members who were about to announce their endorsements pulled back; they were afraid of the police. Which, I think, was what the police union wanted, right?

# Shaking Things Up from Day One

After I won, I got a lot of good advice and reached out to the police chiefs to mend fences. Over time, I sat down with each one of them. We decided that I would do three symposiums with officers on the police force, held in the big ceremonial courtroom. The officers were very angry, but I stood and took their punches. I tried to answer their questions the best I could, and I stood up for myself, saying, "If you're as good as you say you are and you're doing things right, you have nothing to be afraid of with me. You may not like me, but now we have to move on to a new chapter and build bridges and find ways to work together. What things can we work on together? What are you interested in? What would you like to see?"

For months I heard nothing. But over time we've been finding more common ground. In December 2019, we had a meeting about a homicide case that was going to be handed off as I took office and needed attention pretty immediately. We're not going to agree on everything, but I think they realized that I'm not as incompetent as my opponent's campaign said I was.

Here's another story about finding common ground: during my second week on the job, I got a call from a defense attorney. They told me, "My client has been at a mental health hospital being stabilized for the past two weeks. He's about to get out and I think there's an arrest warrant for him. Can you check?" So I confirmed that yes, there was a warrant. And they said, "Okay, I'm worried he'll get arrested as soon as he's released, and I don't want him to decompensate at the jail." I asked, "Do you have a release plan? Is there anywhere he can go?" And they said, "Yes, I'd like him to go to another hospital, and I've made the arrangements. But he's going to end up spending days in jail." And I said, "No, we'll agree to a bed-to-bed transfer."

The defense attorney was silent, and I said, "Hello? Are you there?" And they said, "I'm sorry, what did you say?" I said, "If you have somewhere for him to go, we can just agree to a bed-to-bed. We'll take care of it—it'll all be fine." And they were quiet again. Finally, they just said, "I'm sorry, in my twenty-plus years of practice, I've never had a conversation like this with any prosecutor, let alone a commonwealth's attorney." Here I was worried that I wasn't doing enough; I was almost ready to go pick him up and take him myself! It was clear that something had dramatically changed.

Another easy but dramatic change was about cash bail. On day one we said, "No bail. You either let somebody out on specific conditions of release or we're going to be intellectually honest and ask for them to be held." The judges kept asking, "What's the commonwealth's position?" And we'd say, "No cash bail. These are the conditions under which this person should be released." And the judge would say, "What's the commonwealth's position on bond?" And we'd reply, "He should be released on these conditions." So the really simple things that seemed so obvious were shocking to everybody.

## Transforming "the Capital of the Confederacy"

Another dramatic change in trajectory has been the history of the death penalty in Virginia. If you think about the origin story of the criminal legal system, it was built on this idea that Black people are "bloodthirsty savages" who needed slavery in order to control their behavior. This state was basically the capital of the Confederacy.

I can't talk about ending the death penalty in Virginia without getting emotional. There were laws here that said you could be executed if you were Black and committed a crime that was punishable by three years or more for a white person. And of course, we had Black Codes and executed Black people at a disproportionate rate, and I'm sure we executed people who were innocent.[8] Since 1976, we executed more people than any other state but Texas.[9] I worked on cases where people had pleaded guilty to avoid the death penalty. I worked on the Norfolk Four case, and two of them pleaded guilty for that reason.[10] For Virginia to go from being the head of the Confederacy and number two in executions to abolishing the death penalty in 2021—and doing so because we know that innocent people have been executed and we know it was used in a racially discriminatory way—is an incredible accomplishment.[11]

This reform was long overdue, and so many people fought so hard—including George Kendall, one of my mentors—for so many years. When I started working with George, he was the director of the criminal division of the NAACP Legal Defense Fund; he's probably one of the top five death penalty attorneys in the country. So many of us worked on cases when the client's life was literally in the balance. It's an amazing feeling to be a part of a team like that. I texted George at the beginning of the legislative session in 2021—because I knew the votes were there—and told him, "Virginia's going to abolish the death penalty this year."[12] He wrote back, "I just had a handful of oranges at the grocery store, and I dropped them all."

## Making a Place for *All* of Our Kids

I don't normally talk about my family, but the only commercial I did during the campaign was about my kids, and it was incredibly personal. It was about how I wanted them to grow up in a place where their well-being and safety aren't dependent on what they look like, aren't dependent on what kind of papers they have or don't have, aren't dependent on how much money they have or what they're wearing. It's the building block of why I do anything.

My husband is Black, and my kids are Black. When I was pregnant with my son, who is now a teenager, we went for that ultrasound where you learn the gender. They said, "It's a boy." My first thought—oh, God, I'm getting emotional again—my first thought was overwhelming worry. Like any mother, I knew it was my responsibility to protect my son from the usual dangers children face. But it also hit me—now that I was having a Black son, all the social, political, and legal issues I spent my professional life working on were that much more personal. These issues became personal when I married my husband, but he knows how to navigate this world as a Black man. When it's your child, the worries take root much more deeply, and the responsibility you feel for protecting them is much more serious.

There's really no thought worse than that for a parent. Your joy is hampered because you know your child's race puts them at higher risk for being wrongly accused of a crime, for being followed in a store, for not feeling safe while walking to school, for being harmed by people who are supposed to protect them. Having to get a receipt every single time you buy something and not wearing the clothes you want because you have to look a certain way to assuage the fears of the people you encounter.

One of the things that stuck with me most from the campaign trail—and even before that—was from listening to the parents of children who have emotional and intellectual challenges. What moved me so much is that they knew they couldn't make their kids fit into this world as it was; they couldn't change their kids, so they had to change the world to make a place for them. They were relentless about doing that, and they continue to be. They knew their children were disproportionately likely to become victims of the criminal legal system, a system they wouldn't understand. So those parents had to change it to make sure it would treat their kids fairly. Watching those parents fight for their children taught me to fight to change the world too.

With my kids, I try to model that problem-solving behavior I learned from my mom. I never ask my kids what they want to be when they grow up. I ask them, "What problem do you want to solve? What legacy do you want to leave?"

## Moving from Punishment to Repair, from Prosecution to Protection

To make the world more just, I think the biggest thing we can do to is move from the idea of punishment to repair, and from prosecution to protection. The philosopher John Rawls is fundamental to my thought.[13] The theory is about trying to create a system from the perspective of someone who knows they're going to play a role in it somehow, but they don't know what that role will be. You could be a judge, a prosecutor, a defense attorney, the defendant, or the victim. Given that "veil of ignorance," what kind of system and what kind of world would you create?

To me, justice is the kind of world you would create so that people who have suffered harm have more of a say about what happens to them and what they need to heal. They would be treated fairly and with dignity and would be seen as more than the worst thing they've ever done. Not every social ill should be criminalized, and not everything that's criminalized has to be punished, and not every punishment should be so long and so onerous that it leaves no room for rehabilitation and redemption.

## The "Oxygen" in a Support System

On this path I have a support system of people who have done amazing work as part of the activist community—many of whom ran on the same principles I did and paved the way for me. It's like having oxygen. It's an incredible feeling to know that there are always people I can turn to for emotional and practical support. I remember calling Satana Deberry, the district attorney of Durham County, North Carolina, when I needed advice on how to talk to a victim about something. She spent almost an hour on the phone with me, walking through how she had talked with a family about something similar. I'm also in touch with Rachael Rollins, the former district attorney of Suffolk County, Massachusetts; there's a little group text among those of us who get the most beaten up.[14]

Just being in that community is a huge form of self-care because this work is really isolating. You can't go to your staff about every hurt and every decision. You can't go to the activist community about internal politics and your decision-making process. Having that group of folks nationally—and also the group of reform-minded prosecutors we have in Virginia now—is lifesaving.

Some days it feels as if you can't make anybody happy. Having James Baldwin nearby helps. *The Price of the Ticket* is right here behind my desk.[15] He lit my mind on fire the first time I read his work. Something I would always say to close speeches and in closing arguments was a quote by James Baldwin, from a talk he gave to the Freedom Riders: "The world is before you, and you need not take it or leave it as it was when you came in."[16]

But it's not just Baldwin; I talked about John Rawls earlier. I got sworn in on my law-school copy of Rawls's *A Theory of Justice*, and that's in my office. I have pictures of clients I've exonerated in my office. Everywhere you turn there are symbols that remind me of who I am, so I don't lose my way.

# 4

# Mark A. Dupree Sr.

### District Attorney, Wyandotte County, Kansas

*Mark A. Dupree Sr. became district attorney for Wyandotte County in 2017, the first Black person elected to that office in the state of Kansas. The son of two pastors, he began preaching at twelve years old, became a licensed minister at seventeen, and an ordained elder at twenty-one. He is a graduate of the University of Kansas with a degree in political science and earned his JD from Washburn University School of Law in Topeka. Since taking office, Mark created a community integrity unit, the first of its kind statewide, and has led an office that emphasizes community engagement and involvement. He was reelected to a second term in 2020.*

Tameca Cole
*Mark Dupree*, 2021
Mixed media

**Tameca Cole** is an Alabama-based artist who works in mixed media. After being incarcerated at a young age and spending more than twenty-five years in prison, she is out on parole. She has long used art and writing as an outlet and now leverages these mediums to share her experiences about the criminal legal system and systemic racism. For more on Tameca's work, go to southarts.org/grant-fellowship-recipients/tameca-cole-2021.

## Artist's Statement

*Inspired by the impact of seeing someone who looks like me in an esteemed position, I created a mixed-media piece showing how positive imagery can provide inspiration, opening minds to new opportunities and possibilities. District Attorney Dupree is shown holding the scales of justice, which represent fairness in the judicial process; and a sword, which represents his authority, power, and ability to protect the community.*

## A Preacher's Kid Meets His Mentor

My journey to this office was anything but expected. I grew up in the inner city. My parents were pastors and my father's biggest aim for me was to make sure that I did as much as I could to help as many as I could in my community. Early in my life, everything I knew about doing that was as a pastor, a preacher—spreading our faith.

At the age of fourteen, I had the opportunity through a school program to meet local District Court Judge Cordell Meeks Jr., who has since passed away. Before that, I had never met a judge, a lawyer, or anyone of that sort. My teacher had told me, "Wear your best suit!" As a preacher's kid, that was my black communion suit. I grabbed it and my black tie, and I wore them to school. A bus picked us up in front of the school and I didn't even know who we were going to see until I got off downtown at the courthouse.

I'd never been inside a courthouse before; scared out of my mind, I walked in, and a lady took me into a courtroom. It was full of people, everybody had suits and ties, and I've got to tell you that nobody working in that courtroom looked like me. Everybody in that courtroom was white. And here I was, this young African American guy sitting in the back of the room. I was scared. I didn't know what was going on.

Then out of nowhere I heard someone yell, "All rise!" I looked up and this little, short, African American guy with a mini-Afro came climbing onto the bench. Everyone was standing, but I was still seated, because I was shocked. I said to myself, "Whoa! Who is this guy? He looks like me." I stood up, and ultimately that was the beginning of a seven-year mentor-mentee relationship with the first judge—the first lawyer—I had ever met, let alone one who looked like me.

Judge Meeks encouraged me to be more than what I was, to go

further than I ever thought I could. He encouraged me to get into law. And it was the summer he died, in 2006, that I was able to work as a temporary lawyer in the office where I am now the district attorney. I got to where I am today because a judge showed me what I could be. I still have a picture of him in my office. In that picture, I'm standing behind him as a young, bright-eyed fourteen-year-old boy, and he's sitting on the bench. It keeps me going on a daily basis and reminds me of why I'm here—to help others.

## No Guns in God's House

Growing up, one of the things my parents instilled in us was that everybody is important to God. And if everyone is important to God, then everyone needs to be important to *you.*

Our church was a little storefront building, a Pentecostal church. There was hand-clapping, foot-stomping, and when we would dance and shout, dust would come up from the floor. It wasn't a nice building at all, but we would really praise the Lord. It was in the inner city, right in the core of what I would later come to understand was a high-crime area.

That high-crime area had a lot of different kinds of gangs. But my father, he wasn't just an inside-the-church type of pastor. He would walk the neighborhood with us, and we would witness to young men at the basketball courts, witness to the folks on the corner and encourage them all to come to church.*

---

* In some Christian traditions, the expression "witness to" means sharing one's faith with another person or people, as someone explains how the Gospel and Jesus Christ have transformed their life. The believer "bears witness to" the power of their faith. See Lalsangkima Pachuau and Knud Jørgensen, *Witnessing to Christ in a Pluralistic World: Christian Mission Among Other Faiths* (Oxford, UK: Oxford Centre for Mission Studies, St. Philip and St. James Church, Regnum Edinburgh, 2010), 2, ocms.ac.uk /wp-content/uploads/2021/01/Witnessing-to-Christ-in-a-Pluralistic -final-WM.pdf.

It became common for gang members to come to our church wearing their gang colors with their rags hanging out of their back pockets. The only rule my father had was that you could not bring your guns or your violence inside of God's house. So the Bloods and the Crips would put their guns and their rags in the bushes in front of our church and they would come in together and my father would give a sermon to all of us. He would pray and preach and put forth the altar calls, then everyone would come down and hold hands together in front of the church. It was phenomenal because you'd have members of different gangs holding hands and praying—and then they would leave. And they'd all go back to their separate bushes, get their separate guns and their separate do-rags, and go their separate ways.

But that's how I grew up. I grew up with folks coming together despite their differences, realizing that just because a person is in a gang doesn't make them a bad person; just because a person carries a gun doesn't make them a hoodlum or a thug. Many of these individuals were the breadwinners of their families. And they were thirteen, fourteen; their parents were already in jail or in prison, so they had to survive. So I learned at a young age not to label individuals simply because of the environment or the economic instability that they come from, or how the criminal legal system has already touched them or their family. That really made an impact on me in how I would later view the system and what I believe needed to be changed in it.

## Standing for What Is Right

I was nineteen years old. I was at the University of Kansas, I was on the dean's honor roll, I had good grades, I was a chaplain for the gospel choir. I had done everything I could to do what was right. I came home for the summer and went to the movies with three of my friends in a neighboring county. And in this county, there were not a lot of African Americans.

We went into the theater and the young lady who was working the ticket booth went to the same college I did and recognized us. We paid for our tickets and went inside; then we went to get popcorn, and as we were going back into the theater we were met by an off-duty police officer. He stopped us and said, "I need to see your ticket stubs." Well, at that time, most folks just threw their ticket stubs in the trash. At this point, two of my friends left, and as they left, a second officer approached us. The two officers pulled out their batons and their pepper spray, and they began hitting and spraying us. That ended with six off-duty police officers hitting us so many times I can't remember—spraying our eyes to the point that it took days for them to clear up.

I went to jail and my friend went to jail. He was charged with a felony; I was charged with three misdemeanors, including battery against a law enforcement officer. I was offered pleas and I was offered deals, but my father told me, "Son, if you did nothing wrong, you stand for what is right, despite what the consequences may be."

I stood for what's right and went to trial. And we won. But it was a battle, because I had to sit there and watch as six police officers got on the stand and lied about the entire situation. As an African American man, I had a tough choice to make. I had to decide to have a bench trial in front of a white judge or a jury trial in a county where, 99 percent of the time, the juries were all white. And at that point, no one believed that I could get acquitted in front of an all-white jury, so I took my chances with a judge. That situation showed me: something has to be done. Something has to change. My defense lawyer believed me, stood up for me, and made arguments on my behalf despite these officers lying, despite them putting their story together perfectly. He fought for me. I wanted to become a prosecutor, but I wanted to pay it forward. I wanted to fight on behalf of individuals as that defense lawyer did for me. So I did.

Throughout a decade working as a criminal defense lawyer, I ran into similar cases, and years later I came across a case where the same officers had done the same thing to another young African American man. By then one officer had been fired and another had retired early—and they were ultimately sued—but the rest of them were still active and thus able to continue repeating the pattern. They could not believe that I was the guy who had beat them in that trial.

## Climbing the Ladder to Change the Rules

But something had to change. I decided to be that change—first from the defense side and ultimately in the prosecutor's role. After a judge I'd clerked for suggested I get prosecutorial experience, I had the opportunity to work as an assistant prosecuting attorney in Jackson County, in the neighboring state of Missouri.

There's a case that stands out in my mind. My supervising prosecuting attorney was handling it, and I was in the courtroom. The defendant had not received an attorney yet and was very irritated, very upset. My supervisor was just hammering and hammering him, and I saw the defendant ball up his fist. I stood up and asked the court if I could speak with the defendant. The judge, seeing that the defendant was really heated, called for a recess. I took the defendant outside, and I talked to him. The defendant simply said he didn't understand what was happening. So I explained the process, explained what the situation was. He calmed down and went back before the court. It was dealt with.

After the hearing was over, my supervising attorney pulled me aside and scolded me like nobody's business. "You are not a defense lawyer," she said. "That was my case. I never gave you permission to speak to any defendant on my case." In that moment, it hit me: the problem in that office was that politics played more of a role than justice did. She was upset because she believed that this young prosecutor had shown her up in front of other folks, and so she wanted to put me back in my place. I talked to the head prosecutor about it and ultimately what I got was "You need to stay in your place. And when you climb the ladder, then you can change the rules."

At that point, I made a decision. I talked to my wife that night and said, "If I'm ever able to get back into a prosecutor's office, I will have to come in as the DA, because the tone starts at the top." If the top is all driven by politics and superiority—and not humility—that rolls all the way down and justice has no place. I left the office, and years later this commitment to change convinced me to run for DA, because I refuse to let politics and tradition stop me from doing what is just, what is right, in any case.

## "If I Run, I'm Gonna Win."

When I decided to run, was I concerned? Yes. Was I intimidated? Yes. The amount of pushback and anger that folks hurled my way the moment I filed for DA was completely unexpected. But folks who knew me in this community said, "We need someone who represents the entire community to get in there and to do something different."

So I filed to run, and I believe that I heard the Lord say, "If you run, you will win." And that was my motto. When anyone asked me, "Do you think you're gonna win?" My response was "Well, the Lord said if I run, I'm gonna win." And when the votes were in, right after they called the election, my quote to the paper was "God said if I run, I'm gonna win." So I was confident I had heard the Lord [*laughing*]—and I'm so glad that it was the Lord speaking.

I won my primary election in August 2016. We celebrated—as preachers do—at the church, and my mother was there in the front row with my father, and they were very happy. It was just one month later that she passed away. From there, I went on to win the DA election in the fall, beating the eleven-year incumbent by twenty points. My father held the Bible at my swearing in, and my brother the judge [Wyandotte County District Court Judge Timothy Dupree], the only African American judge here in our county, swore me in. And just a few months after that, my father passed away as well.

And so, those words of wisdom of fighting for what is right, of staying humble, regardless of your role and your position—and keeping God first—those are the things that lead me and guide me. And then, of course, there's the thought that if I ever stepped out of my lane, if you will, I could hear my mother's voice going off on me, because she did not care about your title [*laughing*].

## Hearing and Understanding the Community

Being elected DA has impacted the community both in ways I can see and in ways I can't. I think it has shown the community that—even being from the inner city and a "high-crime" area, even being from a place many have counted out, saying that nothing good is going to come from there—we've come from there and now we sit in this seat. It has encouraged many people to know that they too can come from a high-crime area, from an impoverished neighborhood, that they too can be a minority and still get into this seat.

What I can't see, but I believe has a great impact, is one benefit of having the first African American elected district attorney in the state; it said to the entire community that justice is for everyone. That regardless of your race, regardless of your ethnicity, regardless of whom you represent, you have a right to be involved on the right side of justice. Because of that, I believe there has absolutely been a deeper connection and a building of trust among the community, specifically Black and brown folks in our community, to believe that *we* can receive justice, that we have someone in that office who understands us, who hears us, and who's not just fighting for public safety of one particular suburban neighborhood, but of the *entire* community.

In the early days on the job, it was a great feeling knowing that, yes, now I'm on the other side, yes, I'm in this chair. But I also felt—and still feel—a huge obligation, this huge weight. I had sat with, I had talked to, I had met with so many people who had been victimized by the system. And I want to make sure I emphasize that they had been victimized—not by crime, but *by the system*. Sitting in this seat, I still feel the weight of trying to change a system that victimized so many people in our community, to make it better for everyone. It still feels like a heavy load. I was told that it's best to start chipping away at it. So from day one we started doing just that: making changes, bringing in the right folks, and doing what I believe was right and what was necessary for this justice system to work for everyone.

## Resistance to the Fight for Justice

I was not prepared for the amount of—I don't really want to use the term *pushback*, because that's the term everyone uses when we're talking about politics. In other contexts, what I received coming into office probably could've been considered a crime, potentially assault, a criminal threat. But because we're in politics, we label it "pushback."

I dealt with flat-footed racism and discrimination. Threats on my home, my person, my church as a pastor. I once had an officer literally go toe-to-toe with me in the middle of a building. He said, "You better not ever have to call the police, because you can rest assured that we're going to remember this." I call that a threat. To see the establishment fight vigorously and assault my character, my family, and my church—I wasn't prepared for that. I didn't know that was something I was signing up for. It took me my first two years to realize that this is a battle. To make the law do what the law is supposed to do, you have to fight with those who are supposed to do what's right. That's something I didn't know until I dealt with it.

A few examples come to mind that show what a battle it is. Once I was fighting for an independent investigation of officer-involved shootings that resulted in death. In my community, when individuals were shot or killed by the police, the policing agency would do their own investigation and ultimately clear their colleagues. When I came in, I spoke with the police department and said, "We need an independent agency to come in and do those investigations." The police chief then fought me tooth and nail. The police chief, the sheriff's department, and the mayor wrote a letter to the [Kansas] attorney general, not only questioning my authority and power to force an independent investigation, but also questioning my authority to create a conviction integrity unit.[†] They all but said "You do not have the authority and we will not listen."

Then there was the time I went before the Board of Commissioners to make a case for the conviction integrity unit. I had just

---

† Fair and Just Prosecution describes conviction integrity units (also called conviction review units) as "internal office practices and structures that can enhance the ability of an elected prosecutor and her office to influence, improve, and monitor staff decision-making and office culture, strengthen community trust, and achieve the highest possible integrity in case outcomes." These units aim to remedy "past individual wrongful convictions and [enhance] community confidence in the justice system, [and can be] a tool for improving office-wide practices in a manner that reduces the likelihood of errors occurring again in the future." Fair and Just Prosecution, *Conviction Integrity Units and Internal Accountability Mechanisms* (San Francisco: Fair and Just Prosecution, 2017), fairandjustprosecution.org/wp-content/uploads/2017/09/FJPBrief .ConvictionIntegrity.9.25.pdf.

given my presentation on why it was necessary, why we had to move forward with funding this. And there were many people who were for it and many who were absolutely against it, because the fraternity of police was against it, the chief was against it. Many of the folks I was speaking to are backed by these unions, are backed by the establishment. And ultimately, when I finished, someone—I can't tell you who—said, "You just need to learn to stay in your place, boy."

A silence came over the room, and in that moment, I had to draw on my father's teachings of peace: "Follow peace with all men." That moment brought up all kinds of anger. Here I am, the only Black man in the room, and you feel comfortable calling me "boy"?! That moment opened the eyes of so many who were watching and those on the commission. It brought a reality, to think, "Oh my gosh. . . . Have we created an environment where that type of comment is okay?" The room stayed quiet, and my only response was, "I was elected by the people, and the place that I am in is in the place of justice. So now you have to do what you believe is right." And ultimately, my plan was unanimously passed.

I've also had my church attacked, I've had my children's names thrown out there and attacked, my wife has been verbally attacked. It's a continuous thing that we've had to deal with, and you realize there are some things you just have to go through to fight for justice. I don't believe that there's any cost too high when you're fighting for real justice.

## Changing the Office Culture

A few months after I came into office, an African American young lady came to me and asked if I knew about the "noose award." There was a tradition that if you received a hung jury, before you came down from court, there was a "noose award." And this award literally had a noose attached to it to show that you had a hung jury, and you had to sign your name to it. The tradition had been carried on for decades in this office. For decades, there were twenty-something-odd Caucasian prosecutors and maybe one African American prosecutor, and so nobody felt like it was a problem, nobody thought it was wrong. If that one African American prosecutor did, he didn't have anyone to take it to, because the boss was one of the ones who started the tradition.

So when I came into office and brought in eight or nine African American assistant district attorneys, it took some education, some cultural competence in the office. Ultimately, I said, "This is ridiculous. It is offensive. Over five thousand African Americans have been lynched in this country and died by a noose. For us to have a noose award in the chief law enforcement official's office is unheard of."

And so our office got rid of that tradition, and we found other traditions and dealt with them similarly. But that was the lack of understanding—or maybe they understood, but nobody ever held them accountable. And they didn't care because they were the chief law enforcement, so who could stop them? That's why diversity is so important. It's so important to not just talk about diversity. And when I say diversity, yes, we need more women, yes, we need more folks who think differently, but we also need people of color in these positions.

## "Thank You for Giving Me My Husband Back."

So it hasn't been easy. When I was going through my first term as DA, my wife asked me, "Are you sure this is what God said for us to do?" [*Laughing.*] I really hold true to my faith. Ultimately, when I was ready to give up, I remember going to my barbershop—that was back when I had hair!—and Lamonte McIntyre was at the front door. He told me he had just been made one of the co-owners of the barber school in the city. And it hit me that if I weren't fighting through all that I'm fighting through, Lamonte would still be in prison.[1]

Lamonte had been wrongfully convicted of a double homicide in my county and spent twenty-three years in prison. When Lamonte went to prison, he was seventeen. At that time, I was a thirteen-year-old boy, and I had not met Judge Meeks yet. Twenty-three years later, I was holding the key to Lamonte's freedom. For me that spoke volumes. It said to me that whatever the struggles, whatever the foes and fights and adversity I have to deal with in this position, so many individuals are out there waiting for someone like me to do right by them. There have been times when I've wanted to give up. And then I've realized that whatever I'm going through doesn't compare to what Lamonte went through and to what many others have gone through, and they're all waiting for me to do my part in this city to make sure justice is done.

Because of Lamonte's case we created a conviction integrity unit, and we began receiving letters from individuals in custody saying that they were wrongfully incarcerated. One of the cases was Pete Coones, who was also convicted of a murder he did not commit.[2] Ultimately, he was released after doing twelve years in prison. The court threw his conviction out, and I dismissed the case. In front of the court, in front of his family, I got up and I walked across the courtroom and I shook his hand, and he looked me in my face and said, "Mr. Dupree, thank you for answering my letter, because if you wouldn't have answered my letter, I would have spent the rest of my life in prison." His wife of forty-seven years said to me, "Thank you for giving me my husband back." And what that said to me was that so many people simply want someone to sit in this seat who's willing to answer that letter. And oftentimes, justice is on the other side of that letter.

## Embracing Second Chances

In my office, as soon as you walk in, I have a sign that reads *Ministers of Justice*. It doesn't say *DA*, just *Ministers of Justice*, because we, as the district attorney's office, are supposed to be ministers of justice, upholding and representing what is fair and just for the entire community.

The Supreme Court has said that a prosecutor's role is twofold: It's one, to make sure that the guilty do not go free, and two, to make sure that the innocent do not suffer.[3] So for me, justice is doing those dual roles. At the end of the day, justice requires us to be willing to sacrifice our comfort so that what is wrong can be made right.

I see ministers of justice as individuals who care about their communities, who care about the children in their communities, and who are willing to continue to fight for what is right, via conviction integrity units, expungements, victim service centers, and so many other things that are out there. For progressive prosecutors like me who are fighting for that change, of course I hope they won't be attacked, that their families are not attacked, that their characters are not attacked, that their livelihood is not threatened. And I hope that kind of change will become the norm, that it will be embraced because it's what's right.

Prosecutors should also prevent crime from happening—and the best form of prevention is education and economic growth. If you want folks to stop robbing people, give them the ability to put money in their own pocket. When I came into office, there had been about one hundred expungements in the entire county in the three previous years. In one summer alone, we got over one hundred expungements done. Giving folks an expungement of their record is giving them an opportunity to have a clean record. There is promising data that shows the positive impact jobs have on communities—and if people get a job, they're less likely to commit crime.[4] Sometimes justice requires that you give individuals that second chance, or even a third chance, and I believe justice requires that we take a holistic view of each case. That's also important for accountability. Accountability means looking at each case separately and looking at the facts and the environment of each case. No one case or one standard fits all.

## Seeking Justice as the Rule, Not the Exception

My hope is that the way I see justice becomes the rule rather than the exception. My hope is that Black, brown, and white folks all feel comfortable with the criminal legal system. My hope is that every person who is touched by the system feels and believes that it is fair and that it is just and that second chances are something we consider without question. That the system isn't automatically focused on jail or prison, but that it *is* automatically asking, "What can we do to rehabilitate?"

Being a part of this movement of reform-minded prosecutors is a breath of fresh air. It reminds me that I'm not alone. It means the world, when you are fighting for what you know is right, to see that others think about justice in a similar way—and that there will always be individuals who push back. But we can never allow the voices of justice to be smothered by those who are fighting against it. I still rely heavily on these like-minded DAs, because at the end of the day we're all humans, and in this battle for justice as humans, we all need somebody to whisper in our ears to let us know that the fight is worth it, and you're not fighting by yourself.

# 5

# Kim Foxx

State's Attorney, Cook County, Illinois

*Kim Foxx was elected as state's attorney in 2016. She ran with a pledge to focus on police accountability and to stand with Chicago's communities that had historically been excluded. The Cook County State's Attorney's Office is the second largest in the country, with more than seven hundred attorneys and one thousand employees. Before leading this office, Kim spent three years as a public guardian in family court, more than a decade as an assistant state's attorney, and three years working with the president of the Cook County Board of Commissioners. In 2020, she won reelection to a second term.*

Antonio Howard
*A Nation Can Rise*, 2021
Digital

**Antonio Howard** is a painter based in Erie, Pennsylvania, who typically works in acrylics. He was incarcerated at the age of fifteen and was released in 2018 after serving twenty-six and a half years. He has contributed to more than ten public arts projects and murals in Pennsylvania, participated in numerous art shows and publications in Erie, and published three books. For more about Antonio's work, see erieartsandculture.org/directory /member/159 or facebook.com/antonio.howard.5095110, or find him on Instagram: @antoniohoward_artist.

## Artist's Statement

*The figure in the artwork holds a brick, symbolizing Kim Foxx as a little girl. From my perspective, the brick her mother gave her from their old building was a foundation, literally and figuratively. And that foundation gave her the vision and agency to produce the adult Kim Foxx who stares back at her in the image.*

## A "Project Kid" from Cabrini-Green

I grew up in one of the most notorious public housing complexes in the country: Cabrini-Green. They were towers on the North Side of Chicago with a concentration of poverty and violence. It was the representation of everything that was wrong with what we would call "the urban ghettos." There was a true deprivation of resources. But it was also a place where I knew some of the most loving, nurturing, kind, and determined people, and there was a real camaraderie among those of us who grew up there.

We call ourselves "project kids." I'm a project kid through and through. And the thing about Cabrini—and neighborhoods like it—is that there are assumptions about the people there, for instance, that we don't have the same love and care for our families. That could not have been any further from the truth.

My mother was eighteen when she had me, and she had my brother a year before. Cabrini was where her mother was, where her sisters were, and where I was raised. There were no lawyers in Cabrini; there were no doctors, no accountants. Historically, people from my neighborhood haven't gone on to be lawyers. There were hustlers and survivors. To some people that may sound derogatory, but you learned to hustle to survive. My grandmother was the ultimate hustler, selling Avon, baking pound cakes, making sweet potato pies and fish dinners, and driving people to and from the grocery store and church. Before there was a gig economy, there was my grandmother and her Buick.[1] I know the determination of the people—the women in particular—of Cabrini.

When I was in third grade I moved from Cabrini just a mile north to Lincoln Park, which was a more affluent neighborhood. We couldn't afford it, but we moved because my mother knew they had better schools there, and she was determined that we were going to get the education that kids in Lincoln Park got. I got into a magnet school, LaSalle Language Academy. And when

I started there, I saw the clearest depiction of disparity. I had to learn Spanish like everyone else. Most, if not all, of the other students had studied it since kindergarten. The expectation was that it didn't matter that I had missed three years. I was expected to be at the level of the other kids from more affluent neighborhoods. People believed that I couldn't learn because of the zip code where I was from. So when I graduated from high school, college, and law school—and when I ran for office—I always held tight to my Cabrini roots.

My mother went back to Cabrini in 2011, when the city was in the final stages of tearing down the projects. It was April 4. She took a brick from our building, etched that date—my grandmother's birthday—into it, and gave it to me for *my* birthday. My mother died the following year. I keep that brick on my desk as a reminder of my roots and who I serve. And even though the buildings are gone, and the people are spread far apart, it is a literal concrete reminder of where I came from.

## Wanting the Power to Say No

I ran a campaign for Cook County state's attorney that was about talking to the people of Cabrini. These races have typically been about appeasing suburban white voters, but mine focused on talking to the people most impacted by the justice system—people who came from neighborhoods like Cabrini. I had worked for twelve years in the very office that I lead now. I had also worked in the Office of the Cook County Public Guardian, which has lawyers who represent the kids in the child welfare system. The state brings petitions to take children into care and the public defender's office represents the parents involved. My job was to advocate for the children. What was really impactful about that work is that so many of the kids I saw in our foster care system were very much like me.

I talk very openly about coming from a single-parent household with a teenage mom, growing up in public housing in Cabrini-Green, my mother's issues related to her mental health and substance use disorder, and how I was a survivor of childhood sexual abuse. But in spite of all the struggles we went through in my childhood, my family was together and intact.

The state's attorney's prosecutors who were doing this child welfare work were not proximate to these issues; the issues weren't real life to them. They were twenty-five, twenty-six, twenty-seven years old, had just gotten out of law school, and were handed the responsibility of determining whether a parent was fit or unfit to take care of a child. The children and families were overwhelmingly Black and overwhelmingly poor, yet the people who were in the state's attorney's office were not. It was the gravity of that work—of kids coming into care, of me feeling frustrated that we were overusing the system—that made me want to work for the prosecutor's office.

I wanted to become a prosecutor armed with the ability to say no. A lot of people want the power to *do*, I wanted the power to *not* do. I wanted the power to not bring kids into the child welfare system who didn't belong there. I did not want poverty, race, all the factors I saw at play, being used against communities like mine. I left the guardian's office after three years to join the state's attorney's office. But the same struggles happened there. Being in that office and having the power of prosecutorial discretion—which I think is our ultimate superpower—was important, but I was one of more than eight hundred lawyers. Yes, I brought my experiences to bear, but ultimately, I was just one person in a system that disproportionately affected communities like mine and young girls like me.

I had left child welfare work and gone into juvenile "delinquency" work at the state's attorney's office, and I thought there was nothing more hypocritical in our justice system than what we were doing there. In handling these cases, the kids I was prosecuting were the same kids I had represented as a public guardian. The kids whose parents I was taking them from were the same kids we were treating like criminals when they threw a rock and broke a window or were smoking weed in the bathroom. There was always cognitive dissonance in doing this work: wanting to be an advocate, wanting to use my discretion, but feeling that so long as certain policies existed, I was a fish swimming upstream.

My decision to run for office was about not only the power to say no for myself and my individual caseload, but for my entire office and the millions of families impacted by our justice system. Cook County is home to 5.4 million people, and it was important to me to not be one fish swimming upstream, but to be at the helm of this work and drive conversations and policy that make a difference, that take lived experience into account. I felt that too many people in these positions have no real personal connection to the work, and that's what drove me to do it.

## "Good People Sometimes Do Bad Things."

I grew up with the notion that people do things that jar us, that hurt us, but that is not the sum of who they are. My grandmother was a Baptist-church–praying grandmother, very much rooted in the church's doctrines about redemption. She had five daughters with three different fathers. My grandfather was married at the time that my grandmother was with him, and I think her history and the assumptions and judgments about who she was always stuck with her, particularly as she got deeper into her faith. She tried hard to overcome that, to show that she was this warm, sweet, compassionate woman who had made mistakes, who had done things she knew had caused harm, but that wasn't the totality of who she was. And even from her "mistakes" came her children and her grandchildren. So my grandmother always had this sense that good people sometimes do bad things, and we have to be able to see them in whole.

My mother suffered from bipolar disorder for years before we knew the name for it. I will never forget one particular episode when I was a child: my mother and grandmother got into an argument and my mother hauled off and hit my grandmother across the face. You have to understand, my grandmother was God-like to me, so watching my mother hit this woman felt like the world was crashing in. How could someone I love do this bad thing? My grandmother sat me down afterward and said, "Daughters don't hit their mothers." But she didn't waver in her love for my mother; she didn't berate her. She understood that there was something else at play.

I was sexually abused between the ages of four and seven by a relative. His mother and my mother were sisters, so he was my grandmother's grandson too. She loved him just as much as she loved me. I've always lived in this really complicated world, with people I love doing bad things and still seeing them beyond their bad actions. My grandmother instilled that in me. And it wasn't just my grandmother. My mother was a victim of domestic violence; the man who beat her once saved my life when I was drowning in a pool. It was horrible, the trauma he inflicted on my mother, on my brother, on me, that I live with to this day. He also had demons with drugs and with his own mental health, but he saved my life at one point. I was not without judgment, but I recognized that judgment was not going to heal him. The drug use, the PTSD, the trauma all required treatment, not merely shaming him. It was clear that he embodied the adage about "hurt people hurting people." I needed him to stop hurting my family and me, to be the man that we had glimpses of him being. And I was amazed by what can happen to people when they are able to overcome the worst thing they have done and have the compassion to give back.

These concepts root me and guide me in all the work I do. I can't use words like *thugs* or *animals* or *monsters* that you sometimes hear in law enforcement. I don't know monsters. I know people who've done monstrous things but who are still people. And I know that personally—my grandmother taught me that.

## Trying to Be Perfect

When I entered the office as the state's attorney, it wasn't entirely new to me; for years I had been a supervisor in the Juvenile Justice Bureau. Many of my young assistant state's attorneys had ascended in the office, so I already had a level of trust with a number of people who were there.

Before taking office, I was fortunate to receive advice from now–Vice President Kamala Harris, who was the California attorney general at the time. She had sent me a letter right after I'd won the primary, and I wondered, "How does this woman know who I am?" She was running for the U.S. Senate then and was respected for having been the first Black woman to lead the DA's office in San Francisco.

What was most interesting to me about VP Harris was that she was the first Black woman to do the work. There were blueprints on how to do my job as chief prosecutor, but I needed to talk to her about doing the job as a Black woman—as the *first* Black woman. That kept me up at night because I knew the standards and expectations would be different. I was not going to be judged by the same standards as my male counterparts—as my *white* male counterparts—and here was the chance to ask a history maker about that.

She was very blunt. She said, "You have to be perfect." I was taken aback. She said, "I know that perfection is often unattainable, but you have to try to attain it, because the margin of error for you as a Black woman doing this work is just not the same." She told me about the challenges she'd had with law enforcement and with other elected officials. She shared a story from early in her tenure about not seeking the death penalty after an officer had been murdered. She talked about being at a funeral and how the senior U.S. senator from California called on her from the pulpit to pursue the death penalty.[2] Harris's stance against it was politically toxic, but she said it was the right position. She pointed out that I would be called on to do difficult things that wouldn't be politically acceptable, that some people in law enforcement would not take kindly to taking orders from a woman, particularly a Black woman. But you've got to roll. You have to do the right things. It is not lost on me that she has continued to be a first as vice president, and I know she follows the same advice that she gave me: You have to be damn near perfect.

## Disrupting the System

Before I put my hand on the Bible to be sworn into office as state's attorney, I was labeled as anti–law enforcement. I still think the most jarring part of taking office was law enforcement's reaction to my election. Assumptions had been made about me. I think race and gender absolutely played a role in it, as I was the first Black woman to be the state's attorney in Cook County. But also, my campaign focused on police accountability and reforming the relationship between police and prosecutors, namely changing the prosecutor's role and not being a rubber stamp for the police.

In my view, none of that was anti–law enforcement, but the police groups were ready to pounce. And I was not expecting that. It wasn't that I hadn't worked with law enforcement before: I had seen some really bad police work and I had seen some incredibly good police work and had established some good relationships. I was just not prepared for my views on prosecution to be considered anti–law enforcement.

The judiciary pushback was also strong. In Cook County, many of the judges on the bench in criminal court are former prosecutors and came from the state's attorney's office. Many came from an era that was rife with abuse. We were the false-confession capital of the United States.[3] We had many wrongful convictions that were overturned, even before I was elected. We had a corrupt police commander who was torturing brown and Black men on the South Side of Chicago.[4] I was giving voice to that horrible history. But many of the history makers were on the bench. And then, when we started saying things like "We're not going to ask for cash bail on certain offenses," judges started coming after me and my office.

For instance, there used to be a law that forbade people who'd come out of prison from congregating with each other. Police would file these cases and I'd tell my people to dismiss them as soon as the cases came into court. In one of those instances, a judge who had worked in the office for a number of years knew there was a reporter in the courtroom, and said, "Kim Foxx doesn't care about criminals or crime." She just went all in. Same thing with our retail theft policy: at $300, Illinois had one of the country's lowest thresholds for retail felony theft. As an office we raised it to $1,000, to be more aligned with the areas around us. Law enforcement and judges teamed up and were really aggressive in their pushback, really aggressive in their rhetoric. I had not girded myself for the stakeholders who did not appreciate my disruption of the system.

## Second Chances for Young People

Prior to running for office, I'd spent two years as the chief of staff for the president of our county board of commissioners, someone who was interested in reforming the criminal legal system. One of the things we worked on was "raising the age" in Illinois.[5] I was the lobbying voice in our state capitol for changing the age of majority—that is, the age when you legally become an adult—for criminal cases, as well as for automatic transfer of fifteen-, sixteen-, and seventeen-year-olds to adult courts for certain charges.[6] And we were successful. Juvenile justice was a priority of mine before I even got into the state's attorney's office.

When *Miller v. Alabama* came out—a Supreme Court decision banning automatic life without parole sentences for juveniles—I knew that once I was in office we were going to have many resentencing cases to review.[7] All of those cases would come to me. One particular case comes to mind, that of Adolfo Davis.[8] He was arrested when he was fourteen for his part in an armed robbery that left two people dead; he was tried as an adult and sentenced to life without parole almost twenty years before the *Miller* decision.

I inherited the review of Adolfo's sentence from my predecessor. When his case was up for resentencing, it was in front of a judge who had previously been a state's attorney supervisor in the juvenile bureau. She rejected the science and data about adolescent brain development. It was stunning to me: here was a judge sitting on a bench, looking at a *Miller* case, rejecting science. I was indignant, not just about what was happening to Adolfo, but about the people who were doing it. The assistant state's attorney who argued [in 2015] to keep the life sentence in place said something to the effect of "I don't care about the life traumas that this kid had; other people who lived through those experiences didn't do what he did." I was personally offended.[9]

We were going to do whatever we could to resolve his case in a way that didn't continue with the appeal, so that he could get on with his life. We said, "How do we work together with the defense attorneys to get the outcome we want, so that he can get out?" Ultimately, we struck a deal to reduce his sentence, and Davis was released from prison in March 2020 after spending twenty-nine years there.

## Changes That Will Last

The thing I'm most proud of—which is actually the least sexy—is our work to enhance data transparency. It hadn't been done before. When I was running for office, I wondered, "How do we know we're safer? What does 'safer' or 'safe' mean? How do I know that the things we're doing are having a real impact?" Data transparency and the ability to show our work to the public were—and obviously still are—important to me.

I wanted to be authentic in my answers to the public; I didn't want to just make stuff up. When it came to reporting, some DAs would focus on their most egregious case and say they'd prosecuted this one killer, but they wouldn't tell you that they had also prosecuted people who were suffering from addiction and saddled them with records that made it challenging to get work, so now they're probably committing crimes to get money for drugs. They wouldn't tell you "Our policies are perpetuating the cycle," but would just highlight the murders instead.

With our data transparency work, we went back seven years and showed what the office had been doing—and that those actions and policies weren't necessarily keeping people safe. We showed the good, the bad, and the ugly.[10] We were able to demonstrate to people in Chicago that even though we have a huge gun problem, most of our resources weren't going toward guns and violence; our resources were going toward drug cases. We saw the racial disparities, the issues with age and overpolicing and arrests in certain zip codes. We really dug into the data of what we were doing—and how and with whom.[11] Whenever I leave office, there will be an expectation about transparency in place so that future generations of prosecutors can't obscure the data. I'm proud of that; I've tried to codify much of my work so the next person can't come in and undo what I've done.

The other things I'm most proud of will also outlast me, things like changing laws. For example, Illinois passed a sweeping criminal justice bill in 2021 that ends cash bail across the entire state, starting in 2023—and I was one of just two state's attorneys who pushed for it. In 2017, we stopped prosecuting people for failure to pay tickets for moving violations. People talk about stop-and-frisk a lot, but they don't talk about the traffic stops made in Black and brown neighborhoods; you end up with people who were choosing between paying their parking tickets or their rent. We aren't prosecuting those cases anymore. And I'm proud of the work we've done on conviction integrity: we've vacated over one hundred convictions, and most of those came from one tainted police officer and his crew.[12]

I also created the position of chief ethics officer; it was a dual position with my chief deputy at first, but now it's a stand-alone position in our office. Any assistant state's attorney can call the chief ethics supervisor about anything they feel uncomfortable about and talk it through. We've had people call with information about police officers and about supervisors and partners—it's something I'm incredibly proud of. When we first rolled it out, people didn't trust it, wondering "What's gonna happen to me?" You talk about a code of silence; that code exists when you have people who've done the right thing and are left out there to fend for themselves.

And there's so much more to do. I aim to take many of my policies and enact new laws to make things uniform, so it doesn't matter what county line you are on: fairness, justice, and equity shouldn't depend on your zip code. We hadn't been prosecuting marijuana cases in Cook County, and I wanted the state law changed to codify this practice. There was a movement in Illinois to do just that, but I was the only prosecutor at the table as they were crafting the legislation. And we were the first in the nation to enact automatic expungement for cannabis possession; individuals don't have to apply for it or pay for it.[13] Now no one in Illinois is prosecuting marijuana cases for small amounts, and everyone across the state is eligible to get their records expunged or vacated. We also stopped prosecuting people for driving on suspended licenses for failure to pay tickets. We did that in 2017, and now it's the law statewide. Those policies that we turned into law will outlive me and my tenure—and they will help bring justice across the state.

## No More Empty Porches

This all comes back to public safety, but how do we measure it? To me, the measurement of safety isn't just a dip in crime numbers. Safety is the ability to feel like you can go out on your porch and have a glass of lemonade and not be concerned, and your children can be there with you, your elders can be pulling weeds in the garden and not worry that harm will come to them. That's what safety feels like. In so many Chicago neighborhoods, kids are peering through the blinds because of the notion that they are safer inside than out. To me, safety is not peering through blinds.

When I was a kid, we used to cower in the bathtub when gunshots would go off, because there was this projects wisdom that bullets didn't pierce porcelain. I remember on the Fourth of July, when things got hot, my mother and grandmother would usher us into the bathtub to take shelter. To me, safety is not needing to take shelter in bathtubs.

Safety means no more empty porches. It's jumping double Dutch while someone's sipping lemonade and watching you learn how to hop on one foot instead of two. For so many families in neighborhoods that have been impacted by violence, that's all they want: to be free in their communities, to do the things that so many of us take for granted, which is to just sit on your porch.

## A Vision of Healing

I hope the criminal legal system looks different in the future—that the laziness in the system ends; that we stop using a legal process to deal with things that don't belong here. The system needs to be rightsized to deal with the small segment of the population that poses real harm to the community, and we need to stop prosecuting people for having substance use disorders or mental health disorders or just for being poor.

Here's a case that broke my heart: A woman seeking shelter with her seven kids was living in a unit that had no heat or water, and she was charged with child endangerment. That's a housing issue, an economic issue. Why on earth would we involve the criminal legal system? Police charged her with a misdemeanor. We shouldn't do that. My office immediately dismissed the case and worked with advocates to secure housing for her.

More broadly, our system needs to think and behave differently when holding folks accountable, to recognize that they are more than the act in question. That we are all better if individuals are able to reach redemption, that we *all* benefit. As I tell people all the time, more than 90 percent of the people who go into our prison system in Illinois are coming back out at some point. We need to be invested in them not going back. They help us, they contribute to our taxes, they can coach Little League, they can even take care of people who have done harm. I know it intimately. In the future, I hope for a justice system that has a small specified mission related to harm, and a response that helps heal harm, not just for the person who was hurt, but also for the person who committed the crime.

## Justice Is Personal

Justice is messy. It is an elusive feeling. I can tell you what accountability is: that's when you've done harm to someone, recognize and own what you've done, and try to make amends. *Justice*, on the other hand, is this aspirational word that I don't think we have a real definition of.

I want us to do the right thing for the right reasons all the time, and I don't equate justice with buildings or bars or numbers. To me, that's not justice. Do I feel like the harm done to me has been acknowledged, has been atoned for, that you're not going to do it again? And am I satisfied with those answers? That's what justice feels like to me. It's personal.

I see justice in this movement of progressive prosecutors, but I think people forget how young the movement is. And for me, it wasn't a movement at first. In my head it was just "I want to do this differently." I didn't know that in other places across the country, other people thought about the justice system in the same way. We're seeing more Black women elected as prosecutors, but there still aren't enough of us: when I ran in 2016, I think we were less than 1 percent and now we might be at 2 percent.[14] And I thought, I want to do this for all the reasons that we started this conversation: lived experience, holding power, the power to say no, and showing that you could win on that platform.

We have to show up and win, and show that we can lead authentically, that we don't have to change who we are or what we've lived, that we welcome people with lived experiences. It was amazing to me that Aramis Ayala, the former state attorney in Florida's Osceola and Orange counties, ran, and her spouse had had contact with the justice system. That Rachael Rollins, the former DA in Boston, talks about her family's contact with the child welfare system. It is amazing to me that you can show up with all of that and that it connects and resonates with people. I'm really proud that by leaning into my personal narrative, unapologetically and without shame, I could open up doors for others to do the same.

I think that is how we're going to get a system of *justice*. Not a system based only on racial demographic changes, but also on lived experiences. We need more people like Chesa Boudin, the district attorney of San Francisco—whose father spent more than forty years in prison—to be in these roles. It's unbelievably exciting to me that this role is no longer defined only as a position for the guy who wants to be senator, that it's not the stereotypical white-guy spot to ascend to something else. That we now have people who are wedded to figuring out the elusive word *justice* for the communities they come from, and they've done it nontraditionally. That brings me the biggest joy in all of this.

## Social Justice Warriors

This movement, this time, this moment of change, has allowed us to step out of just talking about the role of the prosecutor and lift up these bigger issues, things like reproductive rights and immigration. There's been a real resurgence of "Hey, bring those people into the conversation too." We are working on policies to improve the criminal legal system, but we are also talking about the bigger universe of what justice looks like.

I hope we continue to talk about issues beyond the courtroom, in the community, and use the power of the bully pulpit to advocate for harm reduction, for sensible housing, for body autonomy. When former U.S. Attorney General William Barr referred to us as "social justice warriors," he meant it as an insult. But the fact that the prosecutor could be deemed a social justice warrior speaks volumes about how far we've come.

When you get into these roles, you sometimes end up muting yourself, and there's an erasure that can happen when things get really big, really fast. There's room for so many more of us, and it is my hope that as we try to expand the tent, we don't erase the unique experiences that Black women and other women of color bring. It is harder doing this work in this skin, in this body. I have really leaned into what Black women's leadership looks like. I think my progressive policies are rooted in my lived experiences as a Black woman from the projects. None of this is academic for me; every policy initiative I've put forth has come with the bias of knowing somebody who has been impacted by it. Bail, wrongful convictions, marijuana, mental health, all of it. I know someone who's been personally affected by it, and the fact that I get to do this work is a privilege.

## Who Gets to Set the Table?

It's no surprise, but I've thought about quitting many times. A lot of people talk about former President Trump and the energy and rhetoric and divisiveness he brought. I saw that firsthand in my work. We don't talk enough about white supremacy and patriarchy in law enforcement, in criminal justice, in the history that got us here. I'm grateful that there has been more conversation about this, sadly, in the wake of people being murdered by police.

But from the day I got here, there has always been real vitriol, a real hatred—not for my policies alone, but for who gets to set the table. It's so vastly different: So far I'm the only Black elected state's attorney in all of Illinois. In my first term, there was one other woman who was appointed after someone became a judge, and she decided not to run. She said, "I don't know how you do this; I can't do this." The rhetoric around criminal justice in rooms with lawyers who take the same oath as you do—how they talk about these communities, about my communities—it is exhausting. I don't want to be angry and disenchanted at every association meeting or law enforcement meeting or suburban neighborhood watch meeting or newspaper editorial board meeting, but there is so much coded language. I lived in two worlds, in Cabrini and in Lincoln Park. I'm fluent in coded racism.

What has kept me here are all the men and women who have had their records cleared, their convictions vacated, people I apologized to because the system did this to them and they did not believe that anyone acknowledged or cared about them. I'm here because of survivors who have seen accountability and moved toward healing. It's a running joke here: I can't go anywhere without someone who comes from public housing shouting their building number to me. Many people who have been impacted horrifically by this system take real pride seeing me in this role. My community has stood up and said, "We know that you're doing this for us. Don't stop." There's also a real obligation to not let them down, because so many elected officials just maintain the status quo. I wouldn't make enemies if I did things the way they have always been done. It would be easier. But easy isn't always right.

I do this for the people who shout out their building numbers—they get me. I do it for the elders who remind me of the people who came before me—maybe not as prosecutors, but in other difficult roles; and for my daughters who watch me do this work and pass on other more lucrative opportunities and say, "Mom, you could make money." I think about little me and the people at Cabrini who need people like them with their experiences at the table. That's what keeps me here. There are way too many people counting on me.

## Finding Greater Purpose

My daughters are teenagers, and I tell them to find purpose. I say, "When you are living your purpose, that's when you are tested the most." When I was tested, I used to ask, "Why is this happening to me?" When we were homeless, I was sixteen and a straight-A student and asked myself, "Why on earth can't I catch a break? I do everything I'm supposed to do, and here I am." I realize, in my purpose, that when I meet homeless teens, when I meet kids and can see a little something that someone else can't—it affords me an opportunity to have empathy and compassion. When bad things happen, I tell my girls that it's for a greater good, "for a greater purpose you cannot see right now."

I also have two bonus children I've taken guardianship of, whose parents struggle with substance use disorder and mental health issues and entanglement in the justice system. They live with me, and I tell them that—given their experience with their parents—I have more in common with them than I have with my daughters. My daughters have a mother who's a lawyer and an elected official who knows the vice president. That's just wild. But my bonus children whose mother suffered with substance use and mental health issues? I've got more in common there. Looking at me, they see that it is possible for them. Every experience is meant for something greater—that's what I tell them.

# 6

# Sarah George

State's Attorney, Chittenden County, Vermont

*In 2011, Sarah George started as an assistant state's attorney in Chittenden County. Six years later, Vermont Governor Phil Scott appointed her as the county state's attorney after her predecessor was elected as the state's attorney general. George pledged to use the power of prosecutorial discretion to implement evidence-based practices and policies that promote safer and healthier communities, and she won election to a full term in 2018. Since taking office, she has ended the use of cash bail in Chittenden County, stopped prosecuting many drug offenses, and has taken bold stances—such as advocating for overdose prevention sites—to prevent deaths and promote harm-reduction strategies.*

Luis "Suave" Gonzalez
*Sarah George*, 2021
Mixed media, watercolors, and acrylic

**Luis "Suave" Gonzalez** is a Philadelphia artist and activist who uses acrylics and mixed media to craft pop-style imagery, collages, and murals that address themes of social justice. He spent thirty-one years in prison, and since his release has served as a TED Talk presenter, a Reimagining Reentry Fellow through Mural Arts Philadelphia, an instructor at the University of Pennsylvania, and cohost of the podcast *Death by Incarceration*. For more insight into Suave's work, find him on Instagram: @the_mad_artist_chunky_papi.

## Artist's Statement

*Inspired by the compassion and humanity the state's attorney has shown for others, I created a realistic portrait of Sarah George and some of the characteristics that define her.*

## Serving the Community, Literally

I have been a waitress since I was a kid. In 2006 I started at Simon Pearce Restaurant in Quechee, the town I'm from in Windsor County, Vermont. I continued working there even after I became the state's attorney for Chittenden County, until COVID-19 hit in 2020.

I loved working at the restaurant, and I love the people, but I did it to afford my student loan payment every month. Frankly, my student loan payments were unmanageable without the additional income; when I became state's attorney and my income went from $60,000 to $120,000, my monthly loan payment more than tripled.

There is something incredible about service jobs and the service industry. I think everybody should have to do this type of work at some point, especially people who want to run for office or be in politics. It humbles you, it educates you, it forces you to have conversations with people you would never meet otherwise—people from different towns, states, countries. You are "on" all day, talking to hundreds of people, and you find out so much about them. It's a great way to learn what matters to people. We often think we know what people care about, but when you talk to people, you find out that the things you thought they might care about they've never even heard of—or the things that matter to them aren't what you thought.

Working as a waitress has made me a better lawyer and prosecutor. My ability to talk to victims and witnesses, to law enforcement, to judges, and to community partners and community members is a direct result of my years in the restaurant industry. In the criminal legal system, you interact with so many people. You learn from them, listen to them, and educate them. In my opinion, there is no better way to hone those skills than in the service industry.

The owners of Simon Pearce and their family are lifelong friends of mine, and I really care about the company and the people who run the restaurant. Working there, I came to have a second family. The local people who come to the restaurant have known me since I was a kid. They are proud of me, but at the same time could not care less that I am the state's attorney in Chittenden County. I'm able to have really great conversations with constituents there, and they are very honest with me. Hearing their perspectives can get me out of my own bubble and force me to think about things differently.

## Wanting a Better System

I have always been driven by empathy and compassion. At a young age, it physically affected me when I saw people struggle or suffer. I would come home from school upset about others in my class who were being bullied, struggling in school, or had less than ideal home lives. I've always tried to take on that pain for the people in my life and for others I don't know.

Growing up, I saw people struggle with substance use. Some were able to recover and have successful lives, and others passed away when they were young. I've lost classmates to drug over-doses and incarceration. They are people who had been in my home, who I hung out with after school, played sports with, or whose parents or siblings I knew. When you have connections with people who end up involved in the criminal legal system, you start to see that system as something you or your loved ones could be a part of, and you want that system to be better.

I went to college to become a child psychologist for Deaf children. At the time, I knew someone around my age who had a younger sibling who was hearing-impaired and was going through some mental health issues, and there didn't seem to be any resources for her in the therapeutic world. Unfortunately, early in my time at the University of Connecticut (UConn), I couldn't get into the sign language classes; it was such a small thing, but it ended up changing my entire life's course. I teach at a college here in Burlington now, and I tell my students that the smallest things can sometimes totally derail you and send you in a different direction—and that's okay. That was my first derailment.

At UConn, I took a criminal psychology class and became enthralled with the theories on why people do the things they do, specifically why they commit crimes. Before I knew it, I had a new passion; I double-majored in criminal justice and psychology. I went on to get my graduate degree in forensic psychology, and that was when I started to delve into the criminal legal system— not just studying the people in it, but the system itself.

As I learned more about the system's injustices, I quickly discovered that I did not want to be a forensic psychologist; I wanted to be a public defender. I wanted to work with the individuals accused of crimes and help give them a voice in our system, while also bringing real justice to the survivors and victims of crime. So I decided to go to law school.

## Changing Course to Change the System

In my second year at Vermont Law School, I did an internship with the public defender's office in Chittenden County. For the first time I was able to appear in court and had my own clients, two of whom had very similar circumstances. They were both veterans, had PTSD and other mental health issues, and struggled with substance use and housing insecurity. They were committing really low-level offenses like stealing stuff to sell so they could buy alcohol or food.

These two clients were being prosecuted by different attorneys in the Chittenden County office, so I went to each one separately to talk about their respective cases, to see what they would be willing to do for my clients. I asked each one: if I were to get my client connected with services through the VA, would the prosecutor consider dismissing the charges? One of them, Mary Morrissey, who later became my mentor and then a judge, not only said "Yes, I will do that," she also had a contact at the local VA office. We called from her office and got my client an appointment so he didn't have to navigate that complicated world on his own. Within a few months he was engaged in the VA's wraparound services and had stable housing—and he hasn't committed another crime.

By contrast, the other prosecutor refused. He said that though it would be great if my client could get services, he had still committed these crimes and his options were to plead guilty or go to trial. So we went to trial and we lost. The judge imposed a $25 or $50 fine, which of course my client didn't have. He never got connected with services, and years later he died from a drug overdose.

Those two experiences made me realize that if you want to change the system from within and want the power that allows you to do that, you need to become a prosecutor. After graduation, I applied to the Chittenden County State's Attorney's Office and got a job straight out of law school. And that is where I have been ever since.

## Leading with Kindness

In 2015, Mary Harris, a high school student from Moretown, Vermont, was in a car with her friends when a man crashed his vehicle going the wrong way on the interstate. Mary and four other teenagers were killed. The trauma of this unthinkable tragedy has rippled throughout our community and state in ways that can never be adequately measured. It will stay with us all for the rest of our lives.

Months before her death, Mary had written a paper in school and talked about kindness and compassion toward others.[1] At the end of it, she wrote: "It is nice to be important, but it's more important to be nice." This simple phrase has stuck with me as a prosecutor, as a human being, as someone just trying to live and lead with kindness and compassion.

It was remarkable to me that somebody so young really understood that. Mary's mother still leads with this message and started the hashtag #LoveLikeMary to promote the kindness and love that her daughter embodied. The accident victims' families are finding a way through their devastation by doing what they can to honor their loved ones' lives. I think it is a testament to what victims need in our system to feel heard and to feel that there is something good and something compassionate or something beautiful coming out of such desperation. It's especially important in our criminal legal system. We are told from a very young age that people involved in the system don't deserve kindness—and that viewpoint has only made us less safe.

## Looking at What Survivors Need and Want

I have always been interested in the dynamics and repercussions of family violence. I was in an abusive relationship in high school, so I know how complicated the dynamics can be, even at a young age. I went on to write my master's thesis on dating violence among teenagers and how it relates to criminal behavior later. But the criminal legal system has gotten to a place where people working in the system think they know better than survivors do, that by taking control away from survivors, they are helping them. I used to make those presumptions as well.

When I first became a prosecutor, I still thought domestic violence cases were different, that they called for a punitive response every time, that the survivors needed that person in jail. I thought

I knew what was best for them. I came to understand that survivors can want very different things—but also a lot of the same things. They want the abuse to stop, but often they don't want the person in jail. They want the person who harmed them to continue to parent with them or live with them or be in a relationship with them, but they want the abuse to stop. They want to understand why this is happening. They want to go to counseling with this individual. The person may be dealing with substance use issues or trauma; a lot of the people who commit domestic violence have been victims of domestic violence themselves. You start to understand that even those cases we like to think are black-and-white are not. There are so many layers to people, and so many reasons that they do the things they do.

I've started doing more work around a restorative process for these cases, because at the end of the day, our system does not hold people accountable the way restorative justice* does. In the typical prosecutorial approach, the person accused of violence never has a conversation with the survivor about why they did what they did, and they don't really have to have that conversation with themselves, so the abuse doesn't stop. I started to see this cycle over and over again, and realized that even with my best intentions, I was not doing anything to help these survivors or the individuals who were committing these offenses. It forced me to think about it from a different perspective and consider a much more holistic approach.

---

* Restorative justice "brings together those directly impacted by an act of harm to address the impact of the crime, hold the person who did it accountable, and make things as right as possible for those harmed." See Common Justice, "Restorative Justice: Why Do We Need It?," common justice.org/restorative_justice_why_do_we_need_it; and *Fair and Just Prosecution, Building Community Trust: Restorative Justice Strategies, Principles and Promising Practices*, (San Francisco: Fair and Just Prosecution, 2017), fairandjustprosecution.org/wp-content/uploads/2017/12/FJP.Brief_.RestorativeJustice.pdf.

## The Underdog Gets the Job

As an assistant prosecutor I had a large caseload—about three hundred cases at a time—and felt I was making a difference. But then I started to think about this system in a more holistic way: for example, when you are talking about a domestic violence case, you might see that the victim is picking up retail thefts or disorderly conducts or other charges that may be related to the domestic violence she's experiencing at home.

I started to realize that this was not just about my cases—we need more people in the system who look at every single case with the goal of figuring out what we could do differently and what we could do better. With each policy change that affects every case coming into the office, you can actually start to have an impact on the entire caseload and the entire community.

The more I started to recognize that, the more I saw that the things I was able to do on my individual cases weren't enough. There needed to be a much more global change to impact the entire system. When the position of state's attorney was coming open—because T.J. Donovan, who had held that job, was elected in 2016 as the Vermont attorney general—a lot of people asked me whether I was going to seek it. Those who were showing interest in the position weren't really people I trusted to be in it for the right reasons, rather than for political gain or as a stepping-stone. I had to be convinced that this was a good idea for me, and I decided I wanted the position so that I could make some significant changes in the system.

The governor had to appoint an interim state's attorney to complete T.J. Donovan's term.[2] Governor Scott ended up deciding among three of us. I was the most senior prosecutor, with about six and a half years of experience, but I was certainly not considered the front-runner. I was the underdog—but I was appointed.

# A Liberating Two-Year Term

I took office almost two years before the next election. My thinking was that I had two years to do what I wanted to do. It was incredibly motivating and liberating. I did not become a prosecutor with the intention of becoming a state's attorney; that had never crossed my mind. But I thought I could do a good job, and if that meant I had only two years to do it, I was okay with that.

That is a really great way to run an office, because you can embrace the idea of carpe diem. You can do the things you want to do, be transparent about it, and make sure the community knows exactly what you're doing. You're sharing these lessons, ideas, policies, and things you want to do, and by doing that, you're not only changing the system, but you're also giving the community an opportunity to say, "I don't like this. I don't like the way this is going." Or, "I do." I benefited from being bold and starting quickly. I immediately made changes I thought would have an impact on the system. Luckily, two years came and went and nobody ran against me, so I was able to get right back into it after being sworn in again.

Somebody might run against me in the future and I am fine with that. The beauty of this position is that the community gets to decide who they put here. I will happily keep doing everything that I can while I can, and so far that has worked out well, because as soon as you start making decisions for the wrong reasons—like reelection—you make bad decisions. In this job, those bad decisions can have serious consequences and create further harm for the people you claim to want to protect.

## Changing Drug Policies and Saving Lives

One of the first things I did as state's attorney was form a commission to discuss the concept of having a safe injection site in our county; it was made up of local experts in public health and substance use services and law enforcement—people with a lot of different perspectives. At the time, safe injection sites were a new idea in the United States; very few states were talking about it, but of course, it was an old idea in a lot of European countries and has been implemented in Australia and widely in Canada.[3]

I think those conversations, those different perspectives, were eye-opening for everybody in the room. I didn't go into it with a particular agenda; I just knew that what we were doing for people in our communities who were using drugs was not working. It was using a ton of services and resources, but we weren't making a dent in the number of people dying of overdoses. I wanted to figure out—from the experts in the field and from the people on the ground—what we could be doing better. Ultimately, they supported the *idea* of safe injection sites unanimously, but all these other exciting policy ideas emerged about what we could be doing as prosecutors and law enforcement in the meantime, given that we knew it could take years to open a safe consumption space.

Out of that conversation came the idea to stop arresting and prosecuting for the possession of buprenorphine/Suboxone [a medication used to treat opioid use disorder].[4] We had seen research and data about this lifesaving drug that is difficult to find in our communities. Doctors are restricted as to how many prescriptions they can write. We pushed a lot of local partners, including our local hospital, and were able to get more buprenorphine in our community; we essentially wanted to flood the community with buprenorphine, and then promised the community that we would not arrest and prosecute for the possession of it, even if they had it illegally. We were first in the nation to do this, and through that policy—created in partnership with law enforcement, our mayor, and our hospital—our overdose death rates plummeted. They went down by over 50 percent in our county while they went up statewide.[5]

After the decision was announced, I received a lot of emails and calls from individuals thanking me, saying that they had never seen an elected leader, especially a prosecutor, who was so honest about the realities of people who use drugs. They felt like that stigma had been eased for them. Research shows that as soon as somebody feels less stigmatized for their actions, they are more likely to seek help. It seems like such a small thing, that all you need is a prosecutor or another elected leader saying "We want you to survive," but that meant enough for them to get help. We are a part of the problem when we stigmatize people and tell them they are criminals and treat them like criminals if they possess something that can keep them alive.

In a related move, I told my staff that the possession of drugs was not our priority, emphasizing that those individuals and their cases should be sent to service providers in the community; our criminal legal system did not need to be involved. We would either direct these cases to a diversion program designed for people with substance use issues or decline to charge them at all. I wanted to spend our resources on cases we might actually be able to do something about.

## Responding to Disturbing Allegations at a Women's Prison

In Vermont, we have one detention facility for all incarcerated women, and it's in my jurisdiction. In 2020, a report came out with multiple allegations of sexual misconduct, retaliation, and general mistreatment within our women's facility that had been going on for years.[6] It was infuriating to hear about the experiences women had had with correctional officers while incarcerated there. Perhaps even more infuriating was learning that these guards had not been held accountable for their actions. It had been swept under the rug by people in power and these women were not believed.

I was appalled as a woman and as an elected official in the jurisdiction where this facility is located; it's three miles from my office. Even before learning of these allegations, I believed that the facility needed to be closed. We had too many women there to begin with, and the facility itself is incredibly old and awful. There is mold present throughout; it was built on a swamp. It's disgusting. No human being should be living there, let alone the women we incarcerate in this state.

I felt a strong need to take a firm stand about how we treat incarcerated women and to try to get this facility closed. The first thing I did was ask the Department of Corrections for a list of all the women who were currently incarcerated there from my county, cases over which I had control. I got that list and immediately started going through it to determine whether those women needed to be incarcerated at all; if not, we converted their sentences to probation or struck them altogether—or, if they were being held pretrial on bail, we struck their bail and got them out.

Because of the publicity about our efforts, I started getting letters from a lot of other women who were incarcerated there but weren't from my county. I sent every one of those letters to the state's attorneys in those counties, to see whether they wanted to get involved. I also sent the allegations to the Vermont State Police and told them that because the facility was in my jurisdiction, I wanted to be the one to review these cases.[7] It was—and still is—important that these allegations be taken seriously, that these women be heard, and for charges to be filed against the abusers when appropriate. It is also imperative that we acknowledge that incarcerating women comes at a significant cost to the women, their families, and our communities, and we should do our best to avoid this outcome.

## Bringing Evidence into a Room Full of Men

Since the day I got this job, there were articles and interviews and comments on social media about my inexperience—about my being so young, even though I had more prosecutorial experience than the other two people in the running for the state's attorney appointment and I was only a year younger than the front-runner. Both were white men.

I always knew this was going to be an uphill battle, that I was going to have to deal with things that other people in my position would not. In the beginning I was often asked whether I was married, why I wasn't married, if I had kids, if I was going to have kids, and what I would do if I got pregnant while I was in this position. Those are questions that men in these positions *never* have to answer. Whenever I would announce a particular policy or go to law enforcement leaders' meetings—and I was the only woman in the room and the youngest person by twenty-plus years—everything I suggested was challenged or shot down. The response from those people is always, "In my experience. . . ." The assumption or projection is that I don't have experience, so I don't know what I'm doing.

But the reality is that every new policy I announce is based on research and data. I would never announce something without being completely confident that I have the evidence to support it—I know that the people who push back often do *not* depend on evidence, because there is no evidence to support 98 percent of the stuff we do in our legal system. The benefit of knowing you must confront that skepticism is that it makes you do things for the right reasons. Women in these positions, and especially Black women, know going in that they need to have evidence, because they know they're going to face pushback. And over time the community starts to see—one person at a time, one policy at a time—the evidence that supports these decisions and the lack of evidence to support the status quo.

Something I tell young women is that when somebody *shows* you who they are, believe them. Far too often we listen to people tell us who they are and that is not who they turn out to be. Watch what people do, the decisions people make, and how those decisions and actions impact people—not what they say. You can tell a lot about someone when you look at their actions.

I also tell women to believe in themselves. When somebody says you're worth it or you should do a particular thing, don't let it take them seven or eight times to convince you. I think the research says that women need to be told seven times to apply for a job or run for office.[8] When we do apply or run, we often win, but we often don't have the faith in ourselves to do it. So I tell them to take that chance, to really believe in yourself and believe that you are capable—and lead with compassion and kindness and your heart, rather than what this job or that job or this person can ultimately get you.

## Looking Beyond the Numbers

When I first became a prosecutor, I was given a document that outlined the appropriate or expected sentences for crimes. It said that a retail theft should get a $200 fine, an aggravated assault should get five to fifteen years, and grand larceny should get two to five years. This was meant as a guide to help new hires resolve their cases, but in reality, it reduced human beings to arbitrary numbers and desensitized prosecutors to what those numbers mean.

To think about these numbers in a more concrete, meaningful way, I took my entire staff—including my victim advocates and my administration staff—to visit one of our facilities. Not just to the visiting center, but through the entire prison, to see where people were living, where *we* were sending them. To hear the doors slamming behind us, to smell the sterile or musty smells, to see what their "gym" looks like or their free space or their kitchen or their cafeteria. It is much harder to distance yourself from these outcomes once you have seen the inside of these facilities. When you're walking around, seeing people that our office played a part in putting there, you wonder how the community is benefiting from them sitting in a cage.

A lot of my staff left there thinking "What did I do? What did we gain from this? Now he's just sitting in there instead of working or paying back his restitution or whatever it was that we ultimately want this person to do." It was a powerful experience for everyone in the office, including the victim advocates. I think victim advocates are often underappreciated in the justice reform movement; the conversations they have can make or break how that survivor feels about the outcome of their case. If the advocates understand why jail may not be the best outcome, they can better explain to victims why we may not seek it.

## A New Path to Accountability

To me, true justice is having an individual who committed a crime be held accountable in a way that helps heal harm. I think a lot of people confuse accountability with a guilty plea or a sentence; from my perspective, that has nothing to do with accountability. Our system does not hold people accountable; people just plead guilty. For there to be justice, I believe there must be true accountability: taking responsibility and doing what is needed to heal the harm. That means both the harm the victim has suffered and the harm within the person who committed the crime, that may have led them to commit the offense in the first place.

I keep a lot of things around me that remind me why I do this and help keep me grounded. I have photos of homicide victims. I also have photos of individuals I've helped release from prison after being incarcerated for thirty-plus years for crimes that would have gotten them a third of that time today. The pictures are of them with their families or the children or grandchildren they never expected to be able to see and hold in person. I also have pictures of my nieces and nephews—especially my nieces—to remind myself that all the pushback and the hate and the sexism that comes with this work is worth it. That I'm showing younger women and girls that this work is important and that they can do it and that it matters. I do this work for their generation.

I also do this work for my friends and their family members who have died from overdoses, and for everybody's loved ones who have died because of the stigma of drug use and the "war on drugs" that has been an absolute failure. I do it for the Black and brown people in our communities who have been systematically oppressed and caged as an extension of slavery. For every person who has been stigmatized and victimized by our system in the name of justice: I do it for all of them, for all those reasons.

And I do it in hopes that we can decriminalize drug use and drug possession and eliminate cash bail throughout Vermont. I think those things will make a drastic difference. I hope we start to make a shift so that prosecutors actually function as advocates whose job is to partner with people in the community and help them to get services, not unlike the role of a public defender. Ultimately, we need to lift people up within their communities and give them the power and resources they need to thrive, rather than responding only after we've failed them through so many oppressive and bureaucratic systems. That should be every elected leader's goal—but we have a lot of work to do.

# 7

# Eric Gonzalez

### District Attorney, Brooklyn, New York

*In 2013, Eric Gonzalez was the head of one of five trial divisions in the Brooklyn District Attorney's Office. That November, Ken Thompson rocked the local political establishment by unseating the DA who had held the office for twenty-four years. Gonzalez became chief assistant district attorney in 2014, leading the office's Conviction Review Unit and the rollout of a new policy declining to prosecute people for possession of marijuana. In October 2016, following DA Thompson's death just months after receiving a diagnosis of cancer, Gonzalez was appointed as acting district attorney. He was the first DA in the country to hire immigration attorneys to help noncitizens accused of crimes avoid deportation and other collateral consequences. In 2017, he ran for the seat and won. Gonzalez reformed the office with his Justice 2020 initiative, which has reduced pretrial detention, considers incarceration a last resort, focuses on pre-arraignment diversion, and shares power and decision-making with communities impacted by violence and other serious crime.*

Russell Craig
*Eric Gonzalez*, 2021
Oil on canvas

**Russell Craig** is a Philadelphia-based painter and portrait artist whose art often explores social and political topics. He grew up in the foster care system and spent nearly a decade in prison. He is an alumnus of Mural Arts Philadelphia's Restorative Justice Guild program, a 2017 Right of Return Fellow, and a 2018 Art for Justice Fellow. For more about Russell's work, see his Instagram account: @r.craig.t1.

## Artist's Statement

*I was inspired by the notion that Eric Gonzalez is raising his family in the Brooklyn neighborhood where he grew up, allowing the youth in his community to see a man in a suit and tie every day. I painted an oil portrait depicting Eric this way. His upbringing and background give him a deeper understanding of the communities and crimes that make their way to his office.*

# Tough Times in Tough Neighborhoods

I think my upbringing—and coming from where I do—sets me apart from a lot of prosecutors across the country. I'm the first elected Latino district attorney in New York State. As a young Puerto Rican boy, I never thought this opportunity to impact public policy could be in my future.

I grew up incredibly poor. My mom worked in a sweatshop and my parents separated before I was two. My father dropped out of school in second grade; his family members were farmers. My mother eventually got her GED, and the idea that I would go to college, let alone law school, was sort of bodacious thinking. Sometimes I would help her sew garments in the evening after she came home from work. She'd get 20¢ or 25¢ apiece, maybe 75¢ if it was a really complicated item—and that's how we survived.

As a young child, I lived in Brooklyn, including Williamsburg before it was gentrified. People forget this, but in the 1970s, Williamsburg had a lot of drugs and a lot of crime, and the area was very poor; it had New York City's highest rate of people receiving public assistance.[1] Then I moved to East New York, which, in the 1980s and 1990s was at the forefront of narcotics: the crack epidemic hit really, really hard there. There was a lot of police activity, a lot of loss of life. It was called the murder capital of New York City.

Growing up, I lost a lot of friends to violence. It was not unusual to learn about a classmate being arrested or shot. The relationship between the police and the community was frayed because the neighborhood was so unsafe. I faced a lot of challenges in East New York as a young guy who didn't know a lot of people—having to deal with the streets, but also feeling like our police looked at the community without its best interest at heart. It was a majority-white police department in a community that was almost exclusively Black and Hispanic. There was a lot of distrust of the police, and we had a lot of negative encounters. I was stopped and searched by the police many times, just walking home from a friend's house or from school. The lack of safety in our community was palpable.

I had a sense of what made the streets of East New York tick, and I knew that not everyone being stopped by the police was a bad person. But many of the people doing the most damage and causing the most violence seemed almost immune from prosecution. I also saw a lot of young friends dabble in drugs, including selling them, and by the time I was in high school a lot of them had been arrested. Some of them went to prison, and it seemed a shame that law enforcement was so focused on stopping minor drug transactions.

Their enforcement approach didn't seem to have any real policy or strategy behind it. It was just "Stop everyone you can stop—and if you make enough stops, perhaps you can fight violence." Even as a young person, I thought we needed a much more focused approach to public safety. I had this crazy idea of going to law school: crazy because I did not know a single lawyer. I believed that if people worked and lived in our neighborhood—people who understood the community and what was driving violence—we could improve our lot in life.

## Reckoning with the Harm the System Causes

I believe my work as DA is about lifting communities up and improving lives. It's not about simply punishing folks who make mistakes or commit crimes. People get involved in the criminal legal system for a lot of reasons. It does not make them terrible people—a lot of them are wonderful people who made the wrong decisions because they were trying to feed their families or put some money in their pocket.

A lot of friends I went to school with came home from jail

or prison with trauma. They came home angry, sometimes to homelessness and sometimes to unemployment. None of them got a chance to go to college. They weren't eligible for federal education grants, and that prevented them from moving forward and having economic and social mobility. They got stuck in the system that was allegedly there to improve the community but instead, was harming people.

We never talked about those things during my early years at the Brooklyn DA's office, about how the work we do as prosecutors can harm people, even though the community already knew it. It bothered me, because they were trying to tell us that: people wouldn't show up on subpoenas or they wouldn't want to come in for jury duty. They were telling us, "You're not giving us what we want from our justice system." But our office didn't understand because we weren't intertwined with—or listening to—the people we serve, as we should have been.

## Understanding the Community and Investing in It

In April 2021, we had a terrible domestic violence tragedy in Brooklyn, where a man shot and killed his ex-partner and two of her daughters, and then took his own life.[2] What I saw at that apartment was terrible. Besides the pools of blood and the loss of life, I saw a family who lived in a housing development in Brownsville who did not have adequate food and did not have a lot of clothing. They were sleeping on beanbags; they didn't have beds. I saw incredible poverty. A lot of the failures in our justice system stem from the dire situations and conditions people live in. This man had significant mental health issues and yet there was no system in place to help him. As I understand it, he was dealing with a bipolar episode when he committed these crimes.

As a kid, I saw homelessness and people with mental health

issues, and saw very little being done about it. These challenges still exist and are responsible for much of the crime and violence we have. If we understand that, we'll see the futility of insisting on incarceration when the behavior involved cannot be corrected by a prison sentence.

A lot of prosecutors are attracted to the job because they want to try cases. They care about public safety, but their view of that entails locking people up and separating them from their community. My view of this role is different: if we want public safety, we have to *restore* these individuals to their communities in safe ways, and we need the resources to make sure they succeed.

When I was a kid, I never saw anyone wearing a suit or a tie in my building. When I graduated from law school, I decided to move back to the same block and put on a suit and tie every day, so that other young people could see me. I made the decision to raise my three boys there, to be an active member of my community: to coach Little League and send my kids to Cub Scouts, to invest my energy locally. All so we could show folks that you don't need to move away to be successful. It has made a difference. I've been told many times by people in my neighborhood that they're happy to see me raising my family here, even after being elected DA.

We live on the border of Williamsburg and Bushwick in Brooklyn. My boys are brown-skinned boys, much darker than I am; my wife is Afro-Latina. I want them to live in a society that's safe for them, where they would be treated fairly and with human dignity in our justice system, and where they never feel the need to carry a weapon, as I did, to live safely in their community. That's what keeps me going, 100 percent. I'm a pretty private person, and I protect my family from a lot of this. It's tough being a teenager when your father's the DA, so I try to keep my kids "normalized." My wife does a good job of that by saying, "Come home and do the dishes."

# How Do We Help People *and* Make the Community Safer?

Growing up, my family received public benefits. We were on food stamps and had Section 8 housing. I remember on a few occasions not having sufficient food and having to go to neighbors' houses to eat. My mom was embarrassed, but the community would help. In the summertime I had to go to the free meals program during the day.

My mother and I still joke about this incident: The ice cream truck came by one day, I was a hungry little kid, and all the other kids were getting ice cream. An ice cream cone back then cost 25¢, and I kept saying, "Mom, buy me an ice cream, buy me an ice cream," and she kept saying, "No, no, no, you don't need it. You just ate. You're just being greedy." Ultimately, I kind of had a tantrum: "I just want my ice cream, Mom, can't you buy me an ice cream?" And she broke down. She said she couldn't afford it. And I felt incredibly guilty for putting her through that. So when I see people today living in tough conditions and struggling, I know we still have a lot of work to do.

When people make decisions and put their survival or their self-interest ahead of some of the rules of our society, they may steal or do things they wouldn't otherwise do. I understand that it's not right, and as DA I have a responsibility to deter that and respond to it. But given the incredible poverty, the mental health issues, and other challenges so many of our people are facing, they need a system that is there to assist them rather than just take harsh action. So in our office, when we see people who commit acts related to poverty or homelessness, our response is: "How can we assist them and keep our community safer by preventing them from doing this again?" Not "This is the third time you've stolen food, and now we've lost our patience with you." We need to identify resources for folks.

I've tried to use my life experiences in developing policy. As a young man living in a tough neighborhood and being fairly new to it, I carried what was called a "007 knife." It was illegal, but I carried it every day while I was in high school because I was going through some of the toughest parts of Brooklyn and felt I needed it to keep myself safe. I was fortunate that I never used that knife, though carrying it was probably poor decision-making on my part.

I see young people who've been arrested for possession of a knife or a gun, and they say, "I don't believe that I can go to the police; I don't believe the police can keep us safe. I don't believe I'm going to be safe unless I can protect myself." I understand from experience that it's not just rhetoric or an excuse. The way we're going to prevent that sort of thing from happening is by restoring trust in our justice system, by developing a policing system that people believe in *and* that they believe has their best interest at heart. Until we do that, people will do what they believe is necessary to stay safe.

## Losing a Brother to Violence

Violence has deeply affected my family. My brother lost his life to gun violence when I was a fledgling prosecutor. I was about twenty-five and he was around twenty-one. I felt incredible shame, as a prosecutor and as a Puerto Rican guy. This office did not have a lot of Latinos back then. Latinos are underrepresented working in our criminal legal system, especially in the ranks of prosecutors—and of course, it was the Puerto Rican guy's brother who had been shot and killed. So it was something I kept private. I don't think people realize that victims and survivors of crime are ashamed, because the immediate response is often, "What did they do to get themselves in this position?"

My brother dealt with addiction from the time he was thirteen.

It was a lifelong challenge for him. The family did the best we could to try and get him treatment; he would be good for a while, but then he would relapse. So when he was shot, it immediately opened up this can of worms that he had been a substance user basically his whole life.

For about three years there wasn't even a witness in the case. Then someone came forward and said he had seen the shooting. He was a pizza delivery guy who was from Mexico; he'd been afraid to report it because he was undocumented and didn't want anything to do with the police. He had continued delivering pizza in that neighborhood and kept seeing the two men involved in the killing of my brother, and they threatened him more than once. One day a group of guys were hanging out and called for pizza, and this man wound up delivering it. They threatened him again. He was afraid, but he made a courageous decision: he walked into a police station in a different part of the city and reported the murder.

The police eventually pieced together that he was talking about the killing of my brother. By the time our family was notified, years had passed and I was in a more senior position at the DA's office. I was a brand-new supervisor, and again, I felt ashamed. I was ashamed that my brother's murder was probably related to a debt owed for drugs, so I continued to keep it to myself. But eventually I had to talk about it: there is a rule in the DA's office that you have to notify a supervisor if you are involved in a criminal or civil proceeding. And though my brother wasn't killed in Brooklyn, once arrests were made, I was speaking to the detectives and getting more involved.

# Does the Process Help
# Victims *and* Survivors?

I think a lot of prosecutors don't truly understand the fear that witnesses and survivors go through. During the three years before my brother's case went to trial, our family had trauma from the court proceedings and how much time it all took. The justice system did not provide what we needed as crime victims, as survivors. We had anxiety, uncertainty, and fear of retaliation, particularly after my sister was threatened by friends of the people who'd been arrested. We just wanted this resolved. We did not believe that moving forward with the case was giving the family—especially my sister—the sense of safety and security we needed.

As a prosecutor, I started thinking about what we were doing and what services we were offering the community. Do we actually meet their needs? Is this what makes people feel they're getting justice or that the process works? As a family, we started to feel like it was a joke. What we needed from our justice system was a sense of safety, something the trial could never provide. We needed to understand why this had happened to my brother. Ultimately, we learned that he had been killed over a debt—a forty- or sixty-dollar debt.

Obviously, we thought there should be punishment, that there should be accountability, and we asked the DA who was handling the case for the maximum sentence. The shooter was convicted of manslaughter and served time. As a family we were open to forgiving him. He was just eighteen years old at the time of the shooting, and nobody in our family wanted him to spend his life in prison. A lot of people think survivors want to see a long prison sentence, but what *we* wanted was to make sure our family was safe—and that he wouldn't hurt anyone else. Those experiences have probably better prepared me to talk to the family members of victims. I don't often tell people about my brother, but I do make it my business to go to funerals, to wakes, to hospitals—and speak with crime victims and survivors, to let them know we care.

## Embracing Restorative Justice*

Our office recently had a case involving two friends who were heavy drinkers—sort of a dysfunctional relationship. During one of their "drinking all day" episodes, they got into a fight, really over nothing. The younger man, who was in his forties, killed the older man, who was in his sixties. It was pretty brutal: it was a fight that went three rounds. Ultimately, the younger guy just lost it and beat the older guy to death. These were people who had been friendly, whose families knew each other. We indicted him. It was a terrible case, but we're putting it through a restorative justice program where the families involved try to get the answers that *my* family sought: Why did this happen? Why did you do what you did? How do you feel about it now? How do we know that you're not going to hurt another person?

I think we're going to see more restorative justice practices, but it's rarely used when there's loss of life. In this case the victim's family was initially reluctant to be part of the process, but decided they'd rather have answers than just sit at a trial where

---

\* Restorative justice "brings together those directly impacted by an act of harm to address the impact of the crime, hold the person who did it accountable, and make things as right as possible for those harmed." See Common Justice, "Restorative Justice: Why Do We Need It?," common justice.org/restorative_justice_why_do_we_need_it; and *Fair and Just Prosecution, Building Community Trust: Restorative Justice Strategies, Principles and Promising Practices*, (San Francisco: Fair and Just Prosecution, 2017), fairandjustprosecution.org/wp-content/uploads/2017/12/FJP.Brief_.RestorativeJustice.pdf.

the defendant claimed justification, where they wouldn't get real answers.

## A Groundbreaking Marijuana Policy

In 2013, Brooklyn had had the same prosecutor since the late 1980s. Ken Thompson—an African American lawyer and upstart politician who had spent some time as a federal prosecutor and a civil rights attorney—decided to challenge him on a platform that focused on ending "stop-and-frisk," reviewing convictions, and doing things differently overall. When Ken won the election, it was a shock to a lot of people. Most of the political establishment stood by the previous DA, but I had a sense that Ken would win. Most of the people I knew in my community said they really liked what he promised, and a lot of them told me, "Sorry, Eric, we know you work there, but we're going to vote your boss out."

By the time Ken won, I was a mid-level supervisor in charge of one of the office's five trial divisions. In the courthouse and among the defense attorneys, I had a reputation for being fair and in tune with justice-related issues. After Ken won, a number of people in the field—defense attorneys, private attorneys, and even some judges—told him that he should think about promoting me. I had distinguished myself with the reform-oriented policies and practices I had put in place in my trial division. Ken asked me to take on a senior leadership role in his administration, and I started as counsel to the DA. He asked about my policy ideas: if I were in charge of this office, how would I do things differently?

One of the first things Ken entrusted me with was developing a new marijuana policy. The office was handling almost ninety thousand arrests a year in Brooklyn in the early 2000s.[3] When we looked closely at the data, in some years about fifteen thousand arrests were simply for possessing small amounts of marijuana—and this was at the height of stop-and-frisk in Brooklyn.[4] I witnessed this firsthand in my community. The police would stop young people, put them up against a wall, and tell them to empty their pockets. If they found marijuana, they would charge them with public possession, a misdemeanor—which is ridiculous, because it wasn't in public view until the police asked them to empty their pockets. Nonetheless, that's what made it a crime versus a violation, despite New York State having decriminalized possession of small amounts of marijuana in the 1970s.[5] Back then, in trying to be "color-blind," the DA's office did not track race or ethnicity. But we realized that about 81 percent of the people charged with possession in Brooklyn were African American or Latino.[6] That was shocking, given that marijuana use is pretty similar among racial and ethnic groups. By March 2014, we created a marijuana declination policy for possession: we said that the tactic of making someone empty their pockets and then charging them with public display of marijuana would no longer be tolerated, and we would decline to prosecute those cases.

Today this policy may seem unsurprising, but when we created it in 2014 it was met with the utmost hostility. Bill Bratton, the NYPD commissioner at the time, summoned the DA, who brought another colleague and me to a meeting where Bratton and all of his top brass told us that we could not do this: we could not create a policy for Brooklyn that differed from the rest of New York City. We were told that the police would continue making these arrests for marijuana and the NYPD expected our office to follow the law and prosecute the cases. But it tells you something that 30 percent of people being arrested citywide had never been in trouble with the law before.[7] This was often their first encounter with the justice system.

Our office fought back, and we continued to follow the policy I had outlined for Ken. We started to decline these cases. The media took cracks at us, with headlines like "Smoking It Up in Brooklyn," and said we were jeopardizing public safety.[8] But a strange thing happened from 2015 to 2019: crime decreased tremendously in Brooklyn, including shootings and homicides.

## Keeping a Legacy Alive

In 2014, Ken promoted me to chief assistant; I became his number two. In that position, I started to really understand the power of the DA's office to change policy. I saw that being independently elected meant that what we thought and did should be given at least as much weight as the opinion of the police commissioner, who is appointed but not elected. We were representing the largest county in the state, with 2.5 million people, and the policies we were advancing were things people in our community care about and wanted to see changed.

Unfortunately, when Ken was only fifty years old, he was diagnosed with Stage 4 cancer; he passed away within six months of his diagnosis. I became the acting district attorney, and I felt that the good work Ken had started was too important for me *not* to run for DA.

Given how closely associated I was with the progress our office had made, I believed that people would vote for me. I went into the 2017 race without a penny and hadn't held political office before, unlike some of my competitors. Shockingly, in a city that's 25 percent Hispanic, people said, "A Latino has never won a borough-wide race in Brooklyn—what makes you think you can be the first?"

We built a coalition throughout Brooklyn of people who believe what I believe: that the criminal legal system has to do more than punish people when they commit a crime; it has to make sure that every community and victim feels the system cares about them; and it has to treat everyone accused of a crime fairly and equally under the law. All of the racial disparities in our system had really undermined people's faith in it.

Winning the race was a bit like catching lightning in a bottle. A lot of things came together for me—but the grassroots movement backing my campaign played a big role. Seven people were in the race for DA at some point, but I won 53 percent of the vote and no one else received more than 10 percent.[9] It was a clear mandate that the policies I was talking about had resonated with the people of Brooklyn.

For me, justice means something more than just equality or fairness under the law. As the chief law enforcement officer for Brooklyn, it means serving and protecting the community—and *serving* is a big part of it. It means that when we take any action on behalf of the people, we understand what we're hoping to accomplish. Every time my prosecutors handle a case and charge someone, I ask them: will it make our community safer or will it cause more harm? Will it promote or erode public trust in our justice system? Helping others is why we have government and why we have law enforcement. It's having the mindset as a servant-leader to make sure that people will be treated fairly and equally, regardless of how much money they have, what race they are, or where they live in the borough.

## Community Members as Partners

Not every offense needs to be prosecuted. I'm moving more cases out of the criminal legal system, opting to send people for services instead. The future should be about engaging our communities more as partners in harm reduction, safety, and fairness.

For years the police department talked about crime being down in Brooklyn, but people didn't feel safer in their neighborhoods, and the *perception* of safety matters. Engaging our community members as partners in problem-solving is such an important piece of all this—and so is sharing some of the power that was entrusted to me as the steward of this office. We need to ask our communities, "What do you want to happen in cases like this?"

We completely reoriented our community service unit so that rather than sending someone arrested for a low-level crime to Rikers Island [New York City's main jail complex as of 2022] to clean toilet bowls or into the transit system to scrub off graffiti, as was done in the past, we refer them to community groups that support personal development, like GED or work programs.[10] Instead of being dealt with punitively, they leave the system knowing they've been treated fairly. Otherwise, people would return to their communities, their neighborhoods, their families, their churches, and their mosques, and say, "The system discriminates against us; the system hates us."

I work hard to be fair; it's important to me that people, including those accused of crime, understand that we don't hate them. We love them and we want to see them succeed. We want accountability for what they did wrong, but we don't punish people because we despise them. Most of them will return to our communities, and we want to be able to tell the people of Brooklyn that they're coming back not worse off for what happened, but hopefully better.

## Working with Other Forward-Thinking Prosecutors

Being part of a network of like-minded prosecutors has opened my eyes to a different way of doing this job. Seeing other people who care as much as I do about public safety and fairness is gratifying. It has also encouraged me to be brave, to tackle issues like vacating wrongful convictions and refusing to prosecute certain categories of cases.[†] It's so important to have a group of people who are equally committed to justice and fairness and equity in our criminal legal system—and to people's humanity.

In 2016, I created a policy to protect immigrants in our criminal legal system from deportation. I was still counsel to Ken Thompson at the time, and a motion landed on my desk from a Haitian man who had pleaded guilty to criminal possession of a controlled substance more than a decade earlier, which was a misdemeanor. When he was nineteen, a police officer had stopped him and told him to empty his pockets. Looking at that case in hindsight, it probably wasn't even a good stop-and-search.

He had a small amount of cocaine on him, one tinfoil. He was too afraid and embarrassed to let his family know that he had been arrested and was anxious to get the case over with. So he pleaded guilty to the possession charge, took a Treatment Readiness Program, and moved on with his life. Many years later, after the devastating earthquake in Haiti in 2010, he went there to try to find his aunt. By then he was a college graduate, was married, and had children. But when he tried to come back about a month later, he was denied reentry because he had a drug conviction on his record, even though he had a Green Card. His choices were to stay in Haiti or come into the States and into detention. That's when our office got involved.

The absurdity of this case was clear to me. It was problematic in terms of due process and probable cause, but it was also a distortion of justice: it was unfair that deportation or exclusion from this country would result from that type of contact with our criminal legal system. How ridiculous is it that we would deny someone reentry because he possessed a small amount of drugs twelve or thirteen years earlier! Early in my career as a prosecutor

---

[†]  A vacated conviction is one that is overruled or rendered void, a process established in states' and federal rules of criminal procedure.

we were told that collateral consequences like these weren't our concern, that it was up to defense attorneys to raise these issues. That seemed like a big failure to me. So I created an immigration policy to help protect people from collateral consequences, including deportation.

As far as I know, at that time I was the only DA in the country who was crafting policies to protect immigrants from deportation in criminal cases. A lot of people criticized me and said I was treating undocumented people better than citizens. I hired two immigration attorneys, not only to advise and train my staff, but to help train defense attorneys. Other reform-minded DAs learned of my approach and expressed interest in following suit. They said, "We want to make sure *our* justice system is fair and forward-thinking like this."

## A Shared Vision for Change

It was invaluable to have a group of like-minded prosecutors support me and follow my lead. At the time, Jeff Sessions, the U.S. attorney general, was criticizing me; later on, Attorney General Bill Barr also denounced our policy to protect immigrants. Nevertheless, I believe this work increased public safety. I'm reminded of my brother's case, where a witness did not come forward for years because he was afraid he would be deported if he talked to the police.

In 2016, I decided our office would stop all prosecution of marijuana—not just possession. It was a struggle with the police department, and people were critical that it would open a Pandora's box. When I called for the expungement of marijuana conviction records, twenty-five thousand people were affected through my office in a short period. I realized that if I stood with like-minded prosecutors and we argued for sound criminal justice policy, we could get our legislators to act. We went from having more than four hundred people arrested in Brooklyn for marijuana in 2019 to just ninety people in 2020.[11] In March 2021, New York State finally legalized marijuana and called for the expungement of these convictions.[12] During the arguments in the legislature, representatives from Brooklyn and other parts of New York City pointed to the work our office had done as proof that you could legalize without the risk of crime increasing.

Collectively, reform-minded DAs are transforming the justice system, and it's critical that we support one another and continue to hear from the best thinkers on tough policy topics—from law enforcement and academics and other practitioners. Working with and learning from other progressive prosecutors across the country has been a great source of pride and joy for me. It is especially important for me as a person of color to stand with my colleagues who are Black women—prosecutors who are facing such hatred, discrimination, and misogyny—and that we stand together.

## Looking Back and Moving Forward

We talk about lived experiences all the time with people who were formerly incarcerated or have had other contact with the justice system. I have my own lived experiences with the system. I know how it works and how it helps, as well as how it harms. It's important to talk about all of that—it makes a difference in how we pursue justice in Brooklyn.

In only two and a half years, Ken Thompson made a tremendous impact on justice and fairness here. I have a photo in my office of the two of us shaking hands when he promoted me to be his chief assistant. Every day, it's a reminder of my obligation to fight for the communities in Brooklyn that are still searching for equity, fairness, and safety. Being the chief law enforcement officer here was beyond my wildest dreams. In just a few short years as DA, we drove down the number of cases that this office prosecutes by more than 40 percent.[13] We continue to do pre-arraignment diversion, sending a lot of our cases to services without bringing them into the criminal legal system.[14] That's important because just entering the system has long-term consequences. No one can ever question that I care about public safety—I have spent my life fighting for it. For every action I take, I think about how it relates to safety. Knowing how much you can accomplish in such a short time is what keeps me motivated and moving forward.

# 8

# Mark Gonzalez

District Attorney, Nueces County, Texas

*On election night in 2016, Mark Gonzalez went to sleep thinking he had probably lost the race for district attorney in Nueces County. He woke up to the news that he had won and would represent the jurisdiction where he grew up—in a town so small that "we know everyone." After attending Texas A&M University and St. Mary's University School of Law, the self-described "Mexican biker lawyer covered in tattoos" worked for years as a criminal defense attorney before becoming DA. Mark Gonzalez was reelected to that position in 2020.*

Justin Sterling
*Renegade (after Mark Gonzalez)*, 2021
Found window, fiberglass, bullet casings, insulation foam, caulking

**Justin Sterling** is a contemporary/modern artist who works across a range of mixed media, from sculpture and installations to painting and drawing to music and performance. He is an activist who hopes his work inspires dialogue about social, economic, and political issues, civil disobedience, and what it means to be a citizen. For more about Justin's work, see his website, justintoart.com.

## Artist's Statement

*Mark Gonzalez is an anomaly of a personality. It is admirable and brave to become a DA as a member of a bike club that, unfortunately, is included in a gang database in Texas. Mark is the quintessential example of "don't judge a book by its cover," so this piece juxtaposes pink fiberglass and bullet casings. He is a renegade empowered to show us what empathy is during these times of violence, suffering, and addiction that are inflamed further by mass incarceration.*

## "You're the DA?"

Being a DA and in the "gang database" can definitely be complicated. I've been in a bike club called the Calaveras for over ten
years. I was a biker a long time before I became a DA. I worked in
a bike shop during college; I have always loved motorcycles, and
my family does too. But where I live, the Corpus Christi Police
Department has put anyone who's in a motorcycle club into the
two databases they use to track potential gang members in Texas.[1]

I haven't been arrested in a very long time, but I continue to be
on this list. Every time I travel outside of the country, I get treated
very well. I travel to Mexico—no issues. If I travel overseas—no
issues. It's when I'm coming *back* to my own home, into my own
country, that I get treated like a criminal. Everyone I travel with
knows to expect this. I tell them, "Look, I'm probably going to
get pulled aside to a small room. They're going to look through
my stuff. I'll be out in about ten to fifteen minutes, and I'll meet
you on the other side." And that's what happens: I get detained by
Customs simply because I'm on that list.

One time a Customs agent asked, "So what do you do?" And
I grinned. I said, "I'm the district attorney for Nueces County."
She was skeptical and replied, "You're the DA?" So then four or
five officers were looking at the computer and looking back at me,
and one of them said, "He says he's the district attorney." Eventually they released me. They said, "You would think that being the
DA, you could get off this list." But that hasn't happened.

In this part of Texas, everybody knows who I am, so any time
an officer has stopped me nearby, they've greeted me and gone
on their way. But one time I was in Laredo, which is about four
counties away, and I was stopped by a sheriff. I was speeding. He
said, "Step out of the vehicle." To me that was a red flag right off
the bat. If I ever get stopped, I turn off the engine, roll down the
windows, and put my hands on the steering wheel where they can

see them—out of an abundance of caution, because I don't want to put an officer in fear. If they're in fear, we know bad things can happen. So when he told me to get out of the car, I told my wife, "Just hang tight."

The officer sent me to the back of the car and was being very aggressive with me. He interlocked my hands, went through all my stuff, and I asked, "Hey, what's going on?" because what he was doing to me wasn't warranted. He had me by my back and he said, "Do you have any drugs or weapons?" And I said, "Bro, I don't have no drugs or weapons; I have my pocketknife right here, but that's it." And he said, "Well, can you tell me why you're coming up on the gang database?" I said, "I'm a Calavera, I ride a bike. It's a family club. We're not an outlaw club." I realized that I had made the decision to speed, so I started to get calm and collected. But I still felt violated by the experience—and by being on that list.

Now I'm fighting on behalf of everybody in Texas who is on that list. Given how it affects me personally as a DA, imagine how it affects an everyday person when they come into contact with law enforcement for a minor infraction like speeding or an expired registration sticker. As the DA, I have the authority to try to right those wrongs. I have taken steps to spread information about how to get out of this database if you haven't committed a crime in the past five years—and many, many people on this list haven't. But they shouldn't have to request to be removed from the list; they should be removed automatically. We're trying to right these wrongs, and it starts here with me.

## Coming of Age in Small-Town Texas

I grew up in a small town called Agua Dulce: in English it means "sweet water." It's about forty-five miles west of Corpus Christi. If you blink, you'll pass through it. I graduated high school with twenty-five students in my class, so if somebody is from the town, I know them. Doesn't matter how old they are, I know them. We know everyone.

I had what I thought was a normal upbringing. I lived with my mother and father, and around the eighth grade, my parents got a divorce. I kept living with my dad, who worked at a refinery in a neighboring town, as many of the dads did. It put a lot of food on the table for our community, but by the time I was getting into high school, a lot of those guys had lost their jobs. My dad did shift work, so sometimes he worked nights and sometimes days. When he worked nights, you could say it was pretty wild for my brother and me. He was a year younger than me and we attended the same school; there was just one school in town!

My dad took the separation from my mother really hard. He was out there trying to discover himself, and that meant my brother and I were on our own. It was literally like *Lord of the Flies*. We learned soon that if you want clean clothes, you wash them; if you want food, you make it; if you want to go to school, then go to school; if you don't want to go to school, you don't have to.

Living with my mom was very different; we always had everything we needed. But with my dad, every month we could count on something going out, whether it was the lights, the gas, or the water. And it wasn't like today, when you can pay over the phone and it gets turned on automatically. If it was Friday and the lights went out, they wouldn't be back until Monday. I remember in high school taking showers at the gym because we didn't have hot water, stuff like that. I look back and it's kind of crazy, but we were happy because we got to do whatever we wanted and we always had friends around who felt like family.

When I graduated high school, I didn't know what I wanted to do. A lot of us in our community weren't told or expected to go to college; it wasn't something people talked or bragged about. Most people went off to work in the oil field, and some people wanted to be like their dads and work in the refinery. But my dad kicked me out—with no car, just whatever I had. He said, "You're going to live with your mom in Corpus, and she's enrolled you at Texas A&M." I thank God that she did, because that's where I started this journey that I'm still on today.

I don't even know how my mother did this, but back in the day it was different: she enrolled me, picked my classes, and I was off. During my first year I was still wild, because I was used to living with my father and wasn't used to people telling me what to do. Living with my mom and her husband, it felt weird that she was washing my clothes and preparing my meals and telling me, "Hey, it's eight o'clock! I don't care if you're hungover, you need to go to school."

## A Rude Awakening
## That Changed Everything

One night I went to a party in Kingsville, a neighboring town. I had made a lot of mistakes, but that night I got caught for the mistake I made. I got a DWI, and I think that's why I'm where I'm at now. I was going probably seventy in a thirty-five–mile-per-hour zone, then stopped at a store to meet up with someone I was supposed to stay with. When I got there, she said, "Hey, there's a cop behind you." I was super intoxicated and I told the officer that and I didn't resist. He said I was speeding, and I said, "Yes, sir." He said, "You smell like alcohol," and I said, "Yes, sir." I pretty much gave him my hands and he put me in the back of his car.

I found myself in jail that night. They were pretty generous with the phone calls in Kingsville, and I got to call as many phone numbers as I could remember. I called my dad, my mom, and my cousin, and all three showed up—and luckily, in small places you get bonded out pretty quickly, so I got out of jail. My parents were disappointed in me, I was disappointed in myself, and that was pretty much it. I thought that maybe it would just magically go away, or they'd give me a chance and it would disappear. Well, it didn't.

Many weeks later I got a letter in the mail. My mom opened it and said, "You have to go to court in Kingsville." I asked her what that meant; I'd never been to court. I'd gotten in trouble for other things, but this was different—I had to appear in front of a judge. I asked her what to do. And she said, "*Mijo,* I'll go with you, you'll plead guilty, and they'll be nice to you." Back then I didn't know any lawyers or judges—I didn't even know any college graduates. So that sounded like the smartest thing to do—you know, you take your mom and it shows that you've got family. You don't fight it and they'll be nice to you.

That is *not* what happened. I can't say I was railroaded, but I definitely got the deal that everybody gets when they bring their mom and not a lawyer: I got one year of probation, where you have to give urinalysis, do community service and monthly check-ins, and you can't leave the county without permission.

When I was entering my plea of guilt, I was sitting in this courtroom, and I saw other people who were accused of crimes: some of them were like me—there with their mom, their grandmother, maybe an uncle. Then there were people who were *not* like me; they were there with lawyers. And I saw this Navy pilot, and his lawyer said, "You know what, we have a Navy pilot here, we don't want to ruin this young man's life," and the judge said, "We're going to go ahead and dismiss this case."

To me it was like someone flipped a switch: hold on, he and I did the exact same thing. But with this Navy pilot, they don't want to ruin *his* life. I brought my mom, but he brought a *lawyer* and his case was dismissed. I felt betrayed. And I don't know if it was because of how I looked—the pilot was a white dude, the lawyer was a white dude, the judge was a white dude, and I am definitely not a white dude—or if it was the difference a lawyer made. I didn't want anyone else to go through what I did. And I saw it all close-up.

I decided I wanted to try to be a lawyer so that I could help my friends, so they wouldn't have to take their moms with them to court; they could take me. That's pretty much how I started to *want* to be a lawyer. I was in college, but it wasn't like now, when you can Google "how can I become a lawyer?" It was hard to figure out. But I thought, "Okay, now I know what I want to do." I still think I got the raw end of the deal; I know now that my case almost definitely would have been dismissed if I'd had a lawyer—someone like me. But I also realize that one single event changed my life, and it probably changed a ton of other people's lives too. That incident had an impact on people I don't even know, people I've never even met.

## Just Getting By

I was very lucky to get into law school; I don't know how I did. I applied to St. Mary's University School of Law, in San Antonio, and I got in. But when I looked around, I quickly realized that there was nobody else like me. I was probably the only guy in law school with tattoos; now I'm probably the only DA with this many tattoos.

I worked through law school because it was the only way I could afford to go. I was lucky to get a job at Texas RioGrande Legal Aid, where they helped people who couldn't afford attorneys. Before that I typically worked as a motorcycle mechanic, a laborer; I built fences, roofed, laid brick, landscaped, did irrigation—anything you could think of to do with your hands. I remember interviewing for the Legal Aid job: The woman asked me, "Mark, why should we hire you? You've never had an office job." And I told her, "That's the reason! If you don't hire me, I'm never gonna get an office job! I'm in law school now and that should count for something. And if y'all need something fixed around here, I can fix it." And she gave me an opportunity. I worked there until I graduated.

I was not very good at law school. I had friends who wouldn't even try and were making great grades, and here I was, trying as much as I could—reading all day, every day, studying whenever I wasn't at work—and I would still come up short. My second year I was on academic probation, and I thought, "What happens if I get kicked out?" So I had a letter from my dean, and I put it in my carrel and I would read it every single day to remind myself what was important: just getting through. And by the grace of God, I got through. I graduated 285th in a class of 286, and I'm very proud of that!

Then I took the bar exam and found that I was not good at taking the bar, either. The first time I didn't pass it; I did horribly. The second time I thought, "Okay, I'm going to try really hard," but I did horribly again. By the third time, it had been a whole year—and probably one of the worst years of my life—that I was just studying and didn't know if I was ever going to be good enough. It didn't matter that I got through law school, because without passing the bar I wouldn't be able to practice law and would still be in the same spot. That third time I passed by one point, and it was one of the best feelings in my life. Someone called me that night and said, "Dude, you passed!" We celebrated, and then I thought, "Okay, now what am I going to do?"

## Getting Paid in Shrimp and Decorating the Office

I knew from the get-go that I was going to help people and represent them. At first, I represented my relatives when they got into trouble, and then I started representing my relatives' friends, and before I knew it, I was representing a lot of people. Back in those days, I would represent people for anything. I worked on one huge case in a small town; the guy didn't have money, but I wanted to take the case because I didn't think he did what they accused him of—and I knew it would make a lot of headlines. I wanted to help him out. Ultimately, I think I got a treadmill and a washer as payment.

I had to accept whatever clients were able to pay me. I wasn't going to *not* represent someone because of money; we could work something out. One time I got paid in shrimp; another guy would do oil changes—and it didn't mean that I wouldn't try my hardest. I was very successful as a criminal defense attorney. It's strange how helping people can generate business and provide a life for you, one where you don't have to worry about the lights or gas going off—or anything else.

When I was a young lawyer, I represented this one guy and he owed me some money. He said, "Mark, I know it's Christmas, man, and I can't pay you, but I brought you something." And it was this huge painting—it's probably four by five feet. It's on the wall right behind my desk; it takes up the whole wall. I'd never had any art. He brought me this amazing painting of Emiliano Zapata, and he said, "Man, I thought of you, and I thought of him, and I made you this painting."[2]

I consider myself Mexican American, so I've studied the Mexican Revolution and I've always thought highly of Emiliano Zapata. He felt that the land should belong to the people, and he would say—there's a saying in Spanish—that he would rather die on his feet than live on his knees. Obviously the painter and I were square on the retainer fee. I told him, "This is beautiful; this is priceless. You don't owe me any more money." I've hung it in every office I've ever had, just to remember that the land *does* belong to the people, and personally, I *would* rather die on my feet than ever live on my knees.

In every office I've had, I've hung up two things: my huge

Emiliano Zapata painting and my mug shot. One of my mentors—this attorney I looked up to—had a mug shot in his office of himself when he was a young man. I realized when I saw his photo that there was a mug shot of me out there. I went down to Kingsville to bail somebody out, and I asked the sheriff if I could get my mug shots. They gave them to me and I hung them up in my office, to remind myself what it felt like when I didn't have somebody there by my side who wasn't my mom. Some people may laugh, but it's something I'm—almost—proud of, because going through that helped me get to where I am today.

## A Grassroots Campaign and a Surprise

I went from getting paid in shrimp to having a big caseload and making so much money I almost felt guilty. As a criminal defense attorney, I was angry at the way the DA's office worked. And I never once asked the DA for even a plea offer, because, number one, the pleas they were giving were not fair; and number two, I just felt that they were intent on doing anything to win.

At that time, the DA was up for reelection. I was waiting for somebody to run that I could support, but no one stood up. I took a hard look at myself and said, "I can gripe about the situation or I can try to do something about it." I had an associate working for me, Matt, who later became my assistant; he was a young African American guy who went to Howard University, which is very different from where we live in Texas. And I told him I wanted to run for DA. And Matt said, "Mark, why? We're making a killing here, we're making a lot of money, we're helping a lot of people; let's just stay here in our lane." And I said, "Dude, if we don't do it, then who will?"

So that's how I decided to run in 2016. We ran a grassroots campaign: we went to the flea markets, we registered voters, including people who had been incarcerated who thought they no longer had voting rights. I had a bus—an old Regional Transportation Authority bus—with my face on the side. We would drive around and take people to medical appointments and ultimately take them to go vote in the primaries.

Election Day started early; we got up at 5 a.m. and by 10:30 a.m. I was already exhausted. I told my family, "God knows where he wants us to be. If we win, we win." That night, me and my wife—my girlfriend at the time—went home and I said, "Look, we're going to find out one way or the other; there's nothing we can do." So I locked my door, I turned off my phone, and I just went to sleep!

They called the race super late, at about one in the morning, and my brother and all my friends were celebrating. These guys were out toasting, taking shots, and someone said, "We have to go tell Mark!" My brother had been celebrating a lot and decided to come over. I was still asleep, and he said, "You won! You did it! You're the DA of Nueces County!" I just couldn't believe what he had said. So I checked the local ABC affiliate, and sure enough, I had won. I went to sleep four thousand votes behind and woke up as the next DA of Nueces County.

## Changing Lives with the Stroke of a Pen

I had no real idea what the DA actually does—or the actual power the DA has—until I got sworn in and went into the office that following January. I tried to set up the office to make sure we had the people I wanted there—and that we removed the people I knew I couldn't work well with. It's one thing to fight about a case with someone who would be fair, but it'd be another thing to fight with someone who will do anything to win. So we identified those people, and before even taking the oath, we told them that they were no longer needed. When I walked through the door, we brought our team together and said, "Hey, I want to welcome everybody as we're starting the new year. You see that some people aren't here, and they aren't here for the following reasons." And then we told them point-blank those reasons, the vision for our office, and we hit the ground running.

I think I made some smart choices: I brought Matt with me, my trusted ally and associate, and made him one of two first assistants; I had one for the courts and one on the administration side. I could really trust Matt, though he was hesitant to come. He said, "Mark, you're already setting yourself up for failure. I'm a thirty-year-old African American dude, and you want me to be your number one? People are going to say I don't have the experience, they'll say this and that." And I told him, "I don't care what people say. We're going to do a lot of things that aren't going to make people happy. And I know I can trust you," and that was something I really needed at that point.

Taking office and finding out what it was actually like was a shocker to me; that first week, people were like, "Hey, boss, we've got a murder out here. What do you want to do—what do you want to charge them with?" And that's when the gravity of the responsibility of the office truly hit me. *I* get to decide what happens now, and what cases we charge collectively with my office and the people who are in it. I really had to have trust and faith that they were going to do exactly what I thought was appropriate, because there's no way any DA can oversee every single case that goes through their office.

One day this hit me like a stack of books: I said to Matt, "Why don't we divert marijuana possession cases?" We didn't want to prosecute; I felt right off the bat that people shouldn't have convictions for marijuana, especially with the inequities usually associated with it. I didn't want people to lose their funding if they were in school, to lose their housing or their jobs; I just didn't think it was fair. So I said, "Why don't we just give pretrial diversion programs to everyone who is accused of marijuana possession, whether it's their first or their hundredth time?" Then they'd have an opportunity to keep that off their record. I asked Matt if we could do that, and when he said yes, I was like, "Are you serious? What do I need to do to make that happen?" And he said, "Send out an email and we'll start doing it now!" That's when I realized that with an email, with a signature, with a stroke of a pen, we could change policy for our entire community. And I realized that this job is something more than I thought it was, and more than a lot of the community thinks it is. I also knew that maybe I had only four years to do it, so day after day we've done our best to create policies that would help our community.

## "This *Shouldn't* Be Easy."

Every day you're the DA is a hard one. Getting into the race in 2020 was a hard decision for me and my wife; she didn't want me to run again. But I told her, "God knows where I need to be." I owe it to my community, because the work I've started isn't over yet. I think that this next term we can finish—or catch up or keep moving in the right direction.

It isn't easy. But deciding what's going to happen to somebody shouldn't be easy. When you have to decide on a policy that could hurt somebody—victims or even defendants and the defendant's family—it shouldn't be easy. So most days at the office aren't easy, but I can tell you, I go to the local supermarket and I see people, and it's kind of mind-blowing. Most of the time they call me Judge, because people don't even know what the DA does. And they say, "Judge Gonzalez, Judge Gonzalez! Thank you so much: I didn't get arrested the other day because of your program, and I thanked the officer, who said, 'No, you have to thank the DA, because he's the one who put the cite-and-release program in place.'"[3] You know, those are the things that really keep me going—the small things with huge impact.

So I know what we're doing is what we *should* be doing, and I know now that I don't intend to run again, and I say that openly and honestly, but it also gives me a sense of freedom, because we can do so many great things in this term. We can right these wrongs, even if it's going up against a statewide or local police department. People know that this term is about accountability, whether you're a regular person in the community or somebody who is entrusted to keep us safe.

## A New Vision of Justice

People talk a lot about my tattoos. When I was a defense attorney, I got "Not Guilty" tattooed on my chest, because I believe the state has to prove every single case, to prove when somebody is guilty of a crime.[4] Obviously I believe it so much that I got the tattoo. Once I became DA, people asked me, "What are you going to do now? Are you going to mark out the word 'not'?" And I told them, "Every prosecutor and every DA should have 'not guilty' tattooed on their heart, to remind them what they have to prove." And that's our burden; that's our job. If you were accused of a crime, you would want every prosecutor to have "not guilty" somewhere on them.

For me, justice is very simple: it's fairness. It's making sure that everyone is getting the same opportunity, and for so long that has not been the case. If you are a brown or Black person or somebody who came out of this neighborhood or you took your mom with you to court, you weren't treated the same way as a Navy pilot who had a lawyer. Justice for me also comes in the form of second chances. It comes in consequences when someone learns their lesson and hopefully doesn't commit the same action again. Justice doesn't look like what I think a lot of people think it is. At the end of the day, we just have to do what's right and fair.

# What You Don't Learn in School

It's an exciting time to be a prosecutor. So many people are starting to think about criminal justice, mass incarceration, and the wrongs done to so many. And now with technology and social media, these stories are getting out. The responsibility we have as prosecutors is so much bigger now, and I'm glad to be a part of that. I know that my platform and shelf life will only last so long, so I have an urgency, every single day, to do as much as I can—to tell and share my stories as much as I can.

I've learned so much from other prosecutors, on all levels, whether it's about the death penalty or other issues. I learned so much about racism in the United States, stuff that was not taught to me in high school, and frankly, that angered me and still does. Very early on in my administration—probably before I could even log on to a computer in my office—I was asked if we were going to seek the death penalty in a murder case. It was a brutal murder, and I felt I should leave that decision to the jury. But as the case moved along, I found myself being scared that the jury was going to convict this man and sentence him to death—and what if they did that? Would I have failed as a DA, as a person? Thankfully, the jury felt that he didn't deserve the death penalty, and now we've stopped seeking the death penalty in my county, because we came to the conclusion that it isn't fair and shouldn't be used anymore. That's something I learned from experts, including people in other countries.

Being the DA is something I never thought I would do. I've seen and met people I never would have if I hadn't become the DA. It's been a crazy ride, and I'm very thankful to be on it. I want everyone to say, "He was always fair with all of us; he was always transparent and upfront. You always knew where you stood with him; he always told you where he stood." That's one of the main things I want people to say when they mention me: "He did what he thought was right and he always wanted to be fair." If people can say that, then I'll be happy. Then I'll have done my job.

# 9

# Larry Krasner

District Attorney, City and County of
Philadelphia, Pennsylvania

*In 2017, Larry Krasner defeated six other Democrats and ultimately a Republican candidate to become district attorney of Philadelphia the following January. During his campaign he vowed to upend the city's criminal legal system, which had been one of the most carceral in the country for decades. Once in office, Krasner's policies helped dramatically decrease the local jail population, kept most children charged with a crime out of the adult system, adopted a public health approach to drug use, and took action to hold police accountable. He also established a Conviction Integrity Unit that had helped exonerate twenty-two people as of November 2021. Krasner attended the University of Chicago and Stanford Law School. His first term was the subject of the PBS Independent Lens series* Philly D.A. *He overwhelmingly won the Democratic primary in May 2021 and was reelected six months later.*

James "Yaya" Hough
*Points of Connection (Portrait of Larry Krasner)*, 2020
Acrylic on canvas

**James "Yaya" Hough** is a Pittsburgh-based artist and painter. He was incarcerated at the age of seventeen and served twenty-three years before being released in 2019. While in prison, he took art classes and partnered with Mural Arts Philadelphia as a muralist. He has contributed to more than fifty murals and was the inaugural artist in residence at the office of Philadelphia District Attorney Larry Krasner. For more on James's work, see his Instagram account: @hough9459.

## Artist's Statement

*As the artist in residence at the office of Philadelphia District Attorney Larry Krasner, I crafted a collection of portraits,* Points of Connection, *to humanize people living and working within justice systems through my art-making. For the project, I crafted portraits of formerly incarcerated people, victim advocates, and members of the district attorney's office—all using the same size and technique. I created these images with the hope of offering a window into the larger system, enabling us all to approach the justice system from perspectives of transformation, repair, and growth.*

## The "Gift" of Growing Up Different

I grew up in St. Louis and then Philadelphia, going to public schools. My parents were from very different backgrounds. My father was the son of Russian Jewish immigrants, and my mother was a tent evangelist.* They were both from the St. Louis area and lived through the Depression and World War II. My dad, who had been a postal worker, volunteered for the war, and because of the G.I. Bill, became the first person in his family to go to college. My mother graduated high school at sixteen and advanced through Bible College and then the seminary.

We didn't have a lot in common with people who lived in our area. Things got worse when my dad, who had terrible arthritis, had to be hospitalized while we were still in St. Louis and ended up having both of his hips removed. He spent the last twenty-five years of his life in a wheelchair.

When your parents become unemployed or incapable of working, it can make you feel like an outsider, and we already felt like outsiders. When you're in a relatively nice public school in a working-class area that's also somewhat affluent and you're getting food stamps, that can make you feel like an outsider. We didn't have a car, and when your community doesn't have sidewalks and you have to walk in the street, you can feel like an outsider. Likewise when you have parents who are idealistic, artistic, religious, that sort of thing. And when the only pool in town is

---

* Through the 1960s, traveling evangelist ministers regularly held tent revival services, particularly in the summer and in the South. See Karen Sorensen, "Faith: The Rise and Fall of Tent Revival Church Services," *Taunton Daily Gazette*, June 16, 2010, tauntongazette.com/story/bulletin-tab/2010/06/16/faith-rise-fall-tent-revival/65328623007; and Lloyd D. Barba, "California's Cross: A Cultural History of Pentecostalism, Race, and Agriculture," doctoral thesis, University of Michigan, 2016, deepblue.lib.umich.edu/bitstream/handle/2027.42/133490/ldbarba_1.pdf.

unaffordable to your family, probably by design to keep people out who don't have a lot of money, you can feel like an outsider.

But looking back, I think that feeling turned out to be a gift. That sense of being different, of not being the archetype, can be really helpful if one day you're in a position to make decisions about other people's lives. Today, when I recruit people to work with our office, I look for whether they have ever been an outsider—whether they understand what it is to be marginalized, to be the outsider who's trying to become an insider, or to have been bullied and to have pushed back. I like to see that.

## A Life-Changing Jury Experience

After majoring in Spanish and literature in college, I didn't know exactly what I wanted to do. I had three things in mind: to be a Spanish professor, to go to divinity school, or to go to law school. My younger brother was pretty clear about the direction I should take, though. He said, "What are you talking about? You like to argue with people." He was not completely wrong.

So eventually I made it to Stanford Law School, but first I took a year off and worked as a not-very-skilled carpenter. During that time, I was selected for a death penalty jury in Chester County, just outside of Philadelphia. It was a sequestered jury—meaning that we couldn't have contact with anyone on the outside—and the case took place right after the U.S. Supreme Court had reinstated the death penalty.[1] So it was the first death penalty case in that county in many years. It was a very, very high-publicity case involving the brutal rape and murder of an elderly woman as well as arson.[2] She was the mother of an FBI agent, so right after her murder the area was flooded with FBI agents. They caught the defendant at a motel with the woman's car; his bloody thumbprint was on the rearview mirror and the blood was hers.

During deliberations, one of the jurors was removed when the judge realized that the man had mental health issues that were preventing him from participating capably. The parties wound up reaching a deal: the defense would accept a guilty verdict with just eleven jurors, but only if the death penalty were not an option. Of course, we didn't know that. All we knew was that eleven of us were continuing to deliberate on guilt, and when we delivered our verdict, a lot of us were pretty tense about the idea of going back to deliberate on a death phase. But then we were informed that we could all go home, that it was over.

Being on that jury was a truly transformative experience for me. By the time the case concluded, I was certain that I wanted to be a lawyer and wanted to work in criminal justice. I was drawn to the trial and to the tremendous strengths and weaknesses I saw with juries. I was fascinated by the quality of the investigation. I saw someone picked for the jury to help decide between life or death, yet the system didn't even realize he was seriously impaired. I also witnessed some jurors make racist comments during deliberations on the guilt phase. A white man with a cowboy hat said, "You know what we're here to do: we're here to get this boy"—and the defendant was Black. The foreperson seemed primarily concerned with getting the verdict over with, because he missed his son who had gone off to college and was coming home soon for the holidays. His priority was to finish quickly and get home.

But at the same time, there was something really impressive about the process. Here were twelve people who had really different capacities. Some people remembered everything about the timing; some had really rational, complex thinking around the physical evidence; and others had strong memories of the procedure. In a way it was like a super brain. It was twelve people's thinking at both their best and worst. It was a fascinating experience and a window into some pretty wonderful and some pretty terrifying aspects of the criminal legal system.

# Homing in on Social Justice

I graduated from Stanford Law School dedicated to the idea of doing criminal justice work, but not necessarily to be a defense attorney. I interviewed at public defender and prosecutor offices around the country and had job opportunities with both. But I ended up at the public defender's office in Philadelphia, which, I believe, was the right place for me to be in 1987: all the prosecutors' offices where I interviewed were much too traditional and too punitive.

While I was a public defender, I got involved with various social justice movements and ended up having a close relationship with ACT UP, one of the most effective activist groups I've ever seen.[3] They were responding to the early days of HIV and AIDS by organizing and taking action. They got me onto a mayoral commission to investigate what was effectively a police riot. I had been a lawyer for only three years, but it made me realize that I wanted to do more than just criminal defense. I also wanted to be a civil rights attorney, to address police abuse.

Five years into my career, I set up my own firm and practiced both defense and civil rights law for the next twenty-five years. Criminal defense in state and federal court made up about 80 percent of my work, but the other 20 percent was the only kind of prosecution of police that was happening in Philadelphia. In my opinion, at that time, both the U.S. Attorney's Office and the Philadelphia District Attorney's Office persistently looked the other way when police were involved in brutality, corruption, framing people, and conduct of that sort. It was truly rare for them to make any effort to deal with those practices, and they usually lost whenever they tried. The only way you could really go after police corruption and violence was to sue police and municipalities over violations of constitutional rights as a civil attorney. I found great satisfaction doing that work.

## Standing Up for Fairness

Many of my criminal and civil cases made an impact on me. I remember representing a homeless man who had stolen food for maybe the third or fourth time, and because of the Pennsylvania retail statute, he was charged with a felony because of his past violations. Judges thought that was normal and it was exactly what prosecutors pursued. That struck me as deeply unfair and inherently unjust.

Later in my career I represented "Dinosaur Man." His brother told me that the man thought he was a dinosaur. He was about sixty years old, had a very low IQ, and had faced serious developmental challenges his whole life. He had been arrested in Philadelphia after becoming agitated in front of a public school. Police responded, but not in a way that made sense, especially for someone who had any kind of disability or impairment. They broke his nose and some other bones in his face. They hurt him badly—and then charged him with aggravated assault on police.

Before I met him, Dinosaur Man had been sitting in a jail for a year after a judge found him incompetent to stand trial three times. When I walked into the jail's mental health unit to see him, one of the guards said, "I hope you can get him out of here." As I approached him, I heard this growling noise: he was sitting at a table, growling. I sat down and started talking with him. He explained to me that he was a dinosaur, and what happened on the street was that he'd had a battle with King Kong.

He believed the police were King Kong and he proceeded to act out the entire battle, with growls and pantomime, to explain what had occurred. Then he sat down, and I said, "Well, look, your brother sent me here and wants me to find a way to get you to live with him down in Florida, where they have better facilities." He said he loved his brother and wanted to go see him. Eventually, we got a compassionate judge to release him to his brother. Dinosaur Man wound up in a much better place, but it was not because of anything done by the criminal legal system, which had kept him in a cell for over a year with no mental health treatment.

Dinosaur Man stuck with me, and cases like that led me to represent activists and protestors for free. It was my professional hobby, because what do traditional prosecutors do to them? They lock them up! They prosecute them! What else would you do to nice people trying to change the world in nonviolent ways? I would defend them when I wasn't trying whatever criminal case I had going on, and I really enjoyed that work. I think all of those experiences ultimately had quite a bit to do with my decision to run for DA.

## A City's Troubling History

When I was approached to run for district attorney in Philadelphia, the office had a wonderful reputation in some parts of the city—the parts that were in favor of locking up everybody for as long as possible. But most of the city did not share that view. Most of the people viewed the Philly DA's office as an unfair, cruel place where winning was the only thing that mattered. They were right.

As of November 2021, we had fewer than five thousand people in our jail system.[4] But before I ran, there were thousands more, for decades. Philadelphia had historically had the highest incarceration rate of the country's ten largest cities. It was also a city with one of the highest levels of probation and parole supervision. It was a place where one of the former district attorneys, Lynne Abraham, achieved a death penalty sentence 108 times, which was basically once every two months she was in office.[5] She even bragged about her "passion" for the death penalty.[6]

This was Frank Rizzo's town. He was a cop who became the

police commissioner and then the mayor. Rizzo pretty much sold the city's entire future to fund pay hikes, pensions, and other entitlements for police and firefighters.[7] In many ways he made the police union here the most powerful political entity in the entire city. Mayors didn't mess with them at contract time. Until very recently there was a Frank Rizzo statue near Philadelphia City Hall. It's gone now; it was removed shortly after the protests surrounding George Floyd's murder. I think that reflects how the city has changed, but Rizzo's legacy of unchecked power for the Philadelphia Police Department remains. It's an enduring problem, and one that obviously has to be remedied.

## Slamming the Brakes on Mass Incarceration

I decided to run for DA so that I could pick the building up and shake out everything that was broken. It was an office dreadfully in need of change—in many ways in need of a complete reversal of course. I was frustrated that after thirty years of working hard and getting good results for many of my individual clients, we had more and more incarceration. It no longer felt like enough to pursue only individual justice, client by client, when the entire system was unjust and going in the wrong direction. When I saw the list of candidates in the race, I realized they were mainly in the mold of all the district attorneys I had dealt with during my career. To them, the job was all about being punitive and incarcerating more people.

I started to think that all my years of representing activists and having good relationships with some of the criminal defense attorneys—and some of the ex-prosecutors—might have value. I knew how weak the big city political machines actually were, and how an insurgent candidate could win. I had watched my wife get elected as a judge fifteen years earlier, running from outside the political machine. Over the years I helped a few people I knew to become judges, because when she ran, my wife had kind of cracked the code.

To win the race for DA, I knew things would have to break the right way on all the decisions we'd made. I had learned from past social justice movements about how to communicate with voters. And this is a social movement; this is coming from the grass roots. Our message—that mass incarceration is a direct consequence of a broken criminal legal system in need of fixing—resonated with the public. People wanted progressive prosecution, and we wanted to show that it's possible to slam the brakes on mass incarceration, just as it was possible to slam on the gas thirty or forty years ago.

We won in spite of not being the favorite. In fact, the local media at first referred to me as a "hilarious" candidate and a "liberal unicorn." But we won because we were saying what people had wanted for a long time. We were weak in many different ways, but we were not weak on ideas. We launched our campaign with a ten-minute speech in which we laid out everything we stood for: ending mass incarceration, ending mass supervision, protecting immigrants, and tending to the real needs of victims as opposed to using them as political pawns. We put the video on YouTube and it spread very quickly; in the first week we had something like 25,000 views. We won not because of me, but because people wanted what we were promising. It was the outsiders who liked these ideas: people who hadn't ever voted or hadn't voted in a long time, people who were completely alienated from a political process that they viewed as being a clubhouse of insiders. They were drawn to our message.

## Bringing the Outsiders In

I don't believe you can change old-school prosecution and mass incarceration overnight, but since I took office we have made tremendous progress toward cultural change. We completely redid how we recruit staff, with the understanding that this is a social justice movement. We know how crucial recruiting is, because I will not be DA forever. We have recruited for talent and for hard work. We have recruited for diversity of every type, and we have done so all over the country—at every single law school at historically Black colleges and universities, every one of the top-twenty law schools, and the Philly law schools, and we will consider someone who comes to us from any law school. When you bring in hypertalented mission-driven people from all over, each one with an intact moral compass, that leads to real change.

We've also developed new criminal justice policies, some of which have been very successful. Before the pandemic, we were able to halve the amount of future jail time that Philly courts produce at sentencings—the future years of incarceration—as compared to the prior administration.[†] While I've been in office, the county jail population reached its lowest point since 1985.[8] We have also reduced future excessive supervision on probation and parole by two-thirds.[9] We started the first unit in this office to protect immigrants. And the number of juveniles in out-of-home placements went from over six hundred when we came into office to around one hundred in 2021.[10] Nearly all juvenile cases are resolved in juvenile court, and the approximately 1 percent that *aren't* are extremely serious cases.[11]

For many years, Philadelphia was the epicenter of juveniles sentenced to life without parole, effectively a death sentence.[12] After the Supreme Court ruled that mandatory life sentences for juveniles were unconstitutional, those who were sentenced as juveniles had to be resentenced.[13] About half of them have been

---

† "Years of future incarceration" is calculated by adding the years of incarceration imposed on defendants in all cases that concluded during a given time range. For more information, see related data at Philadelphia District Attorney's Office, "Public Data Dashboard: Future Years of Incarceration Imposed," data.philadao.com/Future_Years_Incarceration_Report .html.

resentenced under our administration, and many have secured their freedom. For me, the most striking thing is just how incredibly successful they have been overall since being released. It is very encouraging and reassuring to see that our philosophy—that people really do change—is correct.

I think we've had some tremendous achievements, but none of them would have been possible without culture change in terms of recruitment and education. We decided early on that we would not only inform our staff of our policies, but we would educate them as to why we believe in them. I'm the coach; they're the team. We call the play—now hit the field and run in the right direction. That's how it has to go. By treating our attorneys like real professionals rather than treating them like robots in a hierarchical system—by informing them of what we're doing, even if they don't agree—they understand where we are coming from and are much more respectful of our reasons for trying to change things. You can write all the policies you want, but if you don't change the culture within the office, none of them are going to be carried out in the courtroom.

## Reviewing Convictions and Apologizing for Past Injustices

We also have a conviction integrity unit that has been very, very active: so far we've exonerated twenty-two people.[14] Probably the one that stands out the most to me is a guy who did twenty-eight years of a life sentence for a terrible murder/robbery of an exchange student in an affluent neighborhood in Philly in 1991. Chester Hollman had rented one of six virtually identical cars from an airport that night.[15] He happened to be driving toward the crime scene after someone else had committed the killing and drove away in one of those six cars: the same year, same model, same color, with the same first three letters on the license plate.

For all those years in prison, he fought his conviction. When we began looking into the case, we immediately found paperwork in the case file that had never been disclosed, which pointed directly to people who had rented one of the other cars from the airport. Police investigators had acted on that information the day after the killing, but this was never disclosed to the defense. In the circle of people connected to that other rental car was a man who is now doing life for murder. The prosecution also kept from the defense a statement from a woman who claimed she had once gotten rid of a gun of the same caliber used in the same killing, because it "had a body on it." Instead of doing a proper investigation at the time, the police hid that there had been a tip and that they had acted on it. They turned none of that over to the defense attorneys. Chester Hollman is out of prison now, thank goodness, but that one small thing—not turning over a piece of paper—led to his wrongful conviction. Our office saying to him, "They hid this from you," made a big difference.

I saw Chester for the first time after he had been out for only about forty-five days. He said he was having trouble sleeping; when I asked why, he said, "For twenty-eight years, they kept the fluorescent lights on all night, and now I'm out and it's dark and I can't sleep. It just makes me scared. Anytime anybody opens a door to the house, I hear a jail door slam, and I gasp because I'm right back where I was, getting ready to die in jail." This is a man who was housed in a state correctional institution where there is, in fact, danger from some of the other incarcerated people, from some of the guards. But it was the buzz of the fluorescent lights on him all night that had such an impact. He came out to a much, much safer world, but it was frightening to him. I've seen him since, and thankfully, he's doing much better.

We have made it part of our practice—and I have to give credit for this to the head of our conviction integrity unit, Patricia Cummings—that in all appropriate cases, we apologize to the person during the proceeding that results in an exoneration. We didn't lock up Chester Hollman—we came in much later—but that apology is something our office as an institution owes him.

Philadelphia had an incredibly flawed death penalty practice. Even before we came into office, 72 percent of all death sentences had been overturned, often because there was zero effort put into death penalty representation; there was no real funding for the court-appointed attorneys who took these cases.[16] The entire system was rigged.

When defense attorneys challenged the constitutionality of the state's death penalty and how it had been imposed in the city of Philadelphia for forty years, our office agreed that it was unconstitutional. And we took that position publicly because the people getting the death penalty were Black people and brown people, the poorest people, the most intellectually impaired people. That's not what the law allows. The death penalty was supposed to be only for "the worst of the worst," and these cases were by no means "the worst of the worst."

## The Movement, Pushback, and Who Gets Pushed Hardest

I was aware of this progressive prosecutor movement before I was elected. Needless to say, I was not the first. There is a history that goes all the way back to Elizabeth Holtzman, who was the district attorney in Brooklyn in the 1980s. More recently, a number of women of color have been elected as chief prosecutors. It is not surprising to me. It makes sense that people have been elected who come from communities adversely affected by a blatantly racist system. These women are well equipped to be DAs because the electorate in their communities has experienced the boot of that system. As you might expect, many of them have received tremendous pushback. Kim Gardner in St. Louis—the city of my birth—has taken tremendous pushback. Rachael Rollins in Boston as well. Kim Foxx in Chicago too. Aramis Ayala, in Orlando, basically had the governor go at her throat because she made decisions about the death penalty that may well have been tolerated if they'd been made by a conservative prosecutor, especially a white man.[17] That's real and it goes on all the time.

There is plenty of pushback for all of us, but it's easier for me because they're not also pushing back at me because of the color of my skin or my gender. Some people in the city of Philadelphia don't like that so much of what we're doing improves the position of women and men of color and of poor people.

## Envisioning a Just and Wiser System

Those committed to progressive prosecution and reform are part of a great social movement. It's very, very gritty on the inside, and yet the daily fight, the slog, the battle—it's so rewarding. We're taking a lot of heat. At any given time, we're getting punched by the media, by the machine and centrist institutional politics, by some of the judiciary, by probation and parole, and by some of the legislators. But they're missing what we have going for us: that we as reform-minded prosecutors have this role to play to bring about change.

If you look at the old pictures of Martin Luther King Jr., they kind of fall into two categories: there's the view from the outside, where he's in his tuxedo receiving the Nobel Prize; there's the image on the postage stamp, the image you see associated with the holiday. That's not really what it was like for him at all. If you look at the photographs that they took from behind, you see him walking along wearing an Elmer Fudd hat in the cold on the "long march"; he's sitting there with Ralph Abernathy and John Lewis, and they've got construction boots on, and their feet are hurting because they've been walking forever.[18] Or you see the photographs of him when he has been pushed—either by the words or hands, and probably both, of police officers—and he's not his usual peaceful, settled self. He has this look of concern and urgency as he's being pushed around. That's what his life was. I mean we ain't King, that is for sure, but we're taking a lot of heat, and we're taking a lot of hate.

The change we are tasked with bringing about is predicated on pursuing our vision of justice, which to me is a kind of individualized fairness to each person that is rooted in equality and requires the measured and restrained use of power. One of the things I've heard over and over from marginalized people in Philly, especially Black people, is, "You're trying to be fair." That means something to them. They say, "You're *trying* to be fair." I realized that their expectation had been that a chief prosecutor was not even going to try to be fair. To them, just our *effort* to be fair signifies a form of justice, even when you make a mistake. I think that speaks to how bad it has been.

I am hopeful that at some point this movement leads to a much less punitive, much more rehabilitative system, one premised much more on prevention than on punishment. This system would admit that people are capable of profound change and, as Bryan Stevenson of the Equal Justice Initiative has said, "You are not the worst thing you ever did."[19] And if you are a victim—and I have been a victim of violent crime—you're also not the worst thing that ever happened to you. It would be a system that is not built on a cracked foundation, the notion that people's criminality is permanent and unchanging. The United States would no longer be the most incarcerated nation in the world—and the outrageously discriminatory racist and classist aspects of the system would be greatly reduced. I would like to say "abolished," though nothing about human history indicates that all racism is going away anytime soon—but hopefully, it would be greatly, greatly, diminished.

What we would see with the shrinking of this excessive, bloated criminal legal system would be the increase and growth of things that build the beloved community, the beloved society. It would be quality public education for everybody. It would be national health insurance so that if you need treatment or have become addicted or you have mental health issues, you can get care. It would mean economic empowerment of a lot of people who have been systematically disempowered for centuries. It would be a system that has wised up.

# 10

## Marilyn Mosby

### State's Attorney, Baltimore City, Maryland

*When Marilyn Mosby was sworn in on January 8, 2015, as the state's attorney in Baltimore, she became the youngest chief prosecutor of any major U.S. city at the time. She had been a Presidential Scholar at Tuskegee University and a Thurgood Marshall Scholar at Boston College Law School. Mosby then went on to work at the Office of the State's Attorney for Baltimore City and in civil litigation in the private sector before being elected state's attorney. Early in her tenure she found herself in the spotlight when she faced the decision of how to charge Baltimore police officers for the death of Freddie Gray Jr., who sustained injuries in police custody and died days later at the age of twenty-five.*

*In January 2022, a federal grand jury indicted Mosby on charges related to personal financial transactions; three weeks later she pleaded not guilty. As this book went to press, the case had not yet been resolved. Regardless of the outcome of her case, it cannot be denied that Mosby's groundbreaking leadership, even in the face of constant attacks, helped spur the bold reforms taking place in prosecutors' offices across the country that will have a lasting positive impact on historically excluded communities. The story of this movement cannot be told without the story of Marilyn Mosby.*

Akeil Robertson
*Her Justice*, 2021
Watercolor and gouache on paper

**Akeil Robertson** is a Philadelphia-based artist who discovered his passion for art while incarcerated. He has been engaged in the work of Mural Arts Philadelphia since 2014 and is a strong believer in the positive power of art. Since being released he has been an assistant teaching artist for Mural Arts, working with people involved in the justice system. To see more of Akeil's work, find him on Instagram: @akeil.r.

## Artist's Statement

*This portrait was created from a photograph I took in 2021 of Marilyn Mosby on the steps of the Baltimore City Circuit Courthouse, across the street from the Battle Monument, colloquially called Lady Baltimore. I wanted the portrait to communicate that Mosby brings dedication and empathy to the city's justice system.*

## Growing Up in the "Police House"

I come from a very close-knit family—we lived in a duplex in Boston, right across the street from my grandparents in Dorchester. My cousin Diron, who was three years older than me, lived next door, and we grew up like brother and sister. When I was fourteen, our family went through a traumatizing event: Diron was killed right outside of my home in broad daylight after being mistaken for a neighborhood drug dealer. He was seventeen. To this day, it's an image that is still branded in my mind: I opened the door and saw him lying in the street after I heard the gunshots.

If it hadn't been for a neighbor who cooperated with police and testified in court, my family wouldn't have received any sort of justice. That was my introduction to the criminal legal system. I had never gone into a courtroom, but I had to for the trial. My cousin—an honor student with dreams and aspirations of going to college—was now going to a grave. I saw the individual responsible for his death, who was also only seventeen years old. While at the courthouse, I saw the number of African American men going in and out, in chains and shackles, and I wondered, "What is this system? And how do you change it?" So it was that traumatizing event that sparked my passion for reforming the criminal legal system.

I come from four generations of police officers. My grandfather was one of the founding members of the first Black police organization in Massachusetts. He had seven brothers and one sister, so we had a huge family and we were well-known in Boston. My uncles, my father, my mom, and my great-uncles were all police officers, and I grew up in what was called "the police house." We would have people at my house all the time, from all across the neighborhood. I would come home and there was always somebody there, and they'd be like, "Hey, cuz, how you doing?" and I'd respond, "I don't know you. Who are you?" And they're like,

"Oh I'm so-and-so from down the street" [*laughing*]. But even when you grow up in "the police house," you're not shielded from the violence that plagues so many urban communities across the country.

I didn't really appreciate what my family meant to the community until more recently. It was probably 2018: I was in a coffee shop and someone walked up to me and said, "Aren't you Marilyn Mosby? I just want to thank you." I said, "Thank me for what?" He said, "I want to thank you for Mr. T." Mr. T. was my grandfather, who died just a month after I was sworn in as state's attorney. The man told me, "You know, I was one of those knuckleheaded kids who used to always be at your house, but I want to thank you, because I wouldn't be the man I am today if it wasn't for your grandfather." And then it really dawned on me—what my family meant to that community and how my family epitomized community policing.

## Bused to the Suburbs

As a girl I was bused an hour out of Boston's inner city to Dover, one of the richest towns in Massachusetts; I was part of METCO, one of the longest-standing desegregation programs in the country.[1] At the age of six, I was the only Black child in the entire school. I recognized early on that a lot of white people's perceptions about Black people came from us "METCO kids" and through the negative light of the media. I had to learn not to respond to or be offended by the stereotypical views of the children who lived in that town. They would walk up to me and say, "You go, girl!" and I'd respond, "I don't talk like that. Why are you talking to me like that?" I learned that certain perceptions of Black people weren't due to maliciousness, but more to lack of exposure. So at the age of six, I took on the responsibility of being a positive representation of Black people. From then until

I graduated high school, I was in honors classes. I graduated top of my class. I was co-editor of the school newspaper. I brought diversity workshops to the school so we could talk about Black history being American history.

I graduated with honors and applied to only three schools: Tuskegee, Spelman, and Hampton. I got a Presidential Scholarship to Tuskegee University and graduated magna cum laude. I didn't perform well on my LSAT, even though I graduated with a 3.8 grade point average. When I was applying to law schools, I called and told them, "My LSAT score is not indicative of my potential. You need to meet me." Even though that's not usually how it's done, I got interviews for several of the law schools I applied to and got into my first choice: Boston College Law School.

## Pursuing Justice

At first I wasn't sure whether I wanted to be a defense attorney or a prosecutor. I knew that when my cousin was killed, the prosecutor's office helped my family, especially through the grieving process. They held our hands, they talked us through the court proceedings, and we had victim witness advocates who sat in court with us. I knew that side of things from the perspective of being next of kin to a homicide victim. My colleagues from law school were making $40,000 a summer in corporate jobs, but I knew that wasn't what I wanted to do. I wanted to follow my heart and my passion, which was to reform the criminal legal system.

It took some time to figure out the best way to pursue that career path. I interned for the U.S. Attorney's Office in Boston one summer; it was an eye-opening experience, in part because of the disparity in sentencing for crack cocaine versus powder cocaine.[2] They charged a young woman with possession of crack cocaine; she was at the scene of an incident involving her boy-friend, who had a felony conviction and was charged with posses-sion of a handgun. It was my introduction to seeing the disparities in the criminal legal system on a federal level. After that experi-ence I remember thinking, "Well, maybe that's not what I want to do."

Later, I met David Meier, a phenomenal prosecutor in the Suf-folk County District Attorney's Office who visited my school. I talked to him about my negative experience at the U.S. Attor-ney's Office. He said, "I would love for you to come and work in my office in the homicide unit," so I ended up interning there and it was a life-changing experience. I thought, "This is what a prosecutor's office is supposed to be like. You're supposed to fol-low your ethics—and your mission is the pursuit of justice."

## Two Standards of Justice

I won't ever forget one particular case David Meier was working on at the time: a fourteen-year-old girl by the name of Chaun-tae Jones was pregnant and was brutally murdered; one of the two men accused was the presumed father of her unborn child.[3] She didn't get the same attention that Laci Peterson did; the case fell under the radar, and that stuck out to me.[4] This child was eight months pregnant and buried alive, and I thought: "Nobody is talking about it? Why isn't the media covering this the same way they did when a pregnant white woman was killed by her husband? And why isn't that bias in the media apparent to every-one?" Working in the district attorney's office with David Meier, I was able to observe him in action in the courtroom, where he made those same points.

And this is a crazy coincidence: around that time, I was doing some legal research and looked up a related case—they were describing and referring to a young man, and it dawned on me that they were talking about my cousin. It was a cousin on my father's side who was convicted of attempted murder, the same year my cousin Diron, on my mother's side, was killed. They were the same age. I wrote a thesis about that—the irony of having one cousin who was killed and another who was convicted of attempted murder. I interviewed the judge, the prosecutor, and one of the police officers in my cousin's case. They didn't know my personal connection to the case; I approached it as a law student. I got to hear their perspectives, and it was eye-opening to realize that the prosecutor really didn't care to consider the life circumstances of the person he prosecuted. I found that problematic; I was taking a prosecutorial ethics course at the time, and as I understood it, the mission of a prosecutor is the pursuit of justice over convictions. To me, this means that as a prosecutor you have to be informed about every aspect of a case, and that includes making a decision or recommendation about a sentence. And in my cousin's case, neither the prosecutor or the judge did that: they didn't consider any of the life circumstances or the mitigating factors they should have.

I realized then the incredible amount of power that prosecutors have. They decide who's going to be charged, what they're going to be charged with, and what sentencing recommendations they're going to make. They're the ones who decide whether someone's going to enter the criminal legal system in the first place. I realized that these critical decisions are the key to systemic reform.

## Making a Home in Baltimore

After I got out of law school, I married Nick [Mosby], my college sweetheart, in 2005. I met him at Tuskegee University and he's from Baltimore. I couldn't convince Nick to move to Boston, and the cost of living was really, really different in Baltimore, so it

was a no-brainer to move here. We bought an old, vacant dilapi-
dated shell in West Baltimore, across from what was referred to as
"murder mall." We felt compelled to move into the area because
we fell in love with the neighborhood and its potential, and we
wanted to be an example for our community.

I started my career as a law clerk in the Baltimore City State's
Attorney's Office. Once I passed the bar, I was sworn in and started
working in the early resolution court, which dealt with nuisance
crimes, but I was quickly moved to traffic and then assigned to
a criminal division. After only six months in the position, they
brought me back to early resolution court as a supervisor, so I was
mentoring newly sworn-in assistant state's attorneys and teaching
them about courtroom decorum and docket management. I did
that for about a year and then went to the misdemeanor unit and
eventually the felony unit, where I did extremely well.

I loved my job, but then there was a change in administration.
When I started, I was working under Patricia Jessamy; she had
been in the office for sixteen years, the first African American
woman who was the Baltimore state's attorney. Then she was
beat by Gregg Bernstein in 2010. When he came into office, he
had a very different perspective about what a prosecutor was;
he fired all of the community liaisons, exacerbating distrust. In
Baltimore—where witness intimidation started, the home of the
"stop snitching" mentality—people were extremely distrustful
of the criminal legal system, including police, prosecutors, and
judges.

I felt that the state's attorney had a role and an obligation as
a minister of justice to break down those barriers. I didn't see
that happening, so I said, "Okay, it's time for me to pack up and
diversify my experience." I left that office and started working for
a Fortune 100 company, Liberty Mutual. I quickly rose through
the ranks there, but my heart and passion were still in reforming
the criminal legal system. My job was not done, so even though

I was working and a mom of two, I decided to run for state's attorney. My husband was already on the city council. Everybody said that I was too young, I was too inexperienced, I couldn't raise enough money—and that running for that position would not only interrupt but potentially destroy my husband's political career. But I had a core group of people who believed in me, my husband included; he was my rock and political genius.

Nobody expected us to win. Gregg Bernstein outraised me three-to-one, but we prevailed. We beat the incumbent—an older white male—and we beat him by double-digit percentage points. I was thirty-four when I won, so I was the youngest chief prosecutor of any major U.S. city. We immediately had to handle very high-profile cases, including a female Episcopal bishop I charged for the death of a bicyclist in Baltimore the day after I was sworn in as state's attorney.[5] Four months into my first term, we were on schedule to fulfill my one-hundred–day plan.

## The Power of a Single Case

Right around that time I was thrust into the international spotlight when an innocent twenty-five-year-old Black man by the name of Freddie Carlos Gray Jr. made eye contact with police.[6] He was unconstitutionally arrested and was placed in a police transport vehicle headfirst, handcuffed and feet shackled. His pleas for medical attention were ignored after his spine was partially severed in the back of that wagon.

I followed the facts and the law, and to this day I wouldn't do anything differently.[7] One of the things I ran on was ensuring that we have a single standard of justice for all, regardless of race, sex, religion, or occupation. If that meant holding the police accountable, even when others across the country were not holding police accountable for the deaths of Black men, I felt that was my role. That's why I'm supposed to be here, that's what justice requires. Clearly, that came with a great deal of backlash.[8] But that accountability led to exposure: a week after I charged those officers, the U.S. Department of Justice came in and called for an investigation of the eighth-largest police department in the country, ultimately leading to reform.[9] We now have a federally enforceable consent decree—and a spotlight on the corruption that has been entrenched in one of the largest police agencies in the country.

My decision to pursue accountability came at a personal and professional sacrifice. I received hate mail and death threats, I was harassed, mocked, ridiculed, and sued. Ultimately, I was forced to drop the charges after a judge repeatedly acquitted the officers; I knew that I could try this same case a hundred times, but without systemic reforms that hold police accountable, we would end up with the same result.

I can point to tangible reforms that are the direct result of my decision to prosecute those officers in the Freddie Gray case. They include new use-of-force and de-escalation policies that emphasize the sanctity of life; the obligation for officers to intervene when their fellow officers cross the line; the mandate for officers to call a medic when someone in their custody requests one; the mandate for police officers to seat-belt prisoners; the full implementation of body cameras on all officers; and software verification systems.[10] What happened in the Freddie Gray case is that officers would get up on the stand and state that they weren't aware of the general orders, the procedures, and the protocols. Now there is a verification process that ensures adherence to those protocols.

But there are still practices that prevent police accountability, like police investigating themselves; changing that is critical, and it's something I've been advocating for. And the Law Enforcement Bill of Rights ties the hands of a police department attempting to get rid of problematic officers.[11] We've got a long way to go, but the Associated Press did a poll in the summer of 2020, and one of the things they found was that the perceptions of police brutality and race relations have changed dramatically since July 2015, a few months after I charged those police officers in the Freddie Gray case.[12] I'm glad the perception has changed, because when I was prosecuting those officers, accountability was not happening in this country.

## From Accountability to Reform, with a Spotlight on Corruption

The city of Baltimore has had a lack of stability: since taking office, I've worked with five police commissioners and four mayors in six years. Whether you like my policies or you don't, the accountability imposed by my office has been the only real stability this city has seen. That accountability has led to exposure, exposure has led to reform, and reform has led to a focus on corruption. My office had to play cleanup on one of the largest police corruption scandals in the country's history: for decades several officers in the Baltimore Police Department were planting guns and drugs on citizens and redistributing drugs on the streets. Those individuals were ultimately convicted federally, but they had an impact on thousands of cases.

We obviously couldn't proceed on those cases that involved corrupt police officers. One of the things we advocated for—and we met with a great deal of resistance—was to vacate convictions for people who were wrongly accused or whose cases relied on the testimony of officers who were not credible. My colleagues across the state testified in opposition to a piece of legislation that would have provided a legal mechanism for prosecutors to be able to vacate those convictions, depending on the circumstances. They also opposed expunging marijuana convictions: they actually told me that their job as prosecutors isn't to right the wrongs of the past, and I had to direct them to the ABA ethical standards.[13]

We succeeded in getting the State's Motion to Vacate statute passed, but my colleagues managed to strike the language pertaining to the marijuana provision.[14] So we have a statute that allows prosecutors to vacate convictions in the interest of fairness and justice, based on certain circumstances or new facts, but not based on new thinking about marijuana decriminalization. Still, as of early 2021 we had overturned and vacated about eight hundred cases related to those officers. We dismissed several hundred cases that were open and pending. And since Freddie Gray, we've also convicted about thirty-three police officers for misconduct in other criminal acts.

This was also when we released our marijuana policy, which, in 2019, was one of the most progressive policies of its kind in the country. I put out a white paper outlining our rationale for no longer prosecuting possession of marijuana, regardless of weight and regardless of criminal history.[15] Based on the data, we knew there was no public safety value in continuing to do that. It was counterproductive, given the limited resources we have in law enforcement—especially in a city like Baltimore, where violent crime plagues our communities. We were and still are solving only one out of four murders a year, and I wanted to ensure that we were putting our resources where they should be: toward solving homicides.

The data also shows that there aren't discrepancies among white and Black people for actual possession and use of marijuana. But if you're an African American in this country, you're almost four times more likely to be arrested for possession of marijuana.[16] And in the city of Baltimore, African Americans were almost *six* times more likely to be arrested for possession.[17] Even after decriminalizing possession of marijuana for amounts of ten grams or less, once police were issuing citations and not making arrests, Black people were still disproportionately targeted. Baltimore City has nine police districts; we learned from the data that 42 percent of the citations police issued in 2017 were in one district, which happens to be 95 percent Black and disproportionately impoverished.[18] Recognizing my power to shape the criminal legal system through my discretion, I said, "I'll never be complicit in discriminatory enforcement of laws against poor Black and brown people," and we decided not to prosecute marijuana regardless of size, weight, or criminal history.

## Dealing with Aggressive Backlash

Following the Freddie Gray case, I experienced a great deal of backlash from the police, including the Fraternal Order of Police; in New York they put my face on the cover of their magazine and referred to me as "The Wolf That Lurks." The local police union mocked and ridiculed me. To this day, my opponents still seek to create an atmosphere of division. But I believe that justice is always worth the price paid for its pursuit. My decision to hold police accountable, when no other prosecutors had the courage to do so, brought this country and our system of justice one step closer to equality. I had the wind to my face. Now progressive prosecutors have the wind to their back. What keeps me inspired is that this movement is so much greater than me.

I have an enormous binder *filled* with hate mail and death threats. They described how my husband would be killed coming out of my house, and how no police officers would respond. They've referred to me as "n★★★★★ b★★★★." "You racist n★★★★★ b★★★★." The hate-filled backlash I received was shocking to me; remember, this was pre-Trump. Unlike the post-Trump era— when everyone has normalized racist, sexist comments on social media—I didn't know how to take it all in at first. I had to learn very early on not to internalize it, and I grew to understand that it was never about me personally.

When I see these reform-minded prosecutors who are now holding police officers to account across the country—when I see these phenomenal prosecutors who were inspired to run because they saw me in this position—it puts the backlash into perspective, and I recognize that it wasn't all in vain. I am so inspired by my colleagues who have come into this movement, where we're applying one standard of justice to everyone. We are exonerating those who were wrongly convicted and incarcerated, we're taking a holistic approach to addressing crime, and we're breaking the school-to-prison pipeline. We're reevaluating the egregious sentences that have been imposed disproportionately on people of color. We're attempting to address how prosecutors contributed to mass incarceration. We're looking to rectify the wrongs of the past and apply that one standard of justice and racial equity as we move forward. It's inspiring, and it's not just in Baltimore City. It's not just in my state. This is happening nationally. It's incredibly rewarding to know that I have colleagues who are in this struggle and in this fight with me.

Going through what I did early on in this movement was an incredibly isolating experience. So many people came up to me saying, "I got your back, I got your back, sis. I got your back," and I'm looking, and I'm like, "Y'all must be *way* back, because I don't see nobody, like what the? I'm out here by myself!" I told myself that I don't want anybody else to have to go through that by themselves, especially with the misogynoir you experience as a young Black woman in this white male–dominated profession.[19]

In this country, 95 percent of the prosecutors are white, and 73 percent are white men. As a woman of color, I represent just over 2 percent of all elected prosecutors.[20] So in 2016, after Kim Foxx won the state's attorney race in Chicago, it was a no-brainer that I would go and help on her transition team as much as I could. When Aramis Ayala—the former state's attorney for Florida's Orange and Osceola counties—ran and won, I reached out because I wanted to assist in whatever capacity I could. It's great, because now I have a sisterhood of prosecutors—and not just a sisterhood. I have brothers too, like Larry Krasner in Philadelphia and George Gascón in Los Angeles. All across this country, people are making major progressive moves toward rectifying this system of injustice. I'm just so thrilled to be a part of this and thrilled that I was there at the start. To see what it has turned into is so incredibly inspiring.

## Advice for the Next Generation

We've also inspired young folks. When I first won as state's attorney—and this is an impression that will always remain with me—a little eight-year-old girl walked up to me and said, "Marilyn Mosby, I voted for you," and I said, "Well, thank you." Clearly, this little baby did not vote for me, but someone had explained the importance of that fundamental right to her and in that moment, she could see herself in me. That's when it really dawned on me—the importance of the role I play and of my representation, and what that means to the community I serve.

As for my own girls, throughout our careers my husband and I have tried to include them. He is the president of the Baltimore City Council, one heartbeat away from mayor. I'm the state's attorney for Baltimore City. We've been in politics since the girls were babies, so they are very politically astute. They know their council folks and what districts they represent; they know their political platforms. They're very knowledgeable about the importance of civic engagement, but the one thing I really try to impress upon my girls is that they can be *bold*. They can be beautiful, inside and out, and they can be brilliant. It's not one or the other—it's *all*.

# Justice Isn't Black and White

Justice is also not one thing or the other. Justice is not black and white. Justice in one case may be a lengthy sentence, and in another case it may mean drug treatment and ensuring that the person doesn't get into the criminal legal system in the first place. Justice is ensuring that we have one standard we're following for *everyone*. Justice is ensuring that we're considering the victim in each and every one of these cases. Justice is ensuring that we're weighing the totality of the circumstances. Justice is ensuring that we're always doing the right thing, regardless of the controversy that may come from it. That is our one mission, and that's what I tell my prosecutors. Justice is the only barometer of our success and it's always going to be justice over convictions.

One way we're changing what justice means in Baltimore is through the Sentencing Review Unit we launched in December 2020. We hired the second-in-command at the public defender's office as the chief. We are reviewing those egregious sentences that have been imposed disproportionately upon poor Black and brown people in the city of Baltimore. We are evaluating and reassessing the sentences that have been imposed upon juvenile lifers and individuals over the age of sixty who have aged out of crime and no longer present a public safety concern. By February 2021 we had released four individuals, including the longest-serving female prisoner in the state of Maryland. We're really excited about that.

My Conviction Integrity Unit, the first one in the entire state of Maryland, is dedicated to reinvestigating claims of actual innocence. Since the start of my administration, we've exonerated ten individuals who have cumulatively served 270 years in jail and prison for crimes they did not commit.

We're also proud of the COVID-19 policies we've implemented. We enumerated several offenses that we would not be prosecuting in light of the pandemic. Jails have been incubators for the virus, and after consulting with public health experts—and given that prosecuting these low-level offenses has no public safety value whatsoever—we decided not to prosecute sex work, drug possession, disorderly conduct, or trespassing. In roughly a year, we saw an 80 percent decrease in the number of drug arrests since March 2020. There's been about a 40 percent decrease in the number of people cycling in and out of the jail. This hasn't impacted public safety. Our violent crime numbers actually went *down*, even while they went up in other cities across America.[21] Our homicide numbers—which are not great—have stayed roughly the same.[22] We know we have a lot of work to do, holistically, to try to tackle that issue, but prosecuting low-level offenses is not the solution. Coming out of a global pandemic with a backlog of cases, our time, attention, and limited law enforcement resources must be spent on violent offenses.

Another incredibly important thing: we are the only state's attorney's office in Maryland with a Crime Control and Prevention Unit that attempts to break the school-to-prison pipeline. We have a youth coordinator who is dedicated to ensuring that our office is in schools and we're getting to these young folks before they might enter the justice system. We've reached more than seven thousand young people through our initiatives. Since 2015 we've run a Junior State's Attorney program that has exposed over 260 young people across the city of Baltimore to positive careers in the criminal legal system and includes a mock trial competition.[23] We have another program in schools that focuses on fourth- and fifth-graders. We also do pop-up events; on Friday nights in the summertime, we have skating, bowling, and laser tag. During COVID we did it online, and even brought in celebrities and had the young people ask them questions.

Youth who do end up entangled in the system should be treated like children, not adults. In one of our Conviction Integrity Unit cases, we had thirteen-, fourteen-, and fifteen-year-olds who were taken out of school without their parents' consent, without their parents' knowledge, and interrogated for hours. We advocated for a piece of legislation that would require that juveniles under the age of eighteen have their parents and their attorney present during any custodial interrogation, and we are optimistic that it will pass.[24]

## Support from the Movement

The progressive prosecutorial movement makes me optimistic too. I can remember when everybody—the police officers and the Fraternal Order of Police and the media—were attacking me, and the police officers sued me. We had the attorney general representing me, but in the face of such challenges, I'm grateful that I had additional assistance and security from other progressive prosecutors and advocates. They gave me the peace of mind to know that everything would be okay.

This movement is so much greater than Marilyn Mosby or any one individual. This is about reforming a system that was designed to dehumanize and denigrate people of color. What keeps me going is knowing that the keepers of the status quo would love for me to throw in the towel, and I will never give them that. I just can't; it's not within me. This movement is playing out all across this country. If I had to withstand all that I've withstood five hundred times over again, I would do it, because it was never about me. It's always been about dismantling the system from within. That's my job.

# 11

# Rachael Rollins

Former District Attorney, Suffolk County, Massachusetts

*When Rachael Rollins was elected in November 2018, she became the first woman of color to serve as district attorney in Massachusetts and the first woman to ever hold the position in Suffolk County. She fought for justice as a student at the University of Massachusetts (UMass) Amherst, then went on to earn a JD from Northeastern University School of Law and a master of laws degree (an LLM) from Georgetown University Law Center. Rollins has worked for the Boston Celtics and served as the chief lawyer for three major state agencies; she also spent a number of years as an assistant U.S. attorney in Boston. She has had family members directly impacted by the criminal legal system, experiences that helped shape her philosophy and thinking as a DA. In July 2021, President Joe Biden nominated Rollins to serve as the U.S. Attorney for Massachusetts, the state's chief federal prosecutor. The U.S. Senate confirmed her in December 2021, and one month later she became the first Black woman to hold the position in Massachusetts—one of the first two U.S. Attorney's Offices opened in the United States.*

Deavron Dailey
*Brilliant Resilience*, 2022
Mixed-media collage on a map

**Deavron Dailey** is a Detroit-born, Pittsburgh-based artist who typically works in mixed media, crafting collages that leverage his experience in screen printing, painting, ceramics, sculpture, and drawing. Much of his work explores social challenges and is designed to foster discussion about these themes. To learn more about Deavron's work, find him on Instagram: @deavron.dailey .art.

## Artist's Statement

*This artwork commemorates the accomplishments of Rachael Rollins in her former role as district attorney of Suffolk County, Massachusetts.*

## "We Are a Mosaic."

My parents got married shortly after the Supreme Court's *Loving* decision, which decriminalized people of different races to loving and marrying each other.[1] My father is a second-generation immigrant from Ireland. My mom is a first-generation immigrant from Barbados. I was born just a few years later, in 1971, and am the oldest of their five children. I am fortunate to have been born into a multicultural working-class family.

I grew up fighting for what we—they—believed was right. So all of that informs who I ultimately became. On my father's side of the family, every one of my male relatives—going back to my great-grandfather—served their country in one of the armed forces. Many of them are wartime combat veterans. Many of them are members of law enforcement, having spent multiple decades in state and local police departments across the Commonwealth of Massachusetts. So I was raised with a huge respect for our military and for law enforcement, which I still have.

But I have a lived experience that is unique because when I went away to college, my two younger brothers began to cycle in and out of the criminal legal system. I also have a sister who has struggled with substance use disorder and mental health issues. I am a guardian of two of my nieces because of these realities. I know firsthand the collateral consequences that mental health issues, substance use disorders, food or housing insecurity, and incarceration cause, and the ripple effects—how they impact people generationally.

I am fully aware that my siblings may be flawed, but just as I am not defined by my best moment, they are not defined by their worst. And we are a mosaic, all of us. So with me being the oldest, being multicultural, having had amazing experiences with the military and law enforcement and the criminal legal system—

but also some not-ideal experiences with those systems as well—I bring that lived experience to work with me every single day.

## Showing Up When Things Are Awful

In high school I was selected for the New England School Girls Elite Lacrosse Team, and we won a national championship. I was fortunate to get an athletic scholarship, and when I got to UMass Amherst and played, our team was good and we had a solid season. But after my freshman year, the athletic director notified us that the women's lacrosse, tennis, and volleyball teams would be cut in an effort to save money. We were not fully funded teams, meaning that we each only had about three full scholarships for the entire team; our men's football team, on the other hand, had seventy-five full scholarships and didn't have a winning season. As the oldest of five, I may not have known any lawyers or judges, but I knew fairness and equity—and this seemed patently unfair. So along with a few fabulous former female athletes, we asked for a meeting with the athletic director. He had no time for us. We got a lawyer and, miraculously, he found time.

Under the threat of a Title IX lawsuit, we got the three women's teams reinstated.[2] A month before our season started, we had to scramble to put together a team—and I went from being a national high school lacrosse champion to the captain of a Division 1 team that lost every single game. I played on the team for two more years. What that experience taught me was character. It taught me that anyone can be excited, upbeat, and hardworking when things are going incredibly well and the wind is at your back. But who are you when things get hard? Do you show up when things are not just hard, but awful? It showed me the importance of standing up and showing up, of celebrating small victories and never giving up.

# A Wake-Up Call

Fast-forward to 2016—before I ran for district attorney. I was forty-five years old and went to get a routine mammogram, then had to go back a number of times to redo the test. I was told I had to have a biopsy, and then there was another biopsy, and then the call. Ultimately, I was told there was almost a 25 percent chance that my left breast had various stages of DCIS cancer, and that they would have to do a single mastectomy.* I ended up saying, "No, you are removing both of these. I am going to beat cancer and have perfect, wonderful, new pornography-quality breasts. And I'm going to remain as optimistic as possible and do everything that I can, because we caught it early."

But I was terrified. I had to have a conversation with my then-twelve-year-old daughter, and when she asked, "Are you going to die?" I had to be honest and say, "I certainly hope not, but I'm not going to lie to you about this." I remember the night before my surgery, writing her a note telling her how proud I was of her and how much I love her, what a wonderful person she had become, even as a pre-teen. That she was my greatest and proudest accomplishment and the love of my life.

I am so lucky to have made it out alive, because there are women and men far better than me who haven't. But one thing cancer makes you realize is that you are promised nothing; you cannot wait for anything that you want in your life, because the phone can ring and everything can change in an instant. That's what we deal with every day as prosecutors. These calls happen in our lives—and in our victims' lives—all the time and they change us.

---

* Ductal carcinoma in situ (DCIS) indicates that abnormal cells are present inside the breast's milk ducts. See Mayo Clinic, "Ductal Carcinoma in Situ (DCIS): Overview," mayoclinic.org/diseases-conditions/dcis /symptoms-causes/syc-20371889.

Beating cancer removed any amount of fear I had in my life. I fear nothing now.

## Deciding to Fix the System from Within

But even without fear, I was exhausted just turning on the television. I saw Trayvon Martin, I saw Freddie Gray, I saw Tamir Rice, I saw Michael Brown, I saw Sandra Bland, and I saw Eric Garner. Each a homicide victim. I also saw law enforcement interacting with communities that look like me in different ways than they interacted with other communities. And I saw district attorneys willfully looking the other way after violent encounters with the police and choosing not to indict or even present to a grand jury or bring charges against members of law enforcement who disgraced and abused their badge.

There have been iterations of this for decades, if not centuries. And I decided that rather than yelling at my television every time it happened, I should try and fix things from the inside. One of the most rewarding decisions I've made was to step forward and run for DA. I had a lot of things stacking up against me: I have the trifecta of being working-class, a woman, and a Black woman at that. People told me that it was impossible, that I couldn't win, that there had never been a woman elected DA in Suffolk County, and a woman of color had never been elected anywhere in the entire Commonwealth. Most people would have heard that and said, "Okay, well, I'm not going to do it." For me, that is a dare. If anything, I think my competitive nature was such that I said, "We're going to do it and we're going to win. Big. And on a progressive platform." And we did!

I didn't win because I'm a woman, and certainly not because I'm a Black woman. I won because I was the most prepared, hardest working, and most qualified person for the job in that moment. I had the best team around me, and we were multicultural, multigenerational, and multilingual. We knocked on more doors, our story was more compelling and relatable to people, and we recognized sooner than others did what the job of DA actually entails and what the most impacted communities wanted from the person serving in that role.

## The Only Woman in the Room

After I was elected district attorney, the first Black commissioner of the Boston Police Department was appointed. Suffolk County already had a Black sheriff. Certainly, that doesn't mean "and therefore there's no racism in Boston," but at least there were people of color, Black people, in leadership roles in law enforcement. We still have a lot of work to do, but what I noticed when I walked into law enforcement rooms as the district attorney is that I was often the only woman in the room. Certainly, I was the only woman in an executive role. I think that's unfortunate. We are more than 50 percent of the population on this planet.

Sometimes my being in the room has changed the conversation significantly. Shortly after I took office, we had a horrific kidnapping and homicide of a young woman celebrating her twenty-third birthday. When we finally had our press conference, there had already been so much shaming of the victim on social media about what she was wearing. Jassy Correia was a beautiful young woman and she looked fabulous that evening when she went out to celebrate her birthday with her friends.[3] In the middle of a press conference, as the only woman on the dais, I said, "We are not going to discuss what she was wearing, and we are not going to discuss whether she was drinking or what her friends were doing. We're going to tell men to stop raping and kidnapping and killing us. We're going to demand that fathers and uncles and grandfathers speak to their sons and nephews and grandchildren about consent and the way they treat women." I can assure you that none of my male counterparts on that stage said anything remotely close to that.

As a multiracial Black woman, race is not an uncomfortable topic for me. Growing up in a multicultural home was a gift. Part of why we find ourselves in this moment of racial reckoning in the United States of America is because people are so uncomfortable talking about race. Racism has infected far too many policy and governmental decisions since 1619, when people were enslaved, kidnapped, and brought to Virginia against their will. I refuse to be silent when I see things that are unjust, unethical, or hypocritical in our legal system, especially when they are based on a protected category.

For example, now we look at the surge of opioid and drug use and addiction as a public health crisis. But it has always been a public health crisis. Unfortunately, back in the 1980s and 1990s, when it was heroin and crack cocaine, and the impacted community looked like me and my family, nobody cared. It was, "Arrest them. They should 'just say no' to drugs." But now, miraculously, because different communities are being harmed and impacted, all of a sudden there is compassion. We have to marinate in the discomfort of "You did not have any compassion when the impacted community didn't look like you."

## "We've Been There Too."

Most of my time as a prosecutor has been as an assistant United States attorney. Shortly after I left the U.S. Attorney's Office for the District of Massachusetts, one of my brothers was charged federally and indicted by the office where I had worked. As I walked into the courthouse as a family member of a criminal defendant, it felt very different than walking in as an assistant U.S. attorney. I'm very friendly; I got to know everyone who works in that building. The court security officers who wanded me down as I entered the courthouse asked me, "What's going on? What are you back for?" and I said, "My brother got arrested and charged." And they said, "Keep your head up. We've been there too." Many people in law enforcement have loved ones who have touched the criminal legal system, no matter the income bracket, no matter the race, the ethnicity, the language capacity, immigration status, or religion. Many of us have someone we love who has struggled or come into contact with the legal system.

When I walked into the courtroom, the judge—someone I knew from my work—sort of cocked his head as if to say, "What are you doing here?" Then my brother walked out in a jumpsuit. We resemble each other very much and the judge immediately knew that this was a family member of mine.

I felt a lot of things in that moment. I felt shame. I felt a profound sadness for my sibling. I felt disappointment. I felt anger. And even though I was fluent in the legal system, I still felt fear, because I didn't know what was going to happen. So imagine if you've never been to the courthouse before, if you aren't a lawyer, if you don't speak English fluently, if you are terrified of ICE [the U.S. Immigration and Customs Enforcement agency] and of potentially being deported, and your loved one was arrested in a raid or a takedown. It opened my eyes to how complicated our criminal legal system really is, how hard it is to understand—and unfortunately, how unhelpful and standoffish we can be at times to the communities we are supposed to be serving.

As DA, I personally interviewed every single detective who was going to be in the Boston Police Department's homicide unit, as well as those assigned to my Homicide and Narcotics units from the Massachusetts State Police. I say to them, "When the FBI or ATF or DEA or state police or Cambridge Police Department knocks on my parents' door—and unfortunately, all of them have at some point—and they treat my parents disrespectfully, they don't know that those same two people are also the parents of the Suffolk County district attorney and the executive director of the Red Sox Foundation."

We all have flaws, and in other circumstances my brothers are exceptional people. But my parents are potential state and federal grand jurors and trial jurors, so every interaction they have with law enforcement informs the way they look at government. That could ultimately result in the district attorney getting a "not guilty" in front of a trial jury or a "no bill" in front of a grand jury, because some member of law enforcement was disrespectful or rude in a previous encounter with a juror or their loved one.[†]

All of that is infused in me—even those negative interactions—to make sure we're working to enable people to feel welcome. When any one of us walks into a courthouse, our tax dollars pay for that courthouse, for the person who wands us down, and for those judges, public defenders, and prosecutors. So we must shift the paradigm. Government must be better when it interacts with communities—and communities include victims, witnesses, and defendants. As the Commonwealth, as the government, we have to remember that we represent *all* of those parties.

## Standing with Our Immigrant Communities

I was inaugurated on January 2, 2019. That was a Tuesday. The following Monday, I received calls from several people that there had been a "kidnapping" in the Suffolk County Superior Court. They said five plainclothesmen pulled a screaming man into an elevator as he yelled in multiple languages for his lawyer. I learned that they were ICE agents who had been waiting for this individual and had detained and arrested him in a public part of the courthouse, traumatizing many who witnessed the encounter.

---

† A "no bill" indicates insufficient evidence/support to warrant criminal prosecution.

I called the attorney general of our state and said I wanted to file a preliminary injunction to get this young man back immediately.‡ I was told that for the past two years the Middlesex County district attorney had been contemplating bringing litigation about ICE's behavior. My response? "I want in on that, but this needs to start happening *now*, because the young man ICE arrested is going to be deported." I'm proud that I am a named party in the litigation we ultimately filed against ICE. I was proud to join the DA in Middlesex County and push the litigation forward. Our preliminary injunction was granted, making Massachusetts the first state in the country that precluded ICE from making civil arrests in or around state courthouses.

Another incident underscores these concerns, in the case of Osman Bilal. ICE was going to deport Mr. Bilal to Somalia—where he spent the first forty-eight hours of his life, in 1992—for a misdemeanor conviction of larceny under $250.[4] He'd paid his debt to society for that offense and was a sous chef with glowing recommendations from his employer and nonprofits he had worked with in the community. My office had to fight all the way up to our state Supreme Judicial Court to vacate the underlying nonviolent offense and then filed a nolle prosequi, dismissing the underlying deportable conviction.§ It is a fight I was happy to have. And we won. As of 2021, Mr. Bilal has started the process of becoming a citizen in our country and continues to thrive.

Sadly, we've seen an increase in hate crimes targeting immigrants, particularly from Spanish-speaking countries; violence

---

‡ Merriam-Webster defines an injunction as "a writ granted by a court of equity whereby one is required to do or to refrain from doing a specified act."

§ "Nolle prosequi" is Latin for "we shall no longer prosecute." It is a statement on the record by a prosecutor (or by a plaintiff in a civil case) declaring that they will no longer pursue the charges. See Cornell Law School, Legal Information Institute, "Nolle Prosequi," July 2021, law .cornell.edu/wex/nolle_prosequi.

against our AAPI [Asian American Pacific Islander] communities; and a growing number of anti-Semitic violence and hate crimes. We need to stand with all of the individuals and communities who are being targeted and harmed, irrespective of whether we are members of that community or protected class. It is my job to speak out against and change things that are unjust. I am proud to say, "In Suffolk County we don't condone hate." We will either prosecute you criminally or we will send those cases to our attorney general or the Massachusetts Commission Against Discrimination. We must stand up for our immigrant community.

We are also making sure that our office has people who are fluent in all of the languages spoken throughout Suffolk County. For criminal matters, I don't want you to understand 67 percent or 76 percent or 82 percent of a criminal proceeding. You need to understand *100 percent* of what is happening if we can take away your liberty or the liberty of a person you love. Are we hiring people with language proficiency? Yes. And I'm proud that we've started to radically turn around those numbers in our office. Halfway through 2021, of the thirty-four victim witness advocates in the office, we had seventeen people who are fluent in at least one of six languages other than English.

## Raising the Bar High

I take pride in holding myself accountable. As a candidate for DA, six weeks before my primary election, I put up a one-pager that said, "If you vote for me, I will switch the presumption from incarceration to declining to prosecute, diversion, or dismissal for a number of nonviolent, nonserious charges." Essentially there are fifteen types of minor crimes that are clogging up the state criminal legal system.[5] I met with police officers, judges, criminal defense attorneys, probation officers, returning citizens, victims, survivors, and prosecutors. I gathered as much data as I could before publishing that one-pager. Within three months of being sworn in as the elected DA, I published "the Rollins Memo," a substantive sixty-six–page document that built out the rebuttable presumption of the "do not prosecute" policies and many others.[6]

We also created the first Discharge Integrity Team (DIT) in the nation. The DIT is a group of four outside experts I convene whenever there's an officer-involved shooting. There's a criminal defense lawyer, a retired judge, a community member who has a public health background, and an active member of law enforcement. I am the fifth member of DIT and I attend all meetings. Together we review all of the officer-involved shooting and excessive-force allegation cases and meet at a location outside of the DA's office.[7]

I am also incredibly proud of our Integrity Review Bureau (IRB).[8] For me, with convictions, it's not just a review for actual innocence; we're looking at wrongful convictions, which include constitutional violations, *Brady* violations, ethical violations, and severely unjust outcomes.[9] In the year and four months since creating our IRB, we corrected and undid more than three hundred and twenty years of wrongful convictions—and counting.[10] Each position we took was ultimately approved by a neutral adjudication entity—the parole board, trial court, appellate court, Department of Corrections, the Attorney General's Office, or the Advisory Board of Pardons.

I have had very hard conversations with some of the surviving families in those wrongful conviction cases, because they were instructed to believe that "this is the person who committed and was responsible for my loved one's murder." I explain to them, for example, that the DA at the time had a policy of striking all Black jurors in cross-racial homicides. That an all-white jury convicted a Black man of the murder of their loved one. That—in violation of our Constitution—the defendant did not have a jury of his peers. I explain that our position and decision does not mean that their loved one's life wasn't valuable, or that their pain and hurt means nothing to us. It simply means that I won't stand behind a conviction that was obtained unethically, unconstitutionally, or unjustly. I have every one of those conversations myself. And if the family chooses not to speak to me, I honor that. They are always encouraged and permitted to offer an impact statement to the court, whether they agree with our position or not. Always. It takes a lot of work to do it this way, but it is so worth it when it's done right.

## What Justice Could Look Like

Justice is complicated. From the moment that awful phone call happens and you're told that your loved one was murdered, or your loved one has been accused of committing a murder, or the person you care for is missing or harmed—justice means that you believe your government is working for you and not against you. To me it means that your government explains things to you, treats you with dignity and respect, and gives you an opportunity to determine what you think accountability means in that awful circumstance. Justice isn't "I'm the DA and I know what you need better than all of you." It means that we are pulling chairs up to tables that have never had chairs at them—in a system that never cared about or included the people who are now sitting in those chairs—and engaging in those conversations. It means we may be doing far more listening than speaking.

Justice is also hard. It's giving people the respect of telling them, "We are vacating this conviction because it was obtained unjustly, unconstitutionally, and unethically. And although that decision is hurting you—because the person you believed this whole time was responsible for the loss of your loved one might now be free—justice is having the district attorney engage in that conversation with you and your family for as long as it needs to happen. It is feeling heard and getting the opportunity to ask me the tough questions."

I've had more conversations like that than you could imagine, when people were not happy with some of the things I said, but they actually felt heard. They felt they had a voice because they were invited to the proceeding. In every letter I've written about parole, whether I supported or opposed it, I always have a section about what the victim's family has said they want, whether it is consistent or inconsistent with what I'm saying, because it is imperative that their voices are uplifted and heard.

I think all of those things are justice. I think—and I hope—that justice, as a definition, continues to evolve and change for me. I ask most victims, "What would justice look like for you in this circumstance?" Because rather than saying "Okay, you can get five to seven years for this" or "You could get eighteen months for this," we explain to them that with certain crimes we could do a restorative justice¶ option; we could make sure that this person gets training or treatment; or we could look at incarceration, but with requirements attached or some sort of pretrial diversion. But I don't think we give victims enough information to make decisions about what justice could look like for them. Every victim and survivor is different. There is no one-size-fits-all solution.

## The Support of Other "Zebras"

Across the country I see reform-minded elected prosecutors who have worked hard to understand what justice means in their spe-

---

¶ Restorative justice "brings together those directly impacted by an act of harm to address the impact of the crime, hold the person who did it accountable, and make things as right as possible for those harmed." See Common Justice, "Restorative Justice: Why Do We Need It?," common justice.org/restorative_justice_why_do_we_need_it; and *Fair and Just Prosecution, Building Community Trust: Restorative Justice Strategies, Principles and Promising Practices*, (San Francisco: Fair and Just Prosecution, 2017), fairandjustprosecution.org/wp-content/uploads/2017/12/FJP.Brief_ .RestorativeJustice.pdf.

cific community and who listen to the community about what *they* believe justice means. The definition is not the same for every person.

There's a scene in one of the *Madagascar* movies where the animals leave the zoo and go back to Africa and the zebra, Marty, gets to meet other zebras in the wild. In this work, it is wonderful being Spider-Man alone or Batman alone or Wonder Woman alone, but when you finally get to meet and be around other people like you, you feel this sense of belonging. It's a Justice League of sorts.

Elected prosecutors have to be really strong *alone* many times in our day. As reform-minded district attorneys, we are fighting against a system that always bends and snaps back to the status quo. We are fighting against the false narrative of being "tough on crime," the "war on drugs," and the broken windows theory. As independent and confident as I might appear externally, it's exhausting to constantly have to be the lone voice saying, "No, that is not right. We are going to do this instead." Sometimes you're even fighting your own staff, who love and support you, and they ask, "Can there be just one day where you don't fight against something?" But the answer is always no, because every time we have an opportunity to right a wrong, we have to, whether it makes people uncomfortable or not. People's lives depend on it, so we don't get to be silent in the face of injustice.

Some people fully believe in my progressive policies but are afraid of having to always challenge the status quo, and they're terrified of losing. But this isn't about wins and losses. It's about people's lives. And doing what's right, every single time. Because we showed the community—immigrant communities, the AAPI community, the Muslim community, the Jewish community, the working-class community, the disability community, the Black and Latino communities, the LGBTQ+ community—we would fight for them. Showing impacted communities that we will fight injustice and hate makes our communities safer. When we stand up and do what is right, it makes people start believing in the system. They will get engaged when they witness a crime or have information that will help law enforcement. Every action is connected.

Standing shoulder to shoulder with other elected prosecutors across the country who do that every day—it fills me. It literally fills me. You can be drained by the day-to-day challenges of this job. But we can pick up the phone and talk to other reform-minded DAs and say, "This is so overwhelming. Have you ever dealt with this issue?" or "What would you do in this circumstance?" I'm lucky that I can call someone like Satana Deberry, the district attorney of Durham County, North Carolina, or Kim Foxx, the state's attorney for Cook County, Illinois. I don't have to explain to them that I am a woman doing this job, that I am a Black woman doing this job. They say, "Yeah, yeah, I get all that. Me too. What happened?"

It has been everything for me to be able to lay down my concerns, my fears, to say, "What if we're not successful?" The other progressive elected DAs in this movement are the ones who remind me—when it gets foggy or starts to fade a little—that we are in the fight of our lifetime. So it means the world to me to have these friendships and to learn from them. We are making the criminal legal system fair and equitable while focusing on public safety.

I want to leave this world better than I found it. I want to have the work we've done as progressive prosecutors matter. I believe that this is the civil rights movement of our time, and I am proud to be fighting on the right side of this battle.

# 12

# Dan Satterberg

## Prosecuting Attorney, King County, Washington

*A lifelong Seattle native, Dan Satterberg studied political science and journalism as an undergraduate at the University of Washington, where he also attended law school. He began his career as a prosecutor in the 1980s, working his way through the ranks of the King County Prosecuting Attorney's Office to become the chief of staff to Norm Maleng for seventeen years. Days after Maleng's unexpected death in 2007, Satterberg was sworn in as the interim prosecuting attorney, assuming his friend and mentor's role. In November of that year he was elected to the position, and he was reelected in 2010, 2014, and 2018. Satterberg has focused on the need to develop community-based alternatives to punitive approaches for young people and adults and helped start the Law Enforcement Assisted Diversion (LEAD) program, which gives police officers the option of directing someone to case management instead of jail to address "unmet behavioral health needs or poverty." When not running the prosecutor's office, Satterberg plays bass and sings in a rock band, The Approximations.*

Deavron Dailey
*Life Has Layers*, 2021
Mixed-media collage on a map

**Deavron Dailey** is a Detroit-born, Pittsburgh-based artist who typically works in mixed media, crafting collages that leverage his experience in screen printing, painting, ceramics, sculpture, and drawing. Much of his work explores social challenges and is designed to foster discussion about these themes. To learn more about Deavron's work, find him on Instagram: @deavron.dailey. art.

## Artist's Statement

*This portrait depicts some of the life experiences of Prosecuting Attorney Dan Satterberg in King County, Washington, and shows Yoda, the dog he adopted after his sister died. It also shows how the totality of these events led to Satterberg drafting his own "Five Pillars" framework for reforming the justice system.*

# The War on Drug Users

Drug policy ought to be the easy part of justice reform, but drugs scare people; even in Seattle, which is a liberal city, people are still fearful about drugs. They often like to blame the prosecutor—"It's your fault!"—because I don't prosecute people for tiny amounts of drugs anymore. But if you look at Gallup polls, for instance, two out of three Americans favor treatment over more law enforcement strategies.[1] It's probably even higher than that now.

My concern about this issue goes beyond the work I do as a prosecutor. My sister Shelley, who was six years younger than me, developed a substance use disorder that marked her life for many years. She was a daily heroin user and I was the county prosecutor. I lost touch with her for a long time, but one day she reached out for help. I was able to take her to a clinic, where she got mental health counseling and substance use counseling and was prescribed buprenorphine.* I saw what that medication-assisted treatment did to help her.[2]

What my little sister needed was not handcuffs. It was not to be in a courtroom. It was to have someone reach out and help her. When I was able to finally arrange that for her, her life changed. When she was on buprenorphine, she didn't need to find heroin every day. It changed her life. But in 2018, Shelley died. I tell her story in part because she did *not* die from a drug overdose. Because she was able to get treatment and help—and not handcuffs—she was not one of the overdose statistics. She died of a massive organ failure that was a consequence of abusing her body for so long.[3]

---

* Buprenorphine is used as part of medication-assisted treatment for harmful opioid use. The drug suppresses opioid withdrawal symptoms, reduces cravings, and eliminates the "high" associated with opioid use, with little potential for overdose when used as prescribed. Fair and Just Prosecution, *Harm Reduction Responses to Drug Use*, 7, August 2019, fairandjustprosecution.org/staging/wp-content/uploads/2019/08/FJP_Brief_HarmReduction.pdf.

For a few years now I've lived with Yoda, a rescue terrier Shelley adopted when she celebrated her one-year anniversary of recovery. He had been abused and discarded, and he and Shelley became constant companions. Yoda gave her a purpose and unconditional love, plus a connection to other dog lovers and the rest of the world.

A lot of families are struggling with what my family struggled with. But the "war on drugs," which is often a war on drug *users*, has meant that most of the cases in our court system involve people like my sister who are struggling with substance use. Our courts are not the ideal path to treatment. We need a new approach.

Years before Shelley's death, I became a partner in helping to start the LEAD program—Law Enforcement Assisted Diversion—which launched in 2011.[4] LEAD continues to evolve in our jurisdiction but has also become a model for other programs around the world. The basic concept is that when the police encounter someone who uses drugs and needs help, they will call a case manager or social worker. We knew that prosecuting people for drug-use issues wasn't helping, so we developed this other approach. But before LEAD, there was nothing. Drug possession cases came to the court system not because it was the best option, but because it was the *only* option. For the past dozen years, we have been working hard to create an alternative to the courtroom; the criminal legal system cannot be the solution to everything.

In 2020 alone, almost ninety thousand Americans died of overdoses. And that undercounts the extent of the damage and collateral issues that go along with substance use disorders. Eventually, I think our society will come to see drug use as the medical issue it is and take it out of the criminal legal system. If there is any silver lining to the overdose and opioid epidemic, it is that more families are learning that the courtroom is not the place to address their loved ones' issues and struggles. My family certainly did.

## An Accidental Politician

My father was a lawyer, and when I was around eight years old, he started taking me with him once a year to the courthouse in King County. I would sit in the back and watch my dad be an attorney. I remember being impressed with the size of everything, the marble everywhere, and the sort of dignified air of the court proceeding. It had an impact, and very early on I knew I wanted to do what my father was doing, to be a lawyer. I got into debate and public speaking. I went from the University of Washington to the law school there with the idea that I was going to go try cases. I didn't really know what that meant, but pretty quickly realized that being a prosecutor or a public defender would allow me to go to court.

In law school I interned with the DA's office in King County and then went on to work there after graduation. It's easy to say that I wanted to be a prosecutor because I wanted to win more than I wanted to lose. I *do* like to win—I'm competitive, like a lot of people—but the bigger thing for me was that I felt satisfied by that kind of work. I knew that it would be a steady, steep learning curve, and that the more I did, the more serious crimes I would be involved in prosecuting. I made that decision early on in my career: I wanted to stay there until I could try the most serious cases in our community.

I was a trial attorney, working my way up from misdemeanors to gang cases and homicides. But then the chief of staff became a judge, and the prosecuting attorney at the time, Norm Maleng, named me as his chief of staff.[5] I was only thirty years old and didn't feel qualified to do anything I was supposed to do, but I learned—and I learned next to him. Norm ended up serving twenty-eight years in office, but in 2007 he had a heart attack and died at a community event. Before I knew it, I was appointed to serve as the interim prosecuting attorney. We buried Norm on a Saturday, and the next Monday was the deadline to file to run for the position. I filed and ran, and in 2007 I was elected as the prosecutor for King County.

I was an accidental politician. I had been happy being the number-two guy in the office for seventeen years for Norm. When he died, it really threw our office, it threw my world, it threw everything into a little bit of shock and disbelief. I didn't have a lot of time to think about it or talk myself out of it. But I was proud to be in the position and to follow Norm. I have so much respect for the people in my office. We have about five hundred and forty employees—half lawyers, half staff—people who are dedicated and smart and really do the hard work for not much money and not much fame or glory. They want to help people and do important work that's meaningful to them. I ran because nobody else in the office would run, and I was afraid that somebody from the outside might not appreciate the office the way it deserved and needed to be appreciated.

## A Different Take on the Law and the Job

Looking back to my time as a young lawyer, I believed that doing justice meant enforcing the law—that if there were a case, I would go prosecute it. But I look back now at some of the cases I tried early on and think, "Why did I try that? Why didn't we resolve that?" For example, I tried people for possessing cocaine in small amounts. We don't even file those cases anymore, but back then I thought that was my job.[6]

I remember a jury trial in 1987 for a possession of cocaine case where we had charged an African American man who had been at a party that the police broke up. He had in his possession about a gram of cocaine. He didn't want to plead, and we didn't want to dismiss it, so I went to trial. Toward the end of the trial, the jurors started looking at me like, "You brought us in here for this?" This man had a lot of problems, and I was one of them at that moment. I wish I had handled that case differently. Back then, we didn't think about the path to treatment or trying to help people. We thought we were just here to enforce the law, and I thought that enforcing the law was the same thing as doing justice. We didn't think about the impact of the case on the individual before us.

My perspective on the death penalty has also changed. Early in my career I was involved in a lot of death penalty cases. Then in 2010 an execution was scheduled, and I went to participate as a witness and be with the family during that long and difficult process of finally seeing somebody put to death by the state. Seeing the entire process made me realize that it was not worth it. We could have resolved the case without the death penalty and not kept this family in limbo for twenty years.

Today I have a much different view of the role and power of the prosecutor. I learned that we need to approach our job with humility and not assume we have the answers to everything. We have to respect our power and the impact we can have on individuals and families—and our entire community. I went into this job excited and eager to do the work. Then the more I did the work, the more I realized that we needed to think about what we were actually doing and not try to do so much, not to criminalize so much. As prosecutors, we can seek to achieve justice in harmony with what the community wants and needs.

That part of the job has been the most rewarding for me: inviting community nonprofits and community leaders into our work and saying, "Help us identify what accountability is, and help us take people who are heading down one path and see if we can steer them onto a different path." The community has powers of persuasion and connection that far exceed anything we can do in the courtroom.

# Using the Power of the
# Office to Reform the System

We are pursuing ambitious diversion plans in partnership with our community, though some may seem small. In our state, until 2021, if a person did not pay a speeding ticket, your license could be suspended without you even knowing about it.[7] An officer could pull you over and say, "You're driving and your license is suspended," and by that point it was a crime. But about ten years earlier, our office had stopped prosecuting driving with a suspended license in the third degree.[†]

It was the only way that a failure to pay a civil infraction could snowball into a crime. The people who got caught up in that—usually young people and disproportionately people of color and people living in poverty—they never got out of it. They rarely got their license back. They just kept getting arrested, because they had to drive to have a job and to be part of society, and there aren't a lot of great mass transit alternatives in our region. People ran the risk of arrest and impoundment of their vehicle every time they drove. This was a crime against poor people, and it accounted for 40 percent of our caseload in the district courts and our misdemeanor courts. It led to a lot of warrants because people wouldn't show up for court—maybe they didn't even know they'd been charged—and then all of a sudden, another warrant was out for them. It wasn't helping anybody. People lost their jobs and their apartments. The whole thing seemed cruel and expensive, and it did a lot of harm. But with literally one signature on a memo to my office, we stopped doing four thousand prosecutions a year. It may seem like a small thing, but it's a big deal to no longer bring those four thousand people a year through our system.

---

[†] In Washington State, a suspended license in the third degree meant that a person was eligible to have their license reinstated, for example, by paying a fine or appearing in court.

That experience helped me realize that I have a lot of power as a prosecutor.

Through prosecutorial discretion, I can decide where to put our resources and where not to. I can ask the questions that need to be asked: Are we doing anybody any good or are we just doing more harm to people who are already marginalized? And those questions have led us to continually shrink the number of cases we prosecute and aim to not bring people into the system for being addicted to drugs or for being poor.

## Rethinking the "Three-Strikes" Law

Washington State was one of the first to have a three-strikes-and-you're-out law. It was a life sentence without the possibility of release for anybody who committed a third crime on this small list of crimes. One of the crimes that would qualify you for that was robbery in the second degree, which, in our state, is "taking by force." It can be a purse snatch, where the victim is pushed to the ground, or it can be shoplifting, where the clerk is punched or something like that—not great things to do, but not the most serious cases we see. Before this law, if you had a third robbery in the second degree, it would earn you a sentence of fifteen to twenty months in prison. But after the law went into effect in 1994, it meant you would be sent to prison to die. We were sending a lot of people to die in prison, usually young men in their twenties who had crack cocaine addictions. I never liked it. It was one-size-fits-all, and one size *never* fits all. I had a difference of opinion about the law with my boss at the time. But because the initiative passed—more than 75 percent of people voted for it—it seemed as if we had to enforce this law.[8]

When I became the elected prosecutor in 2007, one of the first things I did was ask my team to bring all the boxes out of the basement so we could look at these past cases and see who had been in prison. The law went into effect in 1994, so some people had already been incarcerated for more than a decade. We don't have parole in our state, so if the prosecutor didn't look and consider the possibility of release, nobody did.

I went into the prisons and met with some of the people we had sent there for life. I don't think I have any special power to look somebody in the eye and say, "Oh, you'll be safe to be released." And I knew what a risk it would be—for everybody involved—when I asked the governor to release somebody we'd sent to prison for the rest of their life who was on this three-strikes list. But I did it, and I have supported more than thirty people in clemency or resentencing, to get them out from under this "life without the possibility of release" sentence. Because that sentence wasn't right: it was a gross overreaction, and it was used in an extraordinarily racially disproportionate way. Our indifference to the suffering of the people who received these sentences embarrassed me.

We have since established a resentencing unit that is a big part of our office.[9] We have to look backward and reconcile past sentences. There was a level of dissonance, because prosecutors are trained to argue for finality—and as an office, before I was elected, we were opposed to any clemency. I've completely changed the way we look at clemency. To me, clemency is an arm of justice that needs to be used more. It's a way for us to assess the rehabilitation that people have accomplished for themselves under very harsh conditions in prison, where rehabilitation is not really something we nurture.

I still see some of the people I've helped over the years. Stevan Dozier, the first man we ever got clemency for who was sentenced under "three strikes," now works for King County.[10] He's a supervisor of a crew of about forty-five people who clean buildings. He had been married when he was sentenced to life. His wife divorced him while he was in prison—and then eight years later, she married him again. She said, "When he was addicted to crack cocaine and was doing robberies—that's not the guy I married." The governor was impressed by the fact that Mr. Dozier's wife remarried him, even though there was no hope that he was ever going to get out of prison at the time.

It's a story of redemption, but it's also a story of a law that was cruel and unusual. I realized that if I didn't lead the effort to look at these cases, nobody was going to. Stevan sends me a message on my birthday every year, because that was the day he got out. He's a wonderful person, and I'm glad I was able to be part of the process to release him. Thinking about him still being in prison or being told to die there—and nobody caring enough to look back—makes me sad. It makes me feel that we need to do a lot more of this.

I also argued for clemency for a young man who was eighteen when he was convicted of aggravated murder as an accomplice to an adult. After he served about twenty years, I was introduced to him and his case. I believed he had served enough time and that he had changed and was somebody who could be an asset to the community. I told the governor, "Look, we've got to take a chance on this guy"—and he had a lot of community support. Well, now he's the president of the Seattle chapter of the NAACP and has been an upstanding person, a leader, someone a lot of people look up to.[11] He still gives me the ration of grief I deserve as a prosecutor, but at the end of the day he'll also give me a hug and say "thank you," because he knows I took a chance on him.

## The Power of Restorative Justice

I have been fortunate to be able to sit in a peacemaking circle with people who understand the power of restorative justice.‡ It's

‡ Restorative justice "brings together those directly impacted by an act

a dignified way for people to understand each other, understand each other's backgrounds and pressures. It's a way to connect people—particularly young people—with credible messengers, mentors, coaches, and others who care about them. The very personal, very intimate setting stands in contrast with what happens in the courtroom. Courtrooms, while dignified, are not places to share what you're thinking. In fact, the defense attorney tells a defendant, "Don't talk. I'll do the talking for you."

But when we have a young person who has been involved in a crime—a serious crime—we often want to hear from them: "What were you thinking? Why did you do this? Why did you think you had to carry a gun? What are you afraid of? And more important, what do you want to do with your life? What are your aspirations and your hopes?" All of that happens in a restorative justice circle. When someone is talking, everyone's listening; it's the rule. There is no "right to remain silent." We want to hear what's going through your mind and through your heart. How do we keep you from escalating on a predictable path of violence? The first way we do that is by listening to what is going on in your head.

Peacemaking circles are not perfect by any means, but they are much more of an authentic, human experience than the courtroom experience. So we want to continue sending people into the community for that kind of connection and send fewer people to the courthouse. In 2020 we diverted more cases from juvenile court than we filed, and we're going to continue to do more

---

of harm to address the impact of the crime, hold the person who did it accountable, and make things as right as possible for those harmed." See Common Justice, "Restorative Justice: Why Do We Need It?," common justice.org/restorative_justice_why_do_we_need_it; and *Fair and Just Prosecution, Building Community Trust: Restorative Justice Strategies, Principles and Promising Practices*, (San Francisco: Fair and Just Prosecution, 2017), fairandjustprosecution.org/wp-content/uploads/2017/12/FJP.Brief_.RestorativeJustice.pdf.

of that, because I think the community is willing.[12] Part of that effort is building the capacity of local community nonprofits, so they can take hundreds of our cases and work with people individually, people who need help and need to be listened to. Our county and city councils have put a lot of energy into building that capacity and are encouraging us to send more cases into the community—and it works.

In the past, if the person owed restitution, that was sometimes an obstacle to diverting a case. The average restitution amounts are $500 to $1,000. But instead of sending these cases to diversion, we'd spend tens of thousands of dollars appointing defense attorneys and trying the cases. And the individual would get a conviction and the judge would order them to pay money we all knew they would never be able to pay. But because we didn't have any other way to satisfy the victim's restitution, we would just say, "Well, hold on. In a couple of years, maybe this person will pay you back."

Ultimately, we came up with a different idea: Why don't we, as the government, help make the victim whole? Why don't we write them a check, cover the loss, and then we can be free to do something more creative with the person who caused the harm? We developed a victim restoration fund that's made up of public funds, to be able to send more of these cases into the community.

I'm very excited about this work. But achieving these goals requires money for the community nonprofits that are willing to do this. When you think about it, it's a public safety job. It is every bit as important as police work, and we need to pay these community support workers the same kind of living wage we pay police, so that we can retain people to do this for the long haul. We need to uplift those who work with young people who could be headed toward a path of violent crime and interrupt that. And finally, that is going to happen in King County through two programs: Restorative Community Pathways, which is for young people up to age twenty-one; and the Community Diversion Program, which is for adults facing their first nonviolent felony charge.[13]

## Building a Safer, Healthier Community

The job of the prosecutor is a big one, and it has to extend beyond processing individual cases. That's important; you have to do that well. But I think everyone has to ask, "Why do you care about this work?" I care that we send too many people to prison for too long, and I care that what happens to them there often makes them worse and not better. And when they get out, I care that we have set them up to go right back. It's something we should all be concerned about. So the job of being a prosecutor includes building partnerships, finding money to develop things that don't already exist, and caring about the need for change.

If you don't build the "instead," then there isn't an alternative. And then it's easy to go back to re-criminalizing things in the courthouse, because at least it's *something*. People often want a response. If you're a business owner and there's somebody in the alleyway who's passed out with a needle in their arm, you may not want the person thrown in jail. But you want to know there is some response. If you're a parent and you find fentanyl in your child's room, you may freak out and you may expect a response, but you don't want your child in jail.

We have to keep building these alternatives, because for the most part, all we offer now is the police and the courtroom as solutions, and we know that's not acceptable. Every community has to work together, and prosecutors can lead by being willing to share power, divert cases, and use our bully pulpits to say that we can do better as a community. I think if we're going to get anywhere, we have to accept that the role of the prosecutor is not just to file cases and earn convictions. It is to build a safer and healthier community. You do that in partnership with the government and public health entities—and with the community. Otherwise, it's a lonely job in the prosecutor's office if all you do is process cases and don't think about how people got there or what's going to happen to them when they leave the courtroom. I've enjoyed developing new programs and reaching outside of my little prosecutor's box, and not just sitting in my office and watching as cases are filed and tried.

## Five Steps Toward a Smaller, Fairer System

To me, there are five pillars of criminal justice reform. The first pillar is to divert and deflect as many people's cases as we can. We want to shrink the criminal legal system's footprint by not handling crimes of property, crimes of addiction, and crimes where the community has a better plan than the court system does.

The second pillar is building a public health response to behavioral health crises. Stop the war on drug users. Instead, let's build an alternative response to get people help, to get them access to medication-assisted treatment, to get them off the streets and into housing. Again, that doesn't necessarily exist now, but it's something we have to build if we're going to have a better strategy to deal with substance use disorders than the courts do.

The third area is addressing criminal procedure from soup to nuts, including how you argue for bail, what your pretrial detention looks like, what your discovery policies and your *Brady* policies look like, how you pick jurors, how you plea-bargain cases, and how you address the trial penalty.[14] But if that is *all* you focus on, you're not going to have any impact on mass incarceration.

The fourth pillar is prison reform. What happens when we send people to prison? It's at the end of all this litigation that we do in the prosecutor's office—and most prosecutors don't think about what happens next. What is prison like? I've been visiting prisons since law school, and I've been going as often as I can since I've been the prosecuting attorney. It has repeatedly been eye-opening, how they're really brutal places; they're just warehouses for the most part. We need to do a better job of understanding what happens in there.[15]

And fifth is reentry. After you get out of prison, how are we going to keep you from going back? We have a recidivism problem in Washington State, where almost one of three people released from prison will go back within three years.[16] We can do better. Again, if we're going to shrink mass incarceration, we have to keep cases away from the system, but once we send people to prison, we have to help keep them from returning. It's not rocket science, it's social science, which is a lot harder. We need to provide people with the things they need—that we all need—to succeed. You need some support. You need a place to live. You need a job, a source of income. You may need some help for behavioral health challenges. You need some hope. You need connection to the community. In Washington, when people get out of prison, most of them get $40, a set of clean clothes, and an ID card that says Department of Corrections. They get sent on a bus back to the county where they were convicted. Whether they want to go there or not, that's where they're dropped off. So given the lack of investment and concern about successful reentry, it's really not a surprise that so many people end up back in prison.

I think about justice as that entire horizon. Let's get a smaller system. Let's make sure the system we have is fair and transparent. And when we do punish people, let's make sure we have an agreement about what is going to happen and why. Through clemency or resentencing, let's give people a chance to prove that they're worthy of release. Justice is all of that, and this is how we're going to bring about a greater racial justice in our country *and* shrink mass incarceration to a point where the imprisoned population is no longer an outlier on Earth.

## Strength in Numbers

In November 2016, after Kim Foxx won the race for Cook County state's attorney in Chicago, a number of reform-minded elected prosecutors came together to meet with her, shortly before she took office.[17] It was the first time I'd really sat down with prosecutors and asked the question, "How can we be different?"

I had been part of a national district attorneys association and had sort of soured on it because they were not agents of change; they were defenders of the status quo. That's what lawyers are trained to do: we're trained to defend the status quo and uphold laws and convictions. In fact, we're trained in law school—they use the term *stare decisis*, "the thing decided," a Latin term. It's as if once a case has been decided, that's the way it's going to be forever, and that's obviously not true. The law is dynamic, and the criminal legal system in particular *needs* to be dynamic.

But that conversation in Chicago, it really lit a fire for me. I thought, "There are people across the country who think about this the way I do and want to make changes." And it can be kind of lonely at the top, being a prosecutor. So to have other prosecutors who are going through the same experience and are encountering resistance and overcoming resistance and developing new partnerships in their communities, it is really exciting for me to be part of that. It is clear that there are other people who aspire to do more than just the traditional role of the prosecutor, who are excited to have a vision about a new system of justice and not just defend the old one.

I think an important question for this new generation of prosecutors is "What's politically possible in your jurisdiction?" I've met DAs from very conservative red states who are doing things like not prosecuting small amounts of marijuana—which is great, because that's what's politically possible there. And once they prove that the community doesn't collapse after they change those practices, they can continue to use their discretion and find a way to make an even bigger difference. What can be achieved—and how quickly—often depends on where you are.

## A Lifelong Learning Process

I am over sixty now, and as I get older, it's comforting that I keep learning new things. I continue to think about things in different ways and I'm not stuck in the past. This job has changed me in a lot of ways. I've seen terrible things I wish I hadn't seen. I've sat with crime victims, with families who lost a loved one in a horrific murder. That changes you forever, realizing just how fragile life can be and how the lottery of life can hit somebody out of the blue and change their life in a dramatic and horrific way. Prosecutors see the worst of human nature, but we also see the best. We see examples of courage and grace and humility, and when we do, we say, "Yeah, okay, this job is special." It's a privilege to be with people in the worst moments of their lives and to try to usher them through that.

I hope I continue to be changed by the work. I didn't run on a promise to radically change things. But I think people expect more of the prosecutors they elect now: they expect us to do what legislators are afraid to do and to make bolder moves in criminal justice reform than any other actor could. There was a time when "criminal justice reform" meant getting longer and tougher sentences. Fortunately, that's not what it means anymore. I saw how the old laws were developed and the political nature of them—and a lot of them didn't have a whole lot of thought behind them and certainly didn't include any racial impact analysis. So I don't have reverence for the laws that are on the books. I'm much more interested in imagining what could be, and changing things to adapt to the changing expectations of the community.

Justice is a larger concept than any single outcome. To me, it embodies community recovery and health. It is a concept that involves a response to any harm that was done, but also forgiving the person who caused the harm and coming up with a path for that individual to pay it back, either directly or by improving themselves. Our system of mass incarceration is not sustainable, and ultimately, if we don't do something, it will cause such a divide between the communities that are impacted by crime and the criminal legal system that they won't even be relevant to each other. We have to galvanize ourselves and say, "We can make a difference. We don't have to accept this. We can change it."

# 13

## Tori Verber Salazar

District Attorney, San Joaquin County, California

*Tori Verber Salazar went to work with the San Joaquin County District Attorney's Office in 1988. Twenty-seven years later, she was still there and became the first woman elected to lead that office. As the Republican district attorney in a county that's considered purple, she has expanded services for victims/survivors and witnesses; established a Family Justice Center for people who experience domestic violence, human trafficking, sexual assault, child abuse, or elder abuse; and created a Post-Conviction Review Unit to look at the integrity of past convictions and decades-long sentences and take action as needed. Salazar was reelected in 2018. Toward the end of her second term as DA, she was defeated in the county's June 2022 primary.*

Justin Sterling
*Cycles*, 2021
Found window, organic matter, soil, gravel, and caulking

**Justin Sterling** is a contemporary/modern artist who works across a range of mixed media, from sculpture and installations to painting and drawing to music and performance. He is an activist who hopes his work inspires dialogue about social, economic, and political issues, civil disobedience, and what it means to be a citizen. For more about Justin's work, see his website, justintoart.com.

## Artist's Statement

*Tori Verber Salazar is leading California to a new mindset, turning the status quo upside down after being elected district attorney in San Joaquin County. The dead plant in this work is hemp, and it has been taken over by other new species. For those incarcerated or simply stuck in a familial cycle of delinquency and neglect, this work is a reminder that growth still happens in confined spaces. The past informs the present. What comes next has to be predicated on what was already there—an inequitable and unsustainable racial bigotry based on lies once believed to be core truths regarding the "war on drugs" and the policies that followed.*

## Seeing Desperation Up Close

I had the great honor of growing up in South Side Stockton, part of our community that has always been hit hard economically— and one of the most diverse areas in San Joaquin County. In fact, Stockton is the most diverse city in the United States.[1] I come from an Irish-Italian Catholic family: lots of kids, lots of grand-kids, and no money. I don't know how my grandparents and par-ents made ends meet, but they did; we managed to survive with few resources. I lived in a culturally diverse neighborhood where everybody was together all the time. We played outside together, we cooked together, we shared heartaches and joy. My family had a garden in the backyard for survival, so we'd have food on the table. It felt safe because everybody knew and took care of one another.

Over time, we saw the influx of narcotics into my neighbor-hood. It went from this idyllic place where we played until the streetlights came on, to seeing people who were erratic, difficult, explosive, and violent. Now, looking back, I can see that some of my friends were abused, but as a kid you don't know what it means to have a parent who is addicted. You didn't know that your friends were suffering. You just saw a different kind of harm, and nobody knew what to do or how to treat it.

We saw thriving families in our neighborhood collapse— including my own. We had alcoholism in my family, but we didn't even know about Alcoholics Anonymous, and we sure as heck couldn't afford rehab. Families just collapsed under the weight and the pressure, the shame and the embarrassment, and the fear of the unknown. There were no tools available. I saw people getting even more desperate: the cost of supporting a habit of cocaine, crack, heroin, meth, PCP drove them deep into pov-erty and despair. Even though we were poor, we still had a home.

But there was a whole other level of poverty we didn't even know existed.

## The Difference That Kindness Makes

My dad witnessed firsthand the changes around us—he was a police officer and drove the paddy wagon, mostly transporting people who were struggling with addiction. He would bring them to my grandmother's house for lunch so they didn't have to get booked into jail. He would drive up and say, "Ma, I got four in the back," and she would put together some soup. Her door was always open—and this was a woman who didn't have a penny to spare.

She and my mother would feed anyone who needed help, including any of the other officers who came by or were in the neighborhood. They knew they could always stop by for a meal and that my grandmother was a fabulous cook. We just grew up with that, surrounded by law enforcement. My grandfather was a sheriff; my dad, three uncles, and my brother put in thirty-plus years; and my nephews are just beginning their careers in this field. We'd have a Christmas party and all of the officers' kids were together; we did performances and skits, we vacationed together in the summer, and had picnics in the park. It was a big part of my upbringing.

My dad was ahead of his time; he was very much about community-based policing before anybody even knew what that was. Of course, there are those individuals who are going to go to prison because the harm they caused is so great. But he was not an advocate of jail and prison as a response to addiction, mental health issues, and poverty, because he knew it didn't help people. He didn't think people on the street struggling with those kinds of problems warranted even one night in jail, because, as he said,

"I'm just going to pick them up again tomorrow, and they won't get the help they need."

Both he and my mother would say, "Maybe if you show some kindness, that'll be the difference." My parents also instilled in my brother and me to treat those suffering with mental illness with dignity and respect. My dad always told us that a family member of ours could struggle that way or wind up living on the streets. He said, "There but for the grace of God go I. How would you want them to be treated? And if this were you, would you want to be treated cruelly?"

My parents were divorced. After my dad brought us home to my mother one day, I told her, "I don't know where we went to lunch, but it's the most popular place in town, because it was the longest line I've ever waited in!" Almost immediately I could see my mother—with her Irish temper—fuming. I heard her talking to my dad, and sure enough, we had been in the soup line on skid row. He had told us, "You need to remember that this can happen at any given time—and I want you to see these people as people. This is somebody's husband or wife or son or daughter, and you need to see that. Never drive by and cast judgment."

Those were the best gifts my grandparents and parents gave me: the ability to see the impact of helping others. Sometimes you are going to fall down. It's imperative that we lift people up, give them every opportunity to succeed and every chance to make a difference.

## The Path to the DA's Office

My dad didn't want me to become a police officer. He said, "You see a lot of harm and you see a lot of people do terrible things. If you do not keep yourself balanced and in check, you will believe that there is only evil in the world and that there is no goodness. When you respond to a call, you have to believe that person is

a good person; you have to let them know you have that faith
in them."

Most people get into law enforcement to make a difference.
In this field, we need to remember that we are here to serve and
protect people in our community. We can do that only when we
work *with* them, but I think we've gotten away from learning
from one another. People call the police when something terrible
has happened. The job is high intensity, high stress, high pressure.
The secondary trauma was completely unaddressed in my dad's
generation. Their treatment was alcohol. There was hardly a shift
that didn't end—whether at five in the afternoon or eight in the
morning—at a bar in town that would let cops drink.

My brother went into law enforcement and had an incredible
career—but because I was argumentative in my youth, everyone in my family said I should be a lawyer. So that's why I first
thought about going to law school. I volunteered in the San Joaquin County District Attorney's Office the summer after gradu-
ating from college and really enjoyed it. I went to law school, they
offered me a job, and I came back. That was 1988, and I've been
here ever since.

## Is the Neighborhood Doing Better?

When I came to this office, the culture was one of "tough on
crime." The tougher and meaner you were, the faster you rose.
And I was promoted, fast. But we never had conversations that
came from a moral or economic or spiritual place. We never really
asked ourselves, "What else could we be doing? Are there better
ways to do this?" It was clear when I was a young attorney that if
I didn't demand "maximum justice," meaning the highest charges
and harshest punishment, I would be sidelined. That culture is
something my administration works every day to eliminate.

We have to challenge ourselves and ask, "What role is the justice system playing here?" Not only were we destroying families with those old "tough on crime" practices, we were pushing people further into darkness and harm. We were driving them further into economic disadvantage, driving them into tents on the street with children. We were preventing generations from moving forward, succeeding, getting an education, having secure housing, having simple necessities like food. We have to stop and say, "We played a role in this. This is partly our responsibility and we've got to make it right," and give people better tools to succeed.

My first job in the office was in the child abuse sexual assault unit, which was traumatic and extremely difficult. I prosecuted a case where half the room was filled with church members supporting the defendant, who had been charged with child abuse. The girl walked into the courtroom—where no one was on her side of the room—and testified. She had to look out into the audience, not only at her father, who had committed this terrible harm, but at all these people from the church who supported this man. That is unbelievable courage: to get up there and talk about things that children shouldn't even know about. And for me, to watch a victim walk by everybody she saw on Sunday in church now sitting there, glaring at her in judgment and shaming her for telling her truth, you ask yourself, "Did I make this better?"

Yes, some people are held accountable for their actions, but what did I do for *her*, the survivor? How does she go forward? That is why my whole career has been dedicated to victims. I have quadrupled the number of victim advocates in our Victim-Witness Unit and I built the first Family Justice Center, which provides healing services to more than fifteen hundred people a month.[2] But as district attorneys, we try the case and have to move on to the next one. We meet with crime survivors to get them ready to testify, we see them on a semi-regular basis because of court, and we go with them on part of their journey of healing. But then when the verdict comes in, we most likely won't see them again unless we happen to run into them on the street. We don't know about their lives after the case—but as prosecutors, we *need* to be more involved in the healing journey. But unfortunately, we are limited: in 2020, more than 24,000 cases were referred to my office, with fewer than ninety attorneys to address them.

## The Need to Promote Healing

I moved on to cases involving gang-related homicides, and we would spend a lot of time with the survivors. And when the case was over, I'd think, "Oh, they're going to be so relieved." But that often wasn't the case. I think of one family in particular— we're still good friends to this day. Like so many families, they fought for their loved one to make sure he had a voice and that people knew he mattered and that his life had value. After the guilty verdict, I turned around and looked at them, thinking, "I'm going to be able to deliver some peace to them after this horrible journey." And they looked lost, because, as the sister told me, "I thought this verdict would bring me peace, but it didn't. Now I've got to go home and grieve." I realized an unintended consequence of this process is that it often prevents survivors from having time to focus on healing.

What we did was right, and I stand behind the prosecution of that case, but I thought to myself, "We've got to do better. We shouldn't even be here, because two young men in their early twenties shouldn't be shooting each other." They were friends as children; they lived a block apart. One of the grandmothers had a picture of the defendant and the victim together in her bathtub as little kids. That's how close they were. But fifteen years later, a gang war resulted in one taking the other one's life. And you saw multiple generations impacted, including the two grandmothers who had been friends since they were little girls. And now they no longer talk to each other; they can't even walk down the same street.

In communities that have been hit hard economically—like South Side Stockton—the women run the neighborhood. These two grandmothers were very strong, highly respected, beloved members of the community, both known for keeping their kids in check. But substance use had destabilized their families, and they were caring for their children and raising their grandchildren. The defendant's grandmother was advocating to make sure justice was fair and equal for her grandson; she wanted a different journey and opportunity for him, one I could not provide. You saw their commitment to and love for their grandchildren. But during the lengthy trial, these women would not look at each other. They never spoke a word to each other. Here was this seventy-year relationship—gone.

After that case, part of me was relieved, because I felt that the victim had a voice and he was heard. Part of me thought, "I've done my job. This is what I was tasked to do, and now I can move forward." And yet part of me felt that I hadn't made anything better, other than making sure that this individual couldn't harm anybody else. I couldn't stop thinking of all the people involved. I think most prosecutors feel that, and we compartmentalize it and move on to the next case, starting the whole trajectory all over again.

## Striving for a System That Fails Less

Unfortunately, the justice system has taught our society that the length of a sentence corresponds to the value of the victim's life or harm. Nothing could be further from the truth. Every victim has value and there is no number that can define their worth to their family and the community. People have asked me, "Why is my son's life worth only a few years, and you've got a drug dealer who was shot on the corner and someone's looking at twenty-five to life?" We have to talk about this and do a better job of explaining the law and how people are sentenced. But beyond that, we should vow that every person sent to jail or prison will get the programming and services they need, not only so that they don't come out and harm others, but that they can contribute to the community in some way.

As prosecutors we've been trained to help people by seeking punitive, swift, harsh judgment, often while taking on the survivors' trauma. They look at us as if we're the only thing that can bring them justice or some form of peace. But the research is overwhelming: prison doesn't make people better. And neither the public nor victims believe that prison makes people better.[3] We spend billions of dollars on prisons that are not held accountable for sending people back out in worse shape.

We know that people who come into the criminal legal system are often in crisis and have frequently made decisions that caused harm. We need reentry plans that provide employment, housing, and an opportunity to move forward. If we do not tackle these issues, we will continue to spend enormous amounts of resources with very limited results.

We had a case where a young man committed theft and he pushed the victim and stole his wallet. He ended up serving approximately ten months in the county jail. When he went before the court, he was eighteen years old and had no prior criminal history. Three months after he got out, he killed a man. Did sending him to jail for ten months make him better? No, we made him worse: he went in a thief and came out a murderer, but nobody addressed the fact that he had no rehabilitation or meaningful services. Everybody was upset because the court sentenced him to ten months. More jail time would not have prevented that murder, but maybe services would have. There is an enormous human cost to not embracing change. Every day, the traditional justice system has an opportunity to do better, and to do so, we must be willing to find positive solutions.

## The Promise of Restorative Justice[*]

Years ago we had a series of protests in Stockton, and one of the protestors was arrested for resisting arrest and kicking an officer. We went back and forth on how to resolve this case, and ultimately, she and the officer participated in a restorative justice circle.[4] We brought in a moderator from outside my office and they had the opportunity to hear each other out.

The protester talked about a prior incident in which she was treated poorly by law enforcement—so when *this* officer came at her, she was triggered emotionally, and her response was greater than it might have been otherwise. She had the opportunity to explain to the officer why she did what she did. He explained the risk she had posed to him and the impact it had on him. At the end of this conversation, the two of them hugged and agreed to speak jointly to our community members and youth about their experience.

After the officer understood that the woman had gone through a negative experience in another county, he offered to help her. He said, "You need to go back to the police department and ask them to do an internal affairs investigation." He was advocating for her, and together they helped heal each other. We are trying to do this more often in our PNCC (Project Navigate Constructive

---

[*] Restorative justice "brings together those directly impacted by an act of harm to address the impact of the crime, hold the person who did it accountable, and make things as right as possible for those harmed." See Common Justice, "Restorative Justice: Why Do We Need It?," common justice.org/restorative_justice_why_do_we_need_it; and *Fair and Just Prosecution, Building Community Trust: Restorative Justice Strategies, Principles and Promising Practices,* (San Francisco: Fair and Just Prosecution, 2017), fairandjustprosecution.org/wp-content/uploads/2017/12/FJP.Brief_ .RestorativeJustice.pdf.

Change) program.[5] Crime victims can choose to participate; they seem to understand the need for alternatives to traditional prosecution and are engaging in the process. We hear so often from victims, "I don't want what happened to me to happen to anyone else." But that sentiment is often coupled with "I don't want them to go to prison for a long time, because I know it's not going to make them better." My office has heard the call for change from victims, and through PNCC we are building a pathway for healing and engagement for everyone involved.

## Accounting for Our Discriminatory Past

So many of our laws have harmed communities, in particular women and people of color. I have apologized to my community for the results of laws that contributed to that; as prosecutors we have to accept responsibility and come to terms with our duty to correct past harms.

In 2000, a person in my office found a picture of past DAs, probably from the late 1960s. It showed four men sitting around a desk in the district attorney's office, and there was a lynching rope hanging from the ceiling. When you see that and you're aware of our nation's history, you have to acknowledge that racism has been and continues to be a part of who we are. We need to work every day to change, to create better pathways forward, and to pay back our debts.

Change is always difficult, but even more so when addressing systemic racism. When you talk about systemic racism with people who work in the system, their gut reaction is that you are calling them racist. And they'll often say, "My friend's Black," or "I never look at race. I've never made a decision based on race." But the data is telling us something different. Only 7 percent of my community is Black, but almost 24 percent of the cases referred to my office involve charges against Black people.[6] The criminal legal system drove those results, so we must have the courage to have a conversation about the racism inherent in that system. We cannot keep doing what we're doing.

## The Toll of Taking On Law Enforcement

If, as a district attorney, you prosecute law enforcement, you will receive considerable backlash from police officers and their unions. They are unified, they may hire social media consultants, and they can gather allies in other counties or from across the nation. They may seem as if they have unlimited resources, and they have very devoted followers. The sheer amount of disinformation they have spread about my office and me is staggering and would take us all day, every day, to combat. They have called me "pro-defendant" or "anti-victim." They use comments including misogynistic terminology—for example, that I am "emotionally unstable and unfit"—to try to portray my office as if it's in disarray.

For any other type of case, if I articulated concerns over misconduct, law enforcement would cheer. We would hear statements like "She's tough!" But if I speak up when officers break public trust and betray their oath of office, I'm often labeled as "anti–law enforcement," which is the furthest thing from the truth. Calling for accountability and transparency should not be met with the level of hostility I have received in recent years.

But it's not just what *I* hear. I work out almost every day with my brother. He is one of the hardest-working people I know and one of my heroes, though we do not agree on everything. He has returned to the police force part time, and I know he gets harassed by his colleagues: "What's up with your sister?" "What happened to her?" "How come she's not backing the Blue?" "Can't you talk to her?" I also worry about my nephews because they're young in their law enforcement careers. To avoid any potential harassment they might endure, I don't let people know that we're connected. At the same time, in my home I have the flag the police association gave me at my father's funeral; I have his pictures, I have his uniform, I have his badge. They've always been a part of my home. I taught my children to treat law enforcement with dignity and respect. But now, because of my job and the tense relationships caused by those unwilling to change, my children are afraid.

So far, I have prosecuted more than twenty cases involving officers. Those cases range from narcotics usage and driving under the influence to manslaughter and sexual assault. These are difficult cases for my office and for me. It's heartbreaking that people who wear the same badge my father and my brother wore are committing these harms. It's also frustrating because I see and know great police officers who are in the profession for the right reasons. A few of them have approached me and quietly said, "You're doing the right thing."

## This Movement Is Urgent— and It Isn't Partisan

If you look across the nation, district attorneys in every state are doing incredible work, regardless of political party. We are having similar journeys as we struggle to move our offices in the direction of reform and get pushback from law enforcement. We have to remember that we work for the people. We have to hear their voices. We have to see their wisdom. The people are living with the results of the criminal legal system and their depth of knowledge is as lived as lived can be. When they speak, we better sit down and start listening.

For me, this shift was reflected in my decision to disassociate from the California District Attorneys Association. CDAA opposes criminal justice reform. I could no longer be part of an organization that represents fifty-eight counties yet uses their power to intimidate people about legislation, laws, propositions, and now other elected district attorneys. Instead of fearmongering, I have implemented data-driven practices and policies in my administration.

We have contributed to the harm in our communities—by not hearing people's voices and not taking the time to realize the generational damage that has been done, including the economic impact to families. We must continue to listen to the people, and we have to stop believing that the old way worked when data, research, and the harm we see tell us differently.

A good friend of mine called me out of the blue a couple of weeks ago. He said, "I see what you're doing. I didn't believe in it, but now I know. My son is in prison and we need to create change." He said, "Prison is not making him better, and I need my son to be better."

We owe the people justice. Elected district attorneys have a tremendous ability to create immediate change for the better and give their communities the tools to be successful, healthy, and well. This is not a partisan issue; it cuts across parties. And at the end of the day, it is the right thing to do.

# ACKNOWLEDGMENTS

Even the *idea* for this book couldn't exist without the elected prosecutors who are working every day toward making their systems more just, more equitable, and more humane. That network extends well beyond the thirteen people who tell their stories here, and I am grateful to every member of this growing movement. These leaders inspire me and others with their vision, their boldness, and their efforts to create a criminal legal system that we can all be proud to one day call a "justice" system. They reflect the best of what moral courage is about. And too often they engage in a job that is not only thankless, but also opens them to attack from those who are wedded to doing business as usual. Yet they continue to show up and move forward with needed reforms, even in the face of strong headwinds.

I give my heartfelt thanks, in particular, to all of the prosecutors who took the time to tell us their personal stories for this book. Because of them we have the chance to give a face—in fact, many faces—to this new generation of innovative leaders. I cannot thank them enough. Our team also owes a great debt to their many dedicated executive assistants and other members of their staff, all of whom helped us bring this book and these stories to life. Each chapter reflects hours of scheduling and conducting interviews, reviewing transcripts and drafts, corresponding with artists, lending expertise to the project, hunting down data, fact-checking, and verifying important details. Everything stayed on track due to the committed team in each DA's office.

This book would be a dramatically different one—with less heart and soul—if not for the amazing work of nine talented artists. I am grateful to Tameca Cole, Russell Craig, Deavron Dailey, Luis "Suave" Gonzalez, Antonio Howard, Jared Owens, Akeil Robertson, and Justin Sterling for joining us on this journey and adding the compelling visual depictions that accompany each chapter. I want to give special thanks to James "Yaya" Hough, who, in addition to contributing stunning artwork to the book, was responsible for the related curatorial efforts, bringing diverse artists to the project and supporting them in the creation of their dynamic artworks. These efforts were enhanced by the wisdom of our incredible colleagues at Mural Arts, who provided the "glue" for this project, from the leadership of Jane Golden to the talented team of Nyla Daniel, Ryan Strand Greenberg, Kaitlyn Haney, Kali Silverman, Chad Eric Smith, and Zoriana Strockyj.

But none of this would have happened if not for the connections and insight that came on so many levels from the Art for Justice Fund, a project of Rockefeller Philanthropy Advisors, and in particular from Helena Huang—a partner, leader, and visionary thinker at the intersection of social justice and art. I am also grateful for the generous support of Agnes Gund, who knows, deeply understands, and helps harness the power that comes from combining art and advocacy. Helena and Aggie have cheered us on at every turn, providing input, encouragement, and enthusiasm.

At The New Press, I am thankful for the genius of Diane

Wachtell in helping plant the seeds and nurture the idea of *Change from Within*. If not for Diane, this project would never have left the ground. She brought years of experience (and wisdom!) that helped in ways both large and small to shape the direction of this work and offered her expert feedback and perspective at every step. The New Press has been a thoughtful partner throughout this process, and we are thankful for skillful editing and general guidance from Maury Botton, Ishan Desai-Geller, zakia henderson-brown, Brian Ulicky, and Rachel Vega-DeCesario.

In all I do, I am thankful for a loving family that has always rooted me on in doing work that is often all-consuming. My husband, Glenn (who is an unabashed cheerleader for all I have taken on throughout my career), my daughters Sarah and Hannah (who fill every day with moments of sunshine, even hundreds of miles away), and my son-in-law, Daniel (who is the best husband and brother-in-law anyone could ask for), are my biggest supporters, the bright lights when things at times get dark, and the candid voices that ground me when I need it most. They are the sustenance that gives me the energy to keep fighting for change.

Last but not least, I want to call out the best team imaginable: my colleagues at Fair and Just Prosecution. Creating a book is a lot of work—and this undertaking came on top of everything else we do to fortify the movement. Just as they do in so many other ways, members of the passionate FJP team turned this concept into a reality, and somehow made it seem if not easy, at least not difficult! I am grateful to the many (and I mean *many*) hours of preparing for interviews, doing extensive research, editing, organizing, thinking, brainstorming, scheduling, reading, planning, and so much more. They carried out these endeavors with the highest level of dedication to the project, to the leaders whose stories we sought to convey, and to the readers we hope to educate and inspire.

The end product was the result of the stellar efforts of FJP staffers and consultants past and present, including Rebecca Blair, Emily Bloomenthal, Kacey Bonner, Jessica Brand, Gretchen Burnton, Natasha Camhi, Edda Fransdottir, Liz Komar, Ben Miller, Blaine Miller, Hannah Raskin-Gross, and Amy Weber. Particular thanks go to Jules Verdone for her drafting and editing prowess. (She now knows far more than she ever expected about the lives of a certain group of thirteen prosecutors.) And FJP is fortunate to have an outstanding leadership team, whose members, as always, provided invaluable guidance, insights, and contributions to this book. I am grateful to work alongside this multitalented group: Craig Cichy, Monica Fuhrmann, Kalyn Hill, Alyssa Kress, Rosemary Nidiry, and Greg Srolestar. Finally, I cannot say enough about Stephanie Dolan, who saw to the execution of every detail involved in this project. She is diligent, organized, thorough, perceptive, brilliant, and lovely to work with!

It has been said that one can reach great heights when standing on the shoulders of giants. The members of the FJP team are those giants. The stories and leaders whose work they have helped lift up are a testament to them all—and to every person who made this book possible.

—*Miriam Aroni Krinsky*

# ABOUT THIS BOOK

The people profiled in *Change from Within* are among the many elected chief prosecutors who have been redefining their role and changing the field. This book aims to tell their stories, capture their visions for the future, and describe some of the challenges they face as they seek to shift paradigms.

Working with the dedicated staff of Fair and Just Prosecution, Miriam Krinsky conducted the interviews for *Change from Within* in late 2020 and early 2021. Although some details were updated before the book's publication, the stories here reflect the world at that time, with the 2020 elections recently in the rearview mirror and the COVID-19 pandemic an ongoing crisis.

# ABOUT FAIR AND JUST PROSECUTION

Fair and Just Prosecution (FJP) works to transform the criminal legal system by bringing together elected local prosecutors as part of a network of leaders committed to promoting a justice system grounded in fairness, equity, compassion, and fiscal responsibility. These recently elected leaders—and the vision they share for safer and healthier communities—are supported by FJP's network through ongoing information sharing, research and resource materials, opportunities for on the ground learning, in-person convenings, technical assistance, and access to national experts.

To learn more about this project and stay up to date on Fair and Just Prosecution's work:

- For more on *Change from Within,* visit www. fairandjust prosecution.org/ChangeFromWithin.
- For more on the elected prosecutors profiled in this book, visit https://fairandjustprosecution.org/meet-the-movement.
- Sign up to receive updates at www.fairandjustprosecution .org/contact-us/stay-connected.
- Like and follow us on Facebook: www.facebook.com /fairandjustprosecution
- Follow us on Twitter: www./twitter.com/fjp_org
- Follow us on LinkedIn: www.linkedin.com/company/fjp

# ABOUT MURAL ARTS PHILADELPHIA

Mural Arts Philadelphia is the nation's largest public art program, providing transformative experiences, progressive discourse, and economic stimulus to the city of Philadelphia through participatory public art that beautifies, advocacy that inspires, and educational programming and employment opportunities that empower. Their renowned restorative justice program combats recidivism through innovative art apprenticeships for people impacted by the justice system.

# NOTES

## Introduction: A New Vision for Justice

1. To hear more from the people featured in the book and other reform-minded prosecutors, and to learn about this movement, go to fairandjust prosecution.org/meet-the-movement.

2. Fair and Just Prosecution (FJP), "Joint Statement from Elected Prosecutors on the Murder of George Floyd and Police Violence" (San Francisco: FJP, May 29, 2020), fairandjustprosecution.org/staging /wp-content/uploads/2020/05/George-Floyd-Statement-FINAL .pdf; and FJP, "#JusticeForGeorgeFloyd: DAs For Criminal Justice and Policing Reform" (San Francisco: FJP, June 4, 2020), vimeo.com /426111848?fbclid=IwAR3uYwQ6j6v6vEyDED44xxX3FwplLmp -P6km8NHXQESR99NLMAgvn0Xo6ok.

3. Founded in 1984, the nonprofit Mural Arts Philadelphia is the largest public art program in the United States and is "dedicated to the belief that art ignites change." For more information, see muralarts.org. The Art for Justice Fund, a project of Rockefeller Philanthropy Advisors, supported this collaboration and has made "direct grants to artists and advocates focused on safely reducing the prison population, promoting justice reinvestment and creating art that changes the narrative around mass incarceration." For more information, see artforjusticefund.org.

4. Museum of Modern Art PS1, *Marking Time: Art in the Age of Incarceration*, September 17, 2020–April 5, 2021, moma.org/calendar/exhibitions /5208.

5. Nick Warren, "Antonio Howard: Creating His Own Narrative," *Erie Reader*, February 10, 2021, eriereader.com/article/antonio-howard -creating-his-own-narrative; and Erie Arts & Culture, Member Directory, "Antonio Howard," erieartsandculture.org/directory/member/159%0D.

6. South Arts, "Tameca Cole: 2021 State Fellow," southarts.org/grant -fellowship-recipients/tameca-cole-2021.

7. Jenny DeHuff, "James 'Yaya' Hough: A New Temporary Art Installation at the D.A.'s Office," October 1, 2020, *Dosage Magazine*, dosagemaga zine.com/james-yaya-hough-a-new-temporary-art-installation-at-the-d-a -s-office. To read more about the Art for Justice Fund, see artforjusticefund .org/about.

8. Oliver Roeder, Lauren-Brooke Eisen, and Julia Bowling, *What Caused the Crime Decline?* (New York: New York University School of Law, Brennan Center for Justice, 2015), 1, brennancenter.org/sites/default/files /2019-08/Report_What_Caused_The_Crime_Decline.pdf.

9. Roeder, Eisen, and Bowling, *What Caused the Crime Decline?*, 3, 18–26, 79.

10. For more about "tough on crime" policies and prosecution, see Scott Michels, "Rethinking 'Tough on Crime,'" The Crime Report, Center on Media Crime and Justice at John Jay College, June 28, 2012, thecrimereport .org/2012/06/28/2012-06-rethinking-tough-on-crime; Udi Ofer, "How the 1994 Crime Bill Fed the Mass Incarceration Crisis," American Civil Liberties Union (blog), June 4, 2019, aclu.org/blog/smart-justice/mass -incarceration/how-1994-crime-bill-fed-mass-incarceration-crisis; and Arit John, "A Timeline of the Rise and Fall of 'Tough on Crime' Drug Sentencing," *The Atlantic*, April 22, 2014, theatlantic.com/politics/archive /2014/04/a-timeline-of-the-rise-and-fall-of-tough-on-crime-drug -sentencing/360983.

11. Fair and Just Prosecution, "Over 90 Criminal Justice Leaders Condemn State Voter Suppression Efforts," press release (San Francisco: FJP, June 7, 2021), fairandjustprosecution.org/staging/wp-content/uploads /2021/06/FJP-Voting-Rights-Joint-Statement-Release-June-2021.pdf.

12. Museumsportal Berlin, "House of the Wannsee Conference," mus eumsportal-berlin.de/en/museums/haus-der-wannsee-konferenz.

13. Ian Beacock, "America Doesn't Need Heroes: Why Germany's Concept of Zivilcourage Is One for the Biden Era," *Foreign Policy*, June 20, 2021, foreignpolicy.com/2021/06/20/zivilcourage-biden-rebuild-democracy -germany.

14. Fair and Just Prosecution, "Joint Statement From Elected Prosecutors and Law Enforcement Leaders Condemning the Criminalization of Transgender People and Gender-Affirming Healthcare," (San Francisco: FJP, June 2021), fairandjustprosecution.org/staging/wp-content/uploads /2021/06/FJP-Trans-Criminalization-Joint-Statement.pdf; Rob Abruz-

zese, "Keeping ICE Out of NY Courts: James and Gonzalez Win Lawsuit Against Trump Administration," *Brooklyn Eagle*, June 12, 2020, brookly neagle.com/articles/2020/06/12/keeping-ice-out-of-ny-courts-james -and-gonzalez-win-lawsuit-against-trump-administration; Simon Rios, "DAs Join Lawsuit That Seeks To Bar ICE Arrests At Local Courthouses," WBUR, April 29, 2019, wbur.org/news/2019/04/29/immigration-ice -courthouse-lawsuit-rachael-rollins-marian-ryan; Fair and Just Prosecution, "Joint Statement from Elected Prosecutors and Law Enforcement Leaders on Voting Restrictions," (San Francisco: FJP, June 2021), fairand justprosecution.org/staging/wp-content/uploads/2021/06/FJP-Voting -Rights-Joint-Statement-June-2021.pdf; and Fair and Just Prosecution, "Nearly 100 Criminal Justice Leaders Urge Supreme Court to Protect the Constitutional Right to Abortion Access," press release (San Francisco: FJP, September 20, 2021), fairandjustprosecution.org/wp-content/uploads /2021/09/FJP-Dobbs-Amicus-Release.pdf.

# 1

## Chesa Boudin

1. To read more about the incident in 1981 and developments in recent years, see Michael Hill, "Prosecutor Son Seeks Father's Release in Fatal Brink's Heist," Associated Press, February 19, 2021, abcnews.go.com /Politics/wireStory/da-son-seeks-release-father-imprisoned-fatal-81 -75989493.

2. Unlike the United States and 64 other countries, 144 countries have some provision for parole. See Fair and Just Prosecution, *Lessons Learned from Germany: Avoiding Unnecessary Incarceration and Limiting Collateral Consequences* (San Francisco: Fair and Just Prosecution, 2020), 5, fairandjustprosecu- tion.org/wp-content/uploads/2020/04/FJP_Brief_GermanIncarceration .pdf, citing *Bundesministeriums der Justiz und für Verbraucherschutz*, Ger- man Criminal Code, §57 & §57a, gesetze-im-internet.de/englisch_stgb /englisch_stgb.html#p0354; and Penal Reform International, "Key facts," penalreform.org/issues/life-imprisonment/key-facts.

3. To read more on the use of solitary confinement in the United States and worldwide, see Solitary Watch, "FAQ," solitarywatch.org/facts/faq. For more on violent crime rates, see World Population Review, "Violent Crime Rates by Country 2021," worldpopulationreview.com/country -rankings/violent-crime-rates-by-country.

4. Emily Bazelon and Miriam Krinsky, "There's a Wave of New Pros- ecutors. And They Mean Justice," *New York Times*, December 11, 2018, nytimes.com/2018/12/11/opinion/how-local-prosecutors-can-reform -their-justice-systems.html.

5. Megan Cassidy, "D.A. Chesa Boudin Declines to File Charges in Two 2020 S.F. Police Shootings," *San Francisco Chronicle*, December 10, 2020, sfchronicle.com/crime/article/SFDA-Boudin-declines-to-file-charges -against-15792988.php.

6. Henry Epp, "Why Chittenden County State's Attorney Sarah George Wants to End Cash Bail," Vermont Public Radio, September 18, 2020, vpr.org/post/why-chittenden-county-states-attorney-sarah-george-wants -end-cash-bail#stream/0.

7. See Cook County State's Attorney, "Cook County State's Attorney's Office Releases More Public Data in Foxx's Commitment to Transparency," October 9, 2020, cookcountystatesattorney.org/news/cook-county -state-s-attorney-s-office-releases-more-public-data-foxx-s-commitment -transparency; and Cook County State's Attorney, "A Commitment to Transparency," cookcountystatesattorney.org/about/commitment-transpar ency.

8. Michael Wilson and Jesus Jiménez, "Cuomo Commutes Sentences of 1981 Brink's Robbery Participant and 4 Others," *New York Times*, August 23, 2021, nytimes.com/2021/08/23/nyregion/david-gilbert-brinks-sentence -commuted.html?searchResultPosition=1.

9. Michael Wilson and Ed Shanahan, "Man Convicted in '81 Brink's Robbery Wins Release From New York Prison," *New York Times*, October 26, 2021, nytimes.com/2021/10/26/nyregion/david-gilbert-brinks -parole.html.

# 2

## Satana Deberry

1. To read more about the Youth Steering Committee of the Southern Coalition for Social Justice's Youth Justice Project, see southerncoalition .org/youth-justice-project/youth-steering-committee.

2. In North Carolina, the Governor's School is a "multi-week summer residential program for gifted and talented high school students." For more information, see www.dpi.nc.gov/students-families/enhanced -opportunities/governors-school-north-carolina.

3. STEM stands for science, technology, engineering, and mathematics.

4. To read more about Professor Taylor, see dof.princeton.edu/about /clerk-faculty/emeritus/howard-francis-taylor.

5. To read more about SpiritHouse, the Durham-based nonprofit Nia Wilson founded, see spirithouse-nc.org.

6. For more information about the gender gap in running for political office, see the National Organization for Women, "Why Women Should Run for Office," December 2017, now.org/wp-content/uploads/2017/12/Why-Women-Should-Run.pdf.

7. Statewide, more than 66 percent of young people detained in North Carolina's juvenile system are Black. North Carolina Department of Public Safety, Division of Adult Correction and Juvenile Justice, *Juvenile Justice 2020 Annual Report*, August 9, 2021, 33, files.nc.gov/ncdps/documents/files/2020-Juvenile-Justice-Annual-Report-FINAL.pdf.

8. In February 2015, Deah Barakat, his wife, Yusor Mohammad Abu-Salha, and her sister, Razan Mohammad Abu-Salha, were killed in their home in Chapel Hill, North Carolina. For more information, see Bill Chappell, "N.C. Man Pleads Guilty to Killing 3 Muslim College Students; Video Is Played in Court," National Public Radio, June 12, 2019, npr.org/2019/06/12/731981858/n-c-man-pleads-guilty-to-murdering-3-muslim-college-students.

9. In each of ninety-four federal districts, the U.S. Attorney is the chief federal law enforcement officer. In some cases, the DA and the U.S. Attorney both have interest in and jurisdiction to prosecute the crime. For more information, see U.S. Department of Justice, Offices of the United States Attorneys, justice.gov/usao.

10. Cinnamon Janzer, "Durham, NC Just Finished Erasing $2.7 Million in Traffic Debt," *Next City*, February 17, 2021, nextcity.org/daily/entry/durham-nc-just-finished-erasing-2.7-million-in-traffic-debt.

11. On January 14, 1963, Rabbi Heschel spoke on "The Religious Basis of Equality of Opportunity" at the National Conference on Religion and Race in Chicago, where he said, "The prophet is a person who is not tolerant of wrongs done to others, who resents other people's injuries." See Voices of Democracy: The U.S. Oratory Project, "Rabbi Abraham Joshua Heschel, 'Religion and Race' (14 January 1963)," voicesofdemocracy.umd.edu/heschel-religion-and-race-speech-text; and Stanford University, The Martin Luther King Jr. Research and Education Institute, "National Conference on Religion and Race," January 1963, kinginstitute.stanford.edu/encyclopedia/national-conference-religion-and-race.

12. For more about the Religious Coalition for a Nonviolent Durham, see nonviolentdurham.org.

13. See *Philly D.A.* "Breaking the Cycle." *Independent Lens*. 55:45. April 27, 2021. pbs.org/video/part-3-philly-da-episode-3-9lksp7/

14. To see freedom clay's work, see facebook.com/afrofolkartbyfreedom clay or @freedomclay on Instagram.

# 3

## Parisa Dehghani-Tafti

1. To read more about the case, see Maurice Possley, "Brendan Loftus," National Registry of Exonerations, law.umich.edu/special/exoneration /Pages/casedetail.aspx?caseid=3831.

2. In its 1963 decision *Brady v. Maryland*, the Supreme Court ruled that prosecutors are required to disclose any information that is favorable to the defense; see supreme.justia.com/cases/federal/us/373/83. For more about *Brady* violations, see Jessica Brand, "The Epidemic of Brady Violations: Explained," April 25, 2018, *The Appeal*, theappeal.org/the-epidemic-of -brady-violations-explained-94a38ad3c800.

3. To read more, see The Innocence Project, "Arson and Bad Science," September 14, 2009 (New York: Innocence Project), innocenceproject .org/arson-and-bad-science; and Mark Hansen, "Long-Held Beliefs about Arson Science Have Been Debunked after Decades of Misuse," *ABA Journal*, December 1, 2015 (Chicago: American Bar Association), abajournal.com /magazine/article/long_held_beliefs_about_arson_science_have_been _debunked_after_decades_of_m.

4. When people break a rule and do not meet the conditions of their probation or parole supervision—such as missing curfew or an appointment with a parole officer—it is referred to as a technical violation. Almost 25 percent of people entering prison in 2017 were incarcerated for a technical supervision violation, rather than a new offense. See Miriam Aroni Krinsky and Vincent Schiraldi, "Community Supervision, Once Intended to Help Offenders, Contributes More to Mass Incarceration," *USA Today*, November 19, 2020, usatoday.com/story/opinion/policing/2020/11 /19/supervision-once-intended-help-offenders-ups-mass-incarceration -column/3765824001; citing the Council of State Governments Justice Center, "Confined and Costly: How Supervision Violations Are Filling Prisons and Burdening Budgets," June 2019, csgjusticecenter.org/wp -content/uploads/2020/01/confined-and-costly.pdf.

5. To read more about the case, see Mid-Atlantic Innocence Project, "Troy Burner," exonerate.org/all-project-list/troy-burner; and Maurice Possley, the National Registry of Exonerations, "Troy Burner," law.umich .edu/special/exoneration/Pages/casedetail.aspx?caseid=5802.

6. This parable is widely attributed to the activist and political theorist Saul Alinsky but may have been adapted from a story by the writer and activist Irving Zola. See Gail Smith, "Going Upstream to Help Children," obamawhitehouse.gov, June 18, 2013, obamawhitehouse.archives.gov/blog /2013/06/18/going-upstream-help-children; and Unitarian Universalist Association, "Babies in the River," uua.org/re/tapestry/youth/call /workshop1/171686.shtml.

7. Dehghani-Tafti defeated the incumbent prosecutor Theo Stamos in the Democratic primary in June 2019 and ran unopposed in the general election. She took office in January 2020. See Airey, "What's Next? What Last Night's Primary Election Means for Arlington," June 12, 2019, ARL now.com, arlnow.com/2019/06/12/whats-next-what-last-nights-primary -election-means-for-arlington.

8. For more on the Black Codes, see "Reconstruction: The Black Codes," PBS, ny.pbslearningmedia.org/resource/reconstruction-black -codes/reconstruction-the-black-codes; and Southern Poverty Law Center, "Teaching *The New Jim Crow*: Lesson 4: Jim Crow as a Form of Racialized Social Control," learningforjustice.org/sites/default/files/general/Jim%20 Crow%20as%20a%20Form%20of%20Racialized%20Social%20Control .pdf, 3, citing Michelle Alexander, *The New Jim Crow: Mass Incarceration in the Age of Colorblindness* (New York: The New Press, 2010).

9. Death Penalty Information Center, "Executions by State and Region Since 1976," deathpenaltyinfo.org/executions/executions-overview /number-of-executions-by-state-and-region-since-1976.

10. To read more about the case, see Tom Jackman, "'Norfolk 4,' Wrongly Convicted of Rape and Murder, Pardoned by Gov. McAuliffe," *The Washington Post*, March 21, 2017, washingtonpost.com/news/true-crime /wp/2017/03/21/norfolk-4-wrongly-convicted-of-rape-and-murder -pardoned-by-gov-mcauliffe.

11. Whittney Evans, "Virginia Governor Signs Law Abolishing the Death Penalty, a 1st in the South," National Public Radio, March 24, 2021, npr.org/2021/03/24/971866086/virginia-governor-signs-law-abolishing -the-death-penalty-a-1st-in-the-south.

12. In March 2021, Virginia Governor Ralph Northam signed legislation that abolished the death penalty. Brandon L. Garrett, "Guest Post: How Virginia Ended the Death Penalty," *The Washington Post*, March 24, 2021, washingtonpost.com/crime-law/2021/03/24/va-ends-death.

13. John Rawls, *A Theory of Justice* (Cambridge, MA: Belknap Press, 1971). To read more about the philosopher's description of a "veil of ignorance," also see Julian Coman, "John Rawls: Can Liberalism's Great Philosopher Come to the West's Rescue Again?" *The Guardian*, December 20, 2020, theguardian.com/inequality/2020/dec/20/john-rawls-can -liberalisms-great-philosopher-come-to-the-wests-rescue-again.

14. In July 2021, President Joe Biden nominated Rachael Rollins to serve as the U.S. attorney for Massachusetts, the state's chief federal prosecutor. The U.S. Senate confirmed her in December 2021, and in January 2022 she became the first Black person in Massachusetts to hold the position. To read more about her, see Chapter 11.

15. James Baldwin, *The Price of the Ticket: Collected Writings 1948–1985* (New York: St. Martin's Press, 1985).

16. To read more about the writer and activist James Baldwin, see the Smithsonian National Museum of African American History & Culture, "An Introduction to James Baldwin," July 31, 2017, nmaahc.si.edu/explore /stories/introduction-james-baldwin; to read more about the Freedom Riders, see Marian Smith Holmes, "The Freedom Riders, Then and Now," *Smithsonian Magazine*, February 2009, smithsonianmag.com/history/the -freedom-riders-then-and-now-45351758.

# 4

## Mark Dupree Sr.

1. Rick Tulsky, "Lamonte McIntyre Freed from Prison, 23 Years After Questionable Conviction," Injustice Watch, October 13, 2017, injusti cewatch.org/news/2017/lamonte-mcintyre-freed-from-prison-after-23 -years.

2. Ashley White, McKenzie Nelson, and Sam Hartle, "Wyandotte County DA Dismisses Murder Charge Against Pete Coones," KSHB-TV, November 5, 2020, kshb.com/news/crime/wyandotte-county-da -dismisses-murder-charges-against-pete-coones.

3. In *Berger v. United States*, 295 U.S. 78 (1935), the U.S. Supreme Court said, "The [prosecutor's] interest . . . in a criminal prosecution is not that it shall win a case, but that justice shall be done. As such, he is in a peculiar and very definite sense the servant of the law, the twofold aim of which is that guilt shall not escape or innocence suffer. He may prosecute with earnestness and vigor—indeed, he should do so. But, while he may strike hard blows, he is not at liberty to strike foul ones. It is as much his duty to refrain from improper methods calculated to produce a wrongful conviction as it is to use every legitimate means to bring about a just one." See supreme.justia .com/cases/federal/us/295/78.

4. Research shows that "employment is associated with lower rates of" new criminal activity among people with a past criminal history. See Demelza Baer et al., *Understanding the Challenges of Prisoner Reentry: Research Findings from the Urban Institute's Prisoner Reentry Portfolio* (Washington: Urban Institute, 2006), 4, urban.org/sites/default/files/publication/42981 /411289-Understanding-the-Challenges-of-Prisoner-Reentry.PDF, citing Jared Bernstein and Ellen Houston, *Crime and Work: What We Can Learn from the Low-Wage Labor Market* (Washington, DC: Economic Policy Institute, 2000); and Bruce Western and Becky Petit, "Incarceration and Racial Inequality in Men's Employment," *Industrial and Labor Relations Review* 54, no. 3 (2000), 3–16.

# 5

## Kimberly Foxx

1. Merriam-Webster defines *gig economy* as "economic activity that involves the use of temporary or freelance workers to perform jobs typically in the service sector." See merriam-webster.com/dictionary/gig%20 economy.

2. Phillip Matier and Andrew Ross, "Feinstein's Surprise Call for Death Penalty puts D.A. on Spot," *SFGATE*, April 21, 2004, sfgate.com/bayarea /matier-ross/article/Feinstein-s-surprise-call-for-death-penalty-puts -3313728.php.

3. *Chicago Tribune* staff, "Jon Burge and Chicago's Legacy of Police Torture," *Chicago Tribune*, September 19, 2018, chicagotribune.com/news/ct -jon-burge-chicago-police-torture-timeline-20180919-htmlstory.html.

4. Annie Sweeney and *Tribune* reporter, "Burge Given 4½ Years in Prison," *Chicago Tribune*, January 21, 2011, chicagotribune.com/news/ct-met -burge-sentencing-0122-20110121-story.html; and Chip Mitchell, "Mayor Lori Lightfoot Says Police Tortured 'at Least 100' Black Chicagoans, but Her Law Department Tells a Different Story," WBEZ, June 3, 2021, wbez .org/stories/mayor-lori-lightfoot-says-police-tortured-at-least-100-black -chicagoans-the-city-refuses-to-call-it-a-pattern/7b5eca8c-5089-44a4 -9648-6e720e8fb521.

5. "Raising the age" refers to states legally changing the age at which young people can be charged and tried as adults. Illinois raised the age to eighteen for misdemeanors in 2010 and to age seventeen for felonies in 2013, and then to age eighteen in 2014. Selen Siringil Perker, Lael E. H. Chester, and Vincent Schiraldi, "Emerging Adult Justice in Illinois: Towards an Age-Appropriate Approach," Columbia Justice Lab, January 2019, justicelab.columbia.edu/sites/default/files/content/EAJ%20in%20 Illinois%20Report%20Final.pdf.

6. In 2015, Bruce Rauner, then governor of Illinois, signed a law to stop automatic transfers of children who are fifteen to adult court; the law also limited such transfers for sixteen- and seventeen-year-olds. Bryant-Jackson Green, "New Law Ends Automatic Transfer of Some Juveniles to Adult Court," *Illinois Policy*, August 4, 2015, illinoispolicy.org/illinois-poised-to -update-juvenile-transfer-policy

7. For more about the Supreme Court ruling, see Equal Justice Initiative, "*Miller v. Alabama*," eji.org/cases/miller-v-alabama.

8. To read more about the case, see Patrick Smith, "Sentenced as Teen to Life in Prison, Adolfo Davis Released After Precedent-Setting Legal Fight," WBEZ, March 31, 2020, wbez.org/stories/sentenced-as-teen-to-life-in -prison-inmate-released-after-precedent-setting-legal-fight/d82c1fa0 -a736-4d21-a3ef-c9e9b9f65224; and Steve Bogira, "The Hustle of Kim

Foxx," *The Marshall Project*, October 29, 2018, themarshallproject.org/2018
/10/29/the-hustle-of-kim-foxx.

9. "'I am not suggesting that Mr. Davis had an easy time as a kid,' the
assistant state's attorney told the judge. 'But there are millions of people
throughout this world that have grown up in worse homes, that have grown
up in worse neighborhoods, and they become law-abiding, productive citizens.' To blame the crime on poverty was 'an insult to all the good, decent
people that come from neighborhoods like that.'" Bogira, "The Hustle of
Kim Foxx."

10. To read State's Attorney Foxx's statement on data transparency, see
cookcountystatesattorney.org/about/commitment-transparency.

11. Cook County State's Attorney, "Felony Dashboard," cookcounty-
statesattorney.org/about/felony-dashboard.

12. Cook County State's Attorney's Office, "Foxx Reverses Nine More
Convictions Tied to Corrupt Former Sergeant Ronald Watts," press release,
February 19, 2021, cookcountystatesattorney.org/news/foxx-reverses
-nine-more-convictions-tied-corrupt-former-sergeant-ronald-watts;
and Stefano Esposito, "88 More People Say They Were Framed by Corrupt Ex-Chicago Cop Ronald Watts, Want Their Convictions Tossed,"
*Chicago Sun-Times*, July 20, 2021, chicago.suntimes.com/2021/7/20
/22585625/convictions-challenged-framed-chicago-police-sgt-ronald
-watts-corruption-tactical-unit.

13. For more on expungement in Cook County, see Cook County State's
Attorney, "Cannabis Conviction Relief and Legislation," cookcountystat
esattorney.org/cannabis. For more on expungement in Illinois, see Candice
Norwood, "Historic Marijuana Bill Signed in Illinois," *Governing*, June 26,
2019, governing.com/archive/tns-marijuana-bill-illinois-signed.html.

14. In October 2019, a reported 95 percent of the United States' elected
prosecutors were white, 73 percent were white men, and women of color
represented about 2 percent of all elected prosecutors, as compared to 1 percent in 2015. See Women Donors Network and The Reflective Democracy
Campaign, "Tipping the Scales: Challengers Take On the Old Boys' Club
of Elected Prosecutors," October 2019, wholeads.us/wp-content/uploads
/2019/10/Tipping-the-Scales-Prosecutor-Report-10-22.pdf.

# 6

## Sarah George

1. Liz Mays Harris, "A Mother Reflects on her Daughter's Legacy After
a Tragic Accident," Kids VT, December 5, 2017, kidsvt.com/vermont
/a-mother-reflects-on-her-daughters-legacy-after-a-tragic-accident
/Content?oid=2613275.

2. State of Vermont, Office of Governor Phil Scott, "Governor Phil Scott Appoints Sarah George as Chittenden County State's Attorney," press release, January 19, 2017, governor.vermont.gov/press-release/governor -phil-scott-appoints-sarah-george-chittenden-county-states-attorney.

3. As of 2019, Canada had twenty-five safe consumption sites; see Mattie Quinn, "Safe Drug Injection Sites Are Coming to America. Canada Has Had Them for Years," *Governing*, April 10, 2019, governing .com/archive/gov-supervised-injection-site.html. For more about such programs in Europe, see Cara Tabachnick, "Safe Spaces for Users," *Stanford Social Innovation Review*, Spring 2019, ssir.org/articles/entry /Wary_of_an_Opioid_Epidemic_Europe_Pushes_Safe_Sites_for _Drug_Use. For more on Australia's programs, see Alcohol and Drug Foundation, "Medically Supervised Injecting Centres Save Lives," June 22, 2020, adf.org.au/insights/medically-supervised-injecting-centres.

4. For more about medication-assisted treatment for opioid use disorder, see U.S. Department of Health & Human Services, Substance Abuse and Mental Health Services Administration, "Buprenorphine," 2022, samhsa .gov/medication-assisted-treatment/medications-counseling-related -conditions/buprenorphine.

5. Carolyn Shapiro, "Why Did Opioid Overdose Deaths Drop 50% in Chittenden County?," The University of Vermont Health Network, VTDigger.org, vtdigger.org/sponsored_content/uvm-opioid-overdose -deaths-drop-50-chittenden-county.

6. Paul Heintz, "Vermont Prison Probe Finds 'Disturbing' Number of Sexual Misconduct Allegations," SevenDays, December 23, 2020, sev endaysvt.com/OffMessage/archives/2020/12/23/vermont-prison-probe -finds-disturbing-number-of-sexual-misconduct-allegations.

7. Xander Landen, "Prison Proposals Would Close Women's Facility, but Expand Corrections Capacity," VTDigger, April 14, 2021, vtdigger.org /2021/04/14/prison-proposals-would-close-womens-facility-but-expand -corrections-capacity.

8. For more information about the gender gap in running for political office, see a short piece by the National Organization for Women on "Why Women Should Run for Office," December 2017, now.org/wp-content /uploads/2017/12/Why-Women-Should-Run.pdf.

# 7

## Eric Gonzalez

1. Martin Tolchin, "South Bronx: A Jungle Stalked by Fear, Seized by Rage," *The New York Times*, January 15, 1973, nytimes.com/1973

/01/15/archives/south-bronx-a-jungle-stalked-by-fear-seized-by-rage
.html?searchResultPosition=18.

2. Ashley Southall, Michael Gold, and Matthew Sedacca, "Her Dad Came to Her Birthday Party. Then He Killed Her Family," *The New York Times*, April 6, 2021, nytimes.com/2021/04/06/nyregion/brooklyn -brownsville-murder-suicide.html.

3. New York State, Office of Information Technology Services, "Adult Arrests 18 and Older by County: Beginning 1970," data.ny.gov/Public -Safety/Adult-Arrests-18-and-Older-by-County-Beginning-197/rikd -mt35.

4. New York State, "Adult Arrests 18 and Older."

5. Mary Breasted, "Carey Signs Marijuana Measure Reducing Penalty for Possession," *The New York Times*, June 30, 1977, nytimes.com/1977 /06/30/archives/carey-signs-marijuana-measure-reducing-penalty-for -possession-carey.html.

6. Drug Policy Alliance and Marijuana Arrest Research Project, *Unjust and Unconstitutional: 60,000 Jim Crow Marijuana Arrests in Mayor de Blasio's New York*, (New York: Drug Policy Alliance, 2017), 27, drugpolicy.org /sites/default/files/Marijuana-Arrests-NYC--Unjust-Unconstitutional --July2017_2.pdf.

7. Citing data from the New York State Division of Criminal Justice Services, Harry G. Levine and Loren Siegel wrote, "About 30% of everyone arrested for marijuana possession had never been arrested before for anything; another 40% had never been convicted or pled guilty to anything, not even a misdemeanor. In other words, 70% of everyone arrested had never been convicted of any crime whatsoever." See Levine and Siegel, "Marijuana Madness: The Scandal of New York City's Racist Marijuana Possession Arrests," in *The New York City Police Department: The Impact of Its Policies and Practices*, John A. Eterno, editor (New York: CRC Press, 2015), 147, qcpages.qc.cuny.edu/~hlevine /Marijuana_Madness__NYCs_Racist_Marijuana_Arrests.

8. Michael Lumer, "Smoking It Up in Brooklyn," Fourth and Fourteenth, July 8, 2014, www.fourthandfourteenth.com/2014/07/smoking-it -up-in-brooklyn.html.

9. Alan Feuer, "Eric Gonzalez Wins Primary Election for Brooklyn District Attorney," *The New York Times*, September 12, 2017, nytimes.com /2017/09/12/nyregion/brooklyn-district-attorney.html; Bklyner.com, "NYC General Election 2017: Here's How Brooklyn Voted," November 8, 2017, bklyner.com/nyc-general-election-2017-heres-brooklyn-voted.

10. For more information, see Brooklyn District Attorney's Office, "Brooklyn District Attorney Eric Gonzalez Launches the Brooklyn Community Resource Empowerment Center to Offer Educational and Vocational Opportunities to Those Sentenced to Community Service," press release, June 27, 2019, brooklynda.org/2019/06/27/brooklyn-district

-attorney-eric-gonzalez-launches-the-brooklyn-community-resource
-empowerment-center-to-offer-educational-and-vocational-opportunities
-to-those-sentenced-to-community-service.

11. See New York City Police Department, "Marijuana Arrests and Summons: Marijuana Arrests," www1.nyc.gov/site/nypd/stats/reports-analysis/marijuana.page.

12. Luis Ferré-Sadurní, "New York Legalizes Recreational Marijuana, Tying Move to Racial Equity," *The New York Times*, March 31, 2021, nytimes.com/2021/03/31/nyregion/cuomo-ny-legal-weed.html.

13. From 2016 to 2019, the total number of cases prosecuted in Kings County declined by 42 percent. New York State Division of Criminal Justice Services, "Dispositions of Adult Arrests (18 and Older) 2016–2020: Kings," criminaljustice.ny.gov/crimnet/ojsa/dispos/index.htm.

14. Although pre-arraignment diversion can apply to cases that do not involve drug possession, the Brooklyn District Attorney's Office explains the strategy of one project this way: People "arrested for misdemeanor possession of a controlled substance will be offered the opportunity to receive treatment and other community-based services before their initial court appearance. If they meaningfully participate, the DA's Office will decline prosecution of their cases before they ever appear in court and their arrest record will be sealed." See Brooklyn District Attorney, "Brooklyn District Attorney Announces Project Brooklyn CLEAR to Offer Treatment for Individuals Arrested with Small Amount of Narcotics," press release, March 6, 2018, brooklynda.org/2018/03/06/brooklyn-district-attorney-announces-project-brooklyn-clear-to-offer-treatment-for-individuals-arrested-with-small-amount-of-narcotics.

# 8

## Mark Gonzalez

1. Texas Penal Code §71.01 (2021) defines a *criminal street gang* as "three or more persons having a common identifying sign or symbol or an identifiable leadership who continuously or regularly associate in the commission of criminal activities." See law.justia.com/codes/texas/2019/penal-code/title-11/chapter-71/section-71-01.

2. To read more about the Mexican revolutionary Emiliano Zapata Salazar, see Biography, "Emiliano Zapata," biography.com/political-figure/emiliano-zapata.

3. The Nueces County program gives police the option of issuing people a citation for one of seven misdemeanors instead of arresting them; the citation serves as a summons to appear in court. To read more, see Taylor Alanis, "Nueces County District Attorney's Office Gives Update on Cite and Release Program," KIII-TV, August 28, 2019, kiiitv.com/article/news

/local/nueces-county-district-attorneys-office-gives-update-on-cite-and
-release-program/503-bca8c359-2eff-4ccd-911f-7571cb8fabc5; and State
of Texas, County of Nueces, District Attorney, "Cite and Release Program," nuecesco.com/courts/district-attorney/cite-and-release-program.

4. Timothy Bella, "The Most Unlikely D.A. in America," *Politico*,
May 6, 2018, politico.com/magazine/story/2018/05/06/most-unlikely
-district-attorney-in-america-mark-gonzalez-218322.

# 9

## Larry Krasner

1. The U.S. Supreme Court reinstated the death penalty in 1976; see
American Civil Liberties Union, "Death Penalty 101," aclu.org/other
/death-penalty-101.

2. Meredith M. Henry, "Chesco Man Gets Life in '83 Slaying," *Philadelphia Inquirer*, November 26, 1985, newspapers.com/clip/20454057/emma
-mulholland-1985-sentencing-of.

3. ACT UP stands for AIDS Coalition to Unleash Power. To read more
about the group, go to actupny.com.

4. Philadelphia District Attorney's Office, Public Data Dashboard,
"COVID-19 Impact Report: Jail Population," data.philadao.com
/COVID19_Report.html.

5. Harvard Law School, Fair Punishment Project, "America's Top Five
Deadliest Prosecutors: How Overzealous Personalities Drive the Death
Penalty" (Cambridge, MA: Harvard Law School, Charles Hamilton Hous-
ton Institute for Race & Justice and the Criminal Justice Institute, 2016),
14, https://files.deathpenaltyinfo.org/documents/FairPunishmentProject
-Top5Report_FINAL_2016_06.pdf, citing Robert Brett Dunham, assistant federal defender, Federal Public Defender Office for the Middle
District of Pennsylvania, *Philadelphia Death Row: 1990-2014* (February 23,
2015). Abraham was Philadelphia's district attorney from May 1991 until
January 2010. Archer Attorneys at Law, "Lynne M. Abraham," archerlaw
.com/attorneys/lynne-m-abraham.

6. In 1995, then-District Attorney Abraham said, "When it comes to the
death penalty, I am passionate. I truly believe it is manifestly correct." Tina
Rosenberg, "The Deadliest D.A.," *The New York Times Magazine*, July 16,
1995, nytimes.com/1995/07/16/magazine/the-deadliest-da.html.

7. As a *Vice* article summarized, "Rizzo granted cops pay hikes and
extremely generous pension plans that allowed many to retire with full
benefits after 25 years. Such benefits might be easier to bear with a larger
tax pool, but in a city with a shrinking population and tax base, allowing thousands of officers to retire at . . . age 45 proved a heavy burden."

Jake Blumgart, "The Brutal Legacy of Frank Rizzo, the Most Notorious Cop in Philadelphia History," *Vice*, October 22, 2015, vice.com/en/article/kwxp3m/remembering-frank-rizzo-the-most-notorious-cop-in-philadelphia-history-1022; also see David Gambacorta, Chris Brennan, and Valerie Russ, "Who Was Frank Rizzo? Nearly 30 Years after His Death, Philadelphians Still Don't Agree," *Philadelphia Inquirer*, August 22, 2017, inquirer.com/philly/news/philadelphia-statue-legacy-was-frank-rizzo-racist-20170822.html-2.

8. Data published by the Vera Institute of Justice for Philadelphia County shows the jail population at 3,643 in 1985, and at more than 3,900 in every year reported since then; see Vera Institute of Justice, "Incarceration Trends: Philadelphia County, PA," trends.vera.org/state/PA/county/philadelphia_county. A report by the MacArthur Safety and Justice Challenge and the First Judicial District of Pennsylvania, Department of Research and Development, shows that the jail population dipped into the mid- to high 3,000s in 2020; see First Judicial District of Pennsylvania, Department of Research and Development, "Philadelphia Jail Population Report: July 2015–January 2021," https://www.phila.gov/media/20210216124532/Full-Public-Jail-Report-January-2020.pdf.

9. Philadelphia District Attorney's Office, Public Data Dashboard, "Future Years of Supervision Imposed," data.philadao.com/Future_Years_Supervision_Report_YE.html. In 2014, nearly 47,000 years of future supervision were imposed; in 2019, that had been reduced to about 17,600 (a 62 percent drop), and in 2020 it was reduced further to 6,066.

10. Philadelphia District Attorney's Office, "DA Krasner Highlights Sweeping Changes to Juvenile Justice in Philadelphia," press release, February 8, 2021, medium.com/philadelphia-justice/da-krasner-highlights-sweeping-changes-to-juvenile-justice-in-philadelphia-d24c6b20b304.

11. Philadelphia District Attorney's Office, email correspondence, August 6, 2021.

12. The Defender Association of Philadelphia reports that "Philadelphia has more than 10 percent of all juvenile life without parole cases" nationwide. Defender Association of Philadelphia, "Juvenile Life Without Parole," phillydefenders.org/practice-units/juvenile-life.

13. See *Roper v. Simmons*, 543 U.S. 551 (2005), supreme.justia.com/cases/federal/us/543/551.

14. For data as of June 2021, see Philadelphia District Attorney's Office, "Citing Prosecutor's 'Obligation to Do Justice,' Court Overturns 1991 Murder Conviction," press release, June 25, 2021, medium.com/philadelphia-justice/citing-prosecutors-obligation-to-do-justice-court-overturns-1991-murder-conviction-30d3f49ee7ad.

15. To read more about the case, see Pennsylvania Innocence Project, "Chester Hollman," painnocence.org/chesterhollman.

16. *Philadelphia Sun* staff, "Philadelphia District Attorney's Office Finds Application of Pennsylvania's Death Penalty Unconstitutional," *Philadelphia Sunday Sun*, July 19, 2019, philasun.com/local/philadelphia-district-attorneys-office-finds-application-of-pennsylvanias-death-penalty-unconstitutional.

17. Death Penalty Information Center, "Citing Conflict with Florida Death-Penalty Ruling, Aramis Ayala Will Not Seek Re-Election as State Attorney," May 31, 2019, deathpenaltyinfo.org/news/citing-conflict-with-florida-death-penalty-ruling-aramis-ayala-will-not-seek-re-election-as-state-attorney.

18. See William Lovelace, Daily Express/Hulton Archive/Getty Images, March 1965, gettyimages.com/detail/news-photo/american-civil-rights-activists-john-lewis-ralph-abernathy-news-photo/3322250.

19. Francesca Trianni and Carlos H. Martinelli, "Bryan Stevenson: 'Believe Things You Haven't Seen,'" *TIME*, June 22, 2015, time.com/3928285/bryan-stevenson-interview-time-100.

# 10

## Marilyn Mosby

1. The Metropolitan Council for Educational Opportunity (METCO) was founded in the Boston area in 1965. To read more about METCO's history, see metcoinc.org/about/metco-history.

2. Deborah J. Vagins and Jesselyn McCurdy, "Cracks in the System: Twenty Years of the Unjust Federal Crack Cocaine Law," American Civil Liberties Union, October 2006, aclu.org/other/cracks-system-20-years-unjust-federal-crack-cocaine-law.

3. Jonathan Saltzman, "Jury Convicts Man in Slaying of Teenager, Her Unborn Baby," *The Boston Globe*, October 19, 2004, archive.boston.com/news/local/articles/2004/10/19/jury_convicts_man_in_slaying_of_teenager_her_unborn_baby.

4. Laci Peterson was twenty-seven years old and pregnant when she disappeared in December 2002. Her body was found about four months later, and her husband, Scott Peterson, was convicted of her murder and the murder of the fetus in 2004. In October 2020, the California Supreme Court ordered a review of his convictions, and in December 2021, he was resentenced to life in prison. To read more, see Rachel Swan and Michael Cabanatuan, "Scott Peterson Resentenced to Life in Prison Without Parole for Murder of His Wife and Unborn Son," *San Francisco Chronicle*, December 8, 2021, sfchronicle.com/bayarea/article/Scott-Peterson-resentenced-to-life-in-prison-16685575.php.

5. Jonathan M. Pitts, "The Heather Cook Case: Timeline of Events Surrounding Maryland Bishop's DUI Collision That Killed Cyclist," *The Baltimore Sun*, November 4, 2018, baltimoresun.com/news/crime/bs-md -cook-case-timeline-20181009-story.html.

6. According to Baltimore Police Department (BPD) documents, Freddie Gray "fled unprovoked upon noticing police presence." Officers apprehended him and found a knife in his possession, one the BPD called an illegal switchblade; State's Attorney Mosby disagreed with both descriptions. Eyder Peralta, "Timeline: What We Know About the Freddie Gray Arrest," NPR, May 1, 2015, npr.org/sections/thetwo-way/2015/05/01 /403629104/baltimore-protests-what-we-know-about-the-freddie-gray -arrest. For more on Freddie Gray's death and the aftermath, see Mary Rose Madden, "Since Freddie Gray: Five Years Later, What's Changed?," WYPR, April 24, 2020, wypr.org/wypr-news/2020-04-24/since-freddie -gray-five-years-later-whats-changed.

7. Jonathan Capehart, "Marilyn Mosby's Amazing Press Conference," *The Washington Post*, May 1, 2015, washingtonpost.com/blogs/post -partisan/wp/2015/05/01/marilyn-mosbys-amazing-press-conference.

8. Oliver Laughland and Jon Swaine, "Baltimore: Freddie Gray Police Threaten to Sue State's Attorney Marilyn Mosby," *The Guardian*, May 8, 2015, theguardian.com/us-news/2015/may/08/baltimore-freddie-gray -police-threaten-to-sue-marilyn-mosby.

9. In May 2015, U.S. Attorney General Loretta Lynch announced a federal civil rights investigation of the BPD. See Mike Levine, "Baltimore Police: DOJ Announces Federal Probe of Entire Department," ABC News, May 8, 2015, abcnews.go.com/US/freddy-gray-doj-announces -federal-probe-entire-baltimore/story?id=30899279; in August 2016, the Department of Justice (DOJ) released a report concluding that the department engaged in a "a pattern or practice of (1) making unconstitutional stops, searches, and arrests; (2) using enforcement strategies that produce severe and unjustified disparities in the rates of stops, searches and arrests of African Americans; (3) using excessive force; and (4) retaliating against people engaging in constitutionally-protected expression." The report also stated that the DOJ and the City of Baltimore would negotiate "a comprehensive, court-enforceable consent decree." See U.S. Department of Justice, Civil Rights Division, *Investigation of the Baltimore Police Department,* August 10, 2016, 3, 11, justice.gov/crt/file/883296 /download.

10. Office of the State's Attorney for Baltimore City, "State Legislature Passes Maryland Police Accountability Act of 2021," press release, April 15, 2021, www.stattorney.org/media-center/press-releases/2249 -state-legislature-passes-maryland-police-accountability-act-of-2021.

11. For more on the Maryland Law Enforcement Bill of Rights, see mcp .maryland.gov/Directive%20Manual/5-104.pdf.

12. Kat Stafford and Hannah Fingerhut, "AP-NORC poll: Sweeping Change in US Views of Police Violence," Associated Press, June 17, 2020, apnews.com/article/728b414b8742129329081f7092179d1f.

13. American Bar Association, *ABA Model Rules of Professional Conduct*, "Rule 3.8: Special Responsibilities of a Prosecutor," sections (g) and (h) (Chicago: ABA), americanbar.org/groups/professional _responsibility/publications/model_rules_of_professional_conduct /rule_3_8_special_responsibilities_of_a_prosecutor.

14. Office of the State's Attorney for Baltimore City, "Much Needed Vacatur Legislation Will Become Law October 1, 2019," press release, May 28, 2019, www.stattorney.org/media-center/press-releases/1770 -much-needed-vacatur-legislation-will-become-law-october-1-2019.

15. Office of the State's Attorney for Baltimore City, *Reforming a Broken City: Rethinking the Role of Marijuana Prosecutions in Baltimore City* (Baltimore: Office of the State's Attorney for Baltimore City, 2019), 13, stattorney.org /images/MARIJUANA_WHITE_PAPER_FINAL.pdf.

16. American Civil Liberties Union, "Marijuana Arrests by the Numbers," 2020, aclu.org/gallery/marijuana-arrests-numbers; and Ezekiel Edwards et al., *A Tale of Two Countries: Racially Targeted Arrests in the Era of Marijuana Reform* (New York: ACLU, 2020), 5, aclu.org/sites/default/files /field_document/marijuanareport_03232021.pdf.

17. American Civil Liberties Union of Maryland, "Baltimore City: Racial Disparities in Marijuana Possession Arrests," aclu-md.org/en /baltimore-city; and Sonia Kumar, *The Maryland War on Marijuana in Black and White* (Baltimore: ACLU of Maryland, 2013), 13, aclu-md.org/sites /default/files/legacy/files/aclu_marijuana_in_md_report_whitecover.pdf.

18. Office of the State's Attorney for Baltimore City, *Reforming a Broken System*, 9.

19. The queer Black feminist Moya Bailey first used the word *misogynoir* to describe "the particular brand of hatred directed at black women in American visual and popular culture." Moya Bailey, "They Aren't Talking about Me," Crunk Feminist Collective, March 14, 2010, crunkfeministcol lective.com/2010/03/14/they-arent-talking-about-me.

20. These percentages were reported in October 2019; see Reflective Democracy Campaign, "Tipping the Scales: Challengers Take On the Old Boys' Club of Elected Prosecutors," October 2019, wholeads.us/wp-conte nt/uploads/2019/10/Tipping-the-Scales-Prosecutor-Report-10-22.pdf.

21. Elizabeth Nolan Brown, "Violent Crime in Baltimore Plunges After City Ditches Prosecution of Prostitution, Drug Possession, Other Minor Offenses," *Reason*, April 1, 2021, reason.com/2021/04/01/violent-crime -in-baltimore-plunges-after-city-ditches-prosecution-of-prostitution -drug-possession-other-minor-offenses.

22. See Phil Davis and Phillip Jackson, "With Baltimore Close to the

300-Homicide Mark Again, Leaders Mull New Approaches Amid Some Signs of Improvement," *The Baltimore Sun*, November 20, 2020, balti moresun.com/news/crime/bs-md-ci-cr-300-homicides-2020-20201120 -iwgbid4dezdplkdqz5g3ocr3wu-story.html; and Emily Sullivan, "Baltimore City's Year-to-Date Homicide and Clearance Rates Rise," WYPR, December 15, 2021, wypr.org/wypr-news/2021-12-15/baltimore-citys -year-to-date-homicide-and-clearance-rates-rise.

23. To read more about the Junior State's Attorney program, see www .stattorney.org/community-affairs/crime-control-and-prevention/junior -state-s-attorney.

24. See Maryland State Assembly, HB0315, Juvenile Interrogation Protection Act, mgaleg.maryland.gov/mgawebsite/Legislation/Details /HB0315?ys=2021RS.

# 11

## Rachael Rollins

1. *Loving v. Virginia*, 388 U.S. 1 (1967), law.cornell.edu/wex /loving_v_virginia_(1967).

2. For more about the Title IX statute of the Education Amendments of 1972, see U.S. Department of Education, Office for Civil Rights, "Title IX and Sex Discrimination," www2.ed.gov/about/offices/list/ocr/docs /tix_dis.html.

3. Emily Sweeney and John R. Ellement, "Man Accused of Kidnapping and Causing Death of Jassy Correia Pleads Not Guilty," *The Boston Globe*, April 9, 2019, bostonglobe.com/metro/2019/04/09/man -accused-kidnapping-and-causing-death-jassy-correia-due-federal-court /jNPaEQ0yCJAaB0Ruj53IrM/story.html.

4. To read more about the case, see Kevin G. Andrade, "District Attorney Rachael Rollins Discusses Victory In Osman Bilal Immigration Case," WGBH, January 28, 2020, www.wgbh.org/news/local-news/2020/01 /28/district-attorney-rachael-rollins-victory-in-osman-bilal-immigration -case; and *Commonwealth v. Bilal*, 119 N.E.3d 356 (Mass. App. Ct. 2018), 94 Mass. App. Ct. 1114, casetext.com/case/commonwealth-v-bilal-1.

5. See Rachael Rollins's campaign website, "Charges to Be Declined," rollins4da.com/policy/charges-to-be-declined.

6. Commonwealth of Massachusetts, Suffolk County District Attorney, "The Rachael Rollins Policy Memo," 2019, http://files.suffolkdistrictattor ney.com/The-Rachael-Rollins-Policy-Memo.pdf.

7. Commonwealth of Massachusetts, "Rollins Memo," 28; and John R. Ellement, "Suffolk DA Names 'Discharge Integrity Team' to Probe Fatal

Police-Involved Shooting," *The Boston Globe*, March 11, 2019, bostonglobe
.com/metro/2019/03/11/suffolk-names-discharge-intergrity-team-probe
-fatal-police-involved-shooting/4kFikqc1KEr3FTOTJM5O8O/story
.html.

8. To read more about the Suffolk County District Attorney's Office
Integrity Review Bureau, see suffolkdistrictattorney.com/irbfaqs.

9. A "*Brady* violation" refers to a violation of the Supreme Court's 1963
decision *Brady v. Maryland*, which requires that prosecutors disclose any
information that is favorable to the defense. For more, see *Brady v. Maryland*,
373 U.S. 83 (1963), supreme.justia.com/cases/federal/us/373/83; and Jessica Brand, "The Epidemic of Brady Violations," April 25, 2018, theappeal
.org/the-epidemic-of-brady-violations-explained-94a38ad3c800.

10. Commonwealth of Massachusetts, Suffolk County District Attorney,
"District Attorney Rachael Rollins Releases Mid-Term Report," press
release, August 31, 2021, suffolkdistrictattorney.com/press-releases/items
/mid-term-report-2021.

# 12

## Dan Satterberg

1. "Given two options for approaches to lowering the U.S. crime rate,
more Americans prefer putting money and effort into addressing social
and economic problems such as drug addiction, homelessness and mental
health (63%) rather than putting money and effort into strengthening law
enforcement (34%)." Megan Brenan, "Fewer Americans Call for Tougher
Criminal Justice System," Gallup, November 16, 2020, news.gallup.com
/poll/324164/fewer-americans-call-tougher-criminal-justice-system.aspx.

2. Medication-assisted treatment (MAT) "is the use of medications,
in combination with counseling and behavioral therapies, to provide a
'whole-patient' approach to the treatment of substance use disorders. . . .
MAT is primarily used for the treatment of addiction to opioids such as
heroin and prescription pain relievers that contain opiates, and 'to prevent or reduce opioid overdose.'" U.S. Department of Health & Human
Services, Substance Abuse and Mental Health Services Administration,
"Medication-Assisted Treatment (MAT)," samhsa.gov/medication-assisted
-treatment.

3. Dan Satterberg, "My Sister's Drug Addiction—And What It Taught
Me," Crosscut, May 17, 2018, crosscut.com/2018/05/my-sisters-drug
-addiction-and-what-it-taught-me.

4. To read more, see King County, Prosecuting Attorney, Criminal
Division, "LEAD: Law Enforcement Assisted Diversion," kingcounty.gov
/depts/prosecutor/criminal-overview/lead.aspx.

5. When Norm Maleng died, the *Seattle Times* described him as "one of the most respected leaders in the state's criminal justice system." Steve Miletich and Jennifer Sullivan, "Longtime Prosecutor Norm Maleng Dies," *The Seattle Times*, May 25, 2007, seattletimes.com/seattle-news/longtime -prosecutor-norm-maleng-dies.

6. Justin Jouvenal, "No Charges for Personal Drug Possession: Seattle's Bold Gamble to Bring 'Peace' after the War on Drugs," *The Washington Post*, June 11, 2019, washingtonpost.com/local/public-safety/no -charges-for-personal-drug-possession-seattles-bold-gamble-to-bring -peace-after-the-war-on-drugs/2019/06/11/69a7bb46-7285-11e9-9f06 -5fc2ee80027a_story.html.

7. In June 2021, as the result of a court-ordered moratorium the previous month, the state of Washington stopped "revoking licenses to penalize drivers who fail to pay fines or fail to appear in court." Michelle Baruchman, "Washington State to Halt Driver's License Suspension for Unpaid Tickets, Failure to Appear in Court," *The Seattle Times*, June 7, 2021, seattletimes.com/seattle-news/transportation/washington-state-to-halt -drivers-license-suspension-for-unpaid-tickets-failure-to-appear-in-court.

8. See "Washington 'Three Strikes,' Initiative 593 (1993)," Ballotpedia, ballotpedia.org/Washington_%22Three_Strikes%22, _Initiative_593_(1993); and Nina Shapiro, "Prosecutor Admits Possible Injustice in the 'Three-Strikes' Law," *Seattle Weekly*, January 22, 2008, seattleweekly.com/news/prosecutor-admits-possible-injustice-in-the -%C2%93three-strikes%C2%94-law.

9. Sarah Martinson, "New Wave of Prosecutors Push for Resentencing Laws," LAW 360, July 11, 2021, law360.com/articles/1394847.

10. Kim Murphy, "Three-Strikes Laws May Not Mean You're Out," *Los Angeles Times*, August 11, 2009, latimes.com/archives/la-xpm-2009-aug-11 -na-three-strikes11-story.html.

11. Rebecca McCray, "For a New Breed of Prosecutors, Justice Sometimes Entails a Second Chance," *The Appeal*, November 16, 2017, theappeal .org/for-a-new-breed-of-prosecutors-justice-sometimes-entails-a-second -chance-a10fe0104a1b.

12. Amy Radil, "A 13 Year Old Goes on a Joyride. Thanks to this Program, She Won't Wind Up in Court," KUOW, January 17, 2021, kuow.org /stories/king-county-is-spending-9m-on-programs-to-keep-youth-and -adults-out-of-court.

13. Radil, "A 13-Year-Old Goes on a Joyride."

14. Discovery is "the formal process of exchanging information between the parties about the witnesses and evidence they'll present at trial. Discovery enables the parties to know before the trial begins what evidence may be presented." American Bar Association, "How Courts Work: Steps in a Trial—Discovery," November 28, 2021, americanbar.org

/groups/public_education/resources/law_related_education_network /how_courts_work/discovery. In its 1963 decision *Brady v. Maryland*, the Supreme Court ruled that prosecutors are required to disclose any information that is favorable to the defense; see *Brady v. Maryland*, 373 U.S. 83 (1963), supreme.justia.com/cases/federal/us/373/83. For more about *Brady* violations, see Jessica Brand, "The Epidemic of Brady Violations," *The Appeal*, April 25, 2018, theappeal.org/the-epidemic-of-brady-violations -explained-94a38ad3c800. "The 'trial penalty' refers to the substantial difference between the sentence offered in a plea offer prior to trial versus the sentence a defendant receives after trial. This penalty is now so severe and pervasive that it has virtually eliminated the constitutional right to a trial." National Association of Criminal Defense Lawyers, "The Trial Penalty: The Sixth Amendment Right to Trial on the Verge of Extinction and How to Save It," July 10, 2018, nacdl.org/getattachment/95b7f0f5-90df-4f9f -9115-520b3f58036a/the-trial-penalty-the-sixth-amendment-right-to -trial-on-the-verge-of-extinction-and-how-to-save-it.pdf.

15. Justin Jouvenal, "They Send People to Prison Every Day. Now, They Are Pledging to Visit," *The Washington Post*, November 25, 2019, wash ingtonpost.com/local/legal-issues/they-send-people-to-prison-everyday -now-they-are-pledging-to-visit/2019/11/22/5e0ff274-0d64-11ea-97ac -a7ccc8dd1ebc_story.html.

16. As of 2020, 30.7 percent of people released from the state's Department of Corrections (DOC) in 2017 had returned to DOC institutions. Washington State Department of Corrections, "Fact Card," December 31, 2021, doc.wa.gov/docs/publications/reports/100-RE004.pdf.

17. Hal Dardick and Matthew Walberg, "Kim Foxx Declares Win in Cook County State's Attorney's Race," *Chicago Tribune*, November 8, 2016, chicagotribune.com/politics/ct-cook-county-states-attorney-kim-foxx -election-met-1109-20161108-story.html.

# 13

## Tori Verber Salazar

1. "U.S. News Special Report: Stockton, Calif., Is the Most Diverse City in America," *U.S. News & World Report*, January 22, 2020, usnews .com/info/blogs/press-room/articles/2020-01-22/us-news-special-report -stockton-calif-is-the-most-diverse-city-in-america.

2. The Family Justice Center Alliance describes Family Justice Centers as "multi-agency, multi-disciplinary co-located service centers that provide services to victims of inter-personal violence including intimate partner violence, sexual assault, child abuse, elder or dependent adult abuse, and human trafficking." See Family Justice Center Alli-

ance, "About Family Justice Centers," familyjusticecenter.org/affiliated
-centers/family-justice-centers-2.

3. For more on the effects of incarceration, see Don Stemen, *The Prison Paradox: More Incarceration Will Not Make Us Safer* (New York: Vera Institute of Justice, 2017), 1, vera.org/downloads/publications/for-the-recor d-prison-paradox_02.pdf, citing Don Stemen, *Reconsidering Incarceration: New Directions for Reducing Crime* (New York: Vera Institute of Justice, 2007), 4, perma.cc/T8PJ-QBCD; Oliver Roeder, Lauren-Brook Eisen, and Julia Bowling, *What Caused the Crime Decline?* (New York: Brennan Center for Justice, 2015), perma.cc/NTL9-5Z24; Todd R. Clear, "The Effects of High Imprisonment Rates on Communities," *Crime and Justice* 37, no. 1 (2008), 97–132, vera.org/downloads/publications /veraincarc_vFW2.pdf; and Raymond V. Liedka, Anne Morrison Piehl, and Bert Useem, "The Crime-Control Effect of Incarceration: Does Scale Matter?," *Criminology & Public Policy* 5, no. 2 (2006), 245–276, researchgate.net/publication/337381044_The_Crime-Control_Effect_of _Incarceration_Does_Scale_Matter. For more on the beliefs of crime victims/survivors, see Danielle Sered, *Accounting for Violence: How to Increase Safety and Break Our Failed Reliance on Mass Incarceration* (New York: Vera Institute of Justice, 2017), vera.org/downloads/publications /accounting-for-violence.pdf, citing Alliance for Safety and Justice, *Crime Survivors Speak: The First-Ever National Survey of Victims' Views on Safety and Justice* (Oakland: Alliance for Safety and Justice, 2016), 21, perma .cc/W4XWNQB8. In a 2016 survey, "roughly 52 percent of crime victims" said they "'believe that time in prison makes people more likely to commit another crime rather than less likely.'" Also see Rachel E. Morgan and Grace Kena, "Criminal Victimization, 2016: Revised," U.S. Department of Justice, Office of Justice Programs, Bureau of Justice Statistics, October 2018 bjs.ojp.gov/content/pub/pdf/cv16.pdf.

4. For more information, see Fair and Just Prosecution, *Building Community Trust: Restorative Justice Strategies, Principles and Promising Practices* (San Francisco: FJP, 2017), fairandjustprosecution.org/wp-content /uploads/2017/12/FJP.Brief_.RestorativeJustice.pdf.

5. San Joaquin Office of the District Attorney, "Project Navigate Constructive Change," sjgov.org/department/da/pncc.

6. San Joaquin Office of the District Attorney, *2020 Data Report*, Section 3b, "Demographic Summary: Defendants Charged," sjgov.org/docs/default -source/district-attorney-documents/data-reports/2020_data_report -_sjcda_pub20210629.pdf?sfvrsn=a3b21f6_4.

# ABOUT THE AUTHOR

**Miriam Aroni Krinsky** is the executive director of Fair and Just Prosecution, which supports and interconnects elected prosecutors who are committed to new thinking and innovation aimed at addressing mass incarceration and promoting fairness, equity, compassion, and transparency in the criminal legal system. She has worked in public service, justice system reform, and academia for decades, including fifteen years as a federal prosecutor in Los Angeles and on a strike force in the Mid-Atlantic region.

In 2012, Miriam served as the executive director of the Los Angeles Citizens' Commission on Jail Violence, a high-level body charged with investigating abuse in the largest Sheriff's Department in the nation. She has taught at the UCLA Luskin School of Public Affairs, as well as Loyola and Southwestern Law Schools; served as a national policy consultant on youth violence prevention, juvenile justice, and justice reform issues; and spent five years as the executive director of the Children's Law Center in California. She has also served as president of the Los Angeles County Bar Association, on the Lose Angeles City Ethics Commission (serving as president for three years), on the California Judicial Council and the California State Bar Board of Trustees, and on the advisory groups of the American Law Institute Sentencing and Principles of Policing projects. She has testified before state and national legislative bodies, authored dozens of articles, and lectured nationwide on criminal law, policing, juvenile justice, and sentencing issues.

# PUBLISHING IN THE PUBLIC INTEREST

Thank you for reading this book published by The New Press. The New Press is a nonprofit, public interest publisher. New Press books and authors play a crucial role in sparking conversations about the key political and social issues of our day.

We hope you enjoyed this book and that you will stay in touch with The New Press. Here are a few ways to stay up to date with our books, events, and the issues we cover:

- Sign up at www.thenewpress.com/subscribe to receive updates on New Press authors and issues and to be notified about local events
- Like us on Facebook: facebook.com/newpressbooks
- Follow us on Twitter: twitter.com/thenewpress
- Follow us on Instagram: instagram.com/thenewpress

Please consider buying New Press books for yourself; for friends and family; or to donate to schools, libraries, community centers, prison libraries, and other organizations involved with the issues our authors write about.

The New Press is a 501(c)(3) nonprofit organization. You can also support our work with a tax-deductible gift by visiting www.thenewpress.com/donate.